JAKE LA MOTTA TAKES THE FULL COUNT IN THIS DRAMATIC STORY OF HIS VIOLENT, TURBULENT LIFE . . .

As A Sexual Athlete

"There were times, sometimes months on end, when I couldn't go to bed with a broad. Here you are the world's champ, the symbol of complete masculinity, and you can't even have a woman. Then after I was about ready to commit suicide, I'd be all right again."

As A Teenage Killer

" 'How do you feel, Jake?' he asked. 'I mean inside yourself, knowing you killed a guy?' I waited a moment. 'I think I'm gettin' afraid,' I said. 'I've never been afraid before.' "

As A Brutal-Tempered Husband

"We called the doc. She wasn't dead, thank God."

As Middleweight Champion Of The World

" 'Ladies and gentlemen . . . The winner and new champion . . . Jake La Motta!' I can't describe exactly how I felt. I felt like, you know, God had given me the world."

As Ex-Champ In The Prison "Hole"

"Okay, here I was, in a hole as close to hell as I'll ever want to get, but I knew I was going to get out of there. I was going to fight my way out. But this time I wouldn't be fighting with hate and fear *against* someone but *for* myself. I wouldn't be fighting to destroy anymore but to build."

A ROBERT CHARTOFF–IRWIN WINKLER PRODUCTION
A MARTIN SCORSESE PICTURE

ROBERT DE NIRO
"RAGING BULL"

Produced in association with
PETER SAVAGE

Screenplay by
PAUL SCHRADER and MARDIK MARTIN

Based on the book by
JAKE LA MOTTA with JOSEPH CARTER and PETER SAVAGE

Produced by
IRWIN WINKLER and ROBERT CHARTOFF

Directed by
MARTIN SCORSESE

RAGING BULL

Jake La Motta
with
Joseph Carter and Peter Savage

RAGING BULL
*A Bantam Book/published by arrangement with
author*

PRINTING HISTORY
*Prentice-Hall edition published September 1970
Bantam edition/December 1980*

*Bantam Books are published by Bantam Books, Inc. Its trade-
mark, consisting of the words "Bantam Books" and the por-
trayal of a bantam, is Registered in U.S. Patent and Trademark
Office and in other countries. Marca Registrada. Bantam
Books, Inc., 666 Fifth Avenue, New York, New York 10103.*

To my friend Marty Heller and my beloved children—
Jacklyn, Jack, Joe, Christi, Elisa and Mia

RAGING BULL

ONE

There was this bookie, Harry Gordon. His book was around my neighborhood, ten or fifteen candy and cigar stores, a dozen of those big, old-fashioned Bronx apartment houses that still had a super who would always be within seeing distance of the front door so that tenants would know him enough to tip him a dollar or two at Christmastime. This was thirty or more years ago when with two dollars you could buy a steak dinner. Anyway, the super would pick up the horse bets that the Jewish mothers would give him on their way out for their day's shopping and he'd turn them over to Harry Gordon when Harry dropped by on the day's round. It wasn't much of an operation. Jewish mothers would bet as little as twenty cents on a horse if there was a book who would take it. Harry would take a bet as low as fifty cents, his motto being it wasn't much, but why turn it down? If horseplayers were so smart, would they be living in Bronx tenements? Harry also had a series of taxpayers, five- and six-story buildings where on the first floor would be a machine shop, one flight up a place that made imitation-leather handbags, another flight up a place that made dress forms for the garment industry—you get the idea. Twenty employees maximum in any one of them, including the two brothers who owned the business plus the three nephews. But everybody in the building was an ardent horseplayer, so add all this together and Harry was good for a few hundred bucks a day.

This was when everybody said the Depression was ending, though I couldn't see it. I was sixteen and a hard core, what they now call a juvenile delinquent. What they called them then was a goddamned good-for-nothing bum kid. If

1

I'd been shot by a cop then, stealing the plumbing fixtures out of an empty tenement, they'd have given me a funeral that would have lasted twenty minutes and that would have been the end of it. I was a bum and I lived like a bum in a bum neighborhood.

Now, sometimes, at night, when I think back, I feel like I'm looking at an old black-and-white movie of myself. Why it should be black-and-white I don't know, but it is. Not a good movie, either, jerky, with gaps in it, a string of poorly lit sequences, some of them with no beginning and some with no end. No musical score, just sometimes the sound of a police siren or a pistol shot. And almost all of it happens at night, as if I lived my whole life at night.

I see myself going through a house, looking in the rooms. The rooms are all terrible. The house is naturally a tenement. You come into a shabby hallway where some kid broke the lightbulb a couple of weeks back, or stole it, and the super, who hasn't shaved in three days, says he'll fix it as soon as he gets rid of this pain in his back. If you want to look at any of the nameplates—pieces of cardboard from matchbook covers with the name written in pencil and pushed into the slot—you either have to have a flashlight or what Fred Allen said once, a seeing-eye owl.

What I remember about the tenement as much as anything else is the smell. It's impossible to describe the smell of a tenement to someone who's never lived in one. You can't just put your head in the door and sniff. You have to live there, day and night, summer and winter, so the smell gets a chance to sink into your soul. There's all the dirt that the super never really manages to get clean even on the days when he does an hour's work, and this dirt has a smell, gray and dry and, after you've smelled it long enough, suffocating. And diapers. The slobs who live in tenements are always having kids, and naturally they don't have the money for any diaper service, so the old lady is always boiling diapers on the back of the stove and after a while the smell gets into the walls.

And the food you eat when you're poor. All it does is keep you alive, and it has a smell, too, because it's food like corned beef and cabbage, or food that's cooked in heavy grease, and the smell of it cooking goes all through the building.

And there was the heat in the summer, when I'd try to spend all the time I could out in the street or on the roof or the fire escapes, and the cold in the winter. It seems like I was always cold winters when I was a kid. Being on home relief doesn't do much to keep you warm. Everything piles up on you when you're poor. The super in the building doesn't give a damn and God knows the landlord doesn't, and you call City Hall and get some clerk who doesn't give a damn either because he's on civil service and what the hell difference is it to him if you're freezing your ass off? It's not hurting him any. So winters I remember wearing as many clothes as I could and staying in bed as much as I could, or in the kitchen, which was about the only room in the house that was even halfway warm, unless the old man was in a foul temper like he was a helluva lot of the time, and then the kitchen was off-limits to any kid with a grain of sense in his head.

And the rats! What's a real tenement without rats? Not the kind of rats you probably know that run if they hear a sound. These were rats as big as goddamned alley cats, and if you met them at night you got out of their way. You could hear them at night, too, in the walls, squealing and slamming around, afraid of nothing. *Zoccolas,* we called them, which is Italian slang for a dirty vicious whore.

When you're a kid, you don't think much about it. You don't go around feeling sorry for yourself. Oh, you wish you had it better. You wonder what it would be like to have all the dough you wanted and drive around in a Cadillac and have all the broads falling all over you all the time, and you dream that when you grow up that's how it's going to be, but you don't spend all your time mooning about what you don't have. You didn't back then. Back then you knew that all you would ever get would be what you could steal.

Like I said, when I look back to then it's like looking at a movie. And the strange thing is that it doesn't even seem to be about me. Who's me? I live in Manhattan, I walk down the streets, I go into a decent restaurant, people say,

"That's Jake La Motta." I'm on television, I'm in movies. People say, "He used to be middleweight champ. He beat Sugar Ray Robinson." But I look back to those old years and who am I? I see a fairly decent-looking kid except for the sour look on his face, maybe not Little Boy Blue, but it's thirty years ago and before my nose got to looking like a by-pass on a super highway. Before I took thirty thousand punches. Before I was in reform school. Before I was in jail.

My mother was an Italian girl born in this country but my father was an Italian immigrant from Messina. My father settled down in the Lower East Side, around Tenth Street and First Avenue, right after the first World War, and ended up marrying a girl whose parents had come over from the old country. Who else do you end up marrying on the East Side? After a while my old man worked his way up to being a peddler. That's one of the first things I really remember. I don't think I remember the Lower East Side at all, except for going back there. We moved to Philadelphia when I was a little kid, maybe six-eight years old, where we found another great slum to live in, and that was when I remember my father being a peddler. I don't even know how the old man got the horse and wagon to do the peddling, except I'm sure he didn't own it. Where would an Italian immigrant who could barely speak the language get the money for a horse and wagon? But I do remember the horse and wagon, and we'd peddle whatever was in season—fish, vegetables, fruit, whatever was the cheapest to buy that day.

That's where I first began to learn that if you want to survive in this world, you got to be tough. I was going to school in those days, and my mother always gave me something to eat, a sandwich, something like that, and these other kids, bigger than me, they'd take it away. I'd run home, crying. One day I was blubbering to my mother because I'd been all banged up by some kid because I put up a squawk that he was taking my sandwich right out of my mouth. My father came over to me, hit me a vicious slap across the face and slapped an icepick in my hand. He yelled at me, "Here, you son of a bitch, you don't run away from nobody no more! I don't give a goddamn how many there are. Use that—dig a few of them! Hit 'em with it, hit 'em first, and hit 'em hard. You come home crying anymore, I'll beat the shit outta you more than you ever get from any of them! Ya understand?" He kept yelling and slapped me again, leaving my ear ringing and half-dead, but that phrase, "Hit 'em first, and hit 'em hard," stayed with me. It was the only good thing I ever got from my father, and later it always seemed to push the right triggers at the right time in my brain.

I never let go of that icepick after that. I carried it with me in a leather case hung on my belt. One day three kids ganged up on me. They were working me over pretty good when I remembered what my father had said he'd do if I went home blubbering again, and I remembered the icepick. I whipped it out and ripped into the three of them. I caught one of them across the cheek with it, ripped his skin, and when they saw the blood, you should have heard their screams and the looks on their faces. Talk about fear, they took off like they were being attacked by a monster from outer space. It was the first time I can remember really having someone afraid of me. I can still remember that feeling of power flood through me. An icepick in my hand—and I was boss!

Until the icepick, I was always the kid getting it in the ass. If it wasn't my old man belting me around, it was these kids after me, or a teacher slapping me silly—always someone asking me what right I had to be alive. The icepick showed me what it felt like to make the other guy as afraid as I had always been.

My old man had that figured, too. In a funny way, I got respect for the old bum, even though he was never more than a peddler and he used to beat up my mother and us kids all the time. I don't know why but later, when I was making it big in fighting, I gave him an apartment house. Sometime after that, when I needed money and asked him for a loan, how much did I get? *Niente,* that's what. Nothing. A real son of a bitch. But what the hell. He's back in Italy now, he's a big man there. He sold the apartment house I gave him, which gave him enough money to live on—in Sicily you can live like a king on what you starve on in the Bronx—but he didn't go back with just the

apartment-house money. He waited till he qualified for
Social Security so he could have that, too. Now he must
have around three or four hundred bucks a month income,
which makes him very big in Messina.

You know, all you ever hear about—or read about, anyway—when it comes to immigrants to this country, especially Irish or Italian immigrants, is how they came here
and made good and went home for a visit to show the
folks back home that they had it. If a writer wanted to
have a switch on it, he could take a look at my old man.
He came over here, he moved from one slum on the
Lower East Side to another in Philadelphia to another in
the Bronx, and he didn't make it except the way I just
mentioned, with what I gave him, and Social Security.
And when the ending of his life came into sight, he didn't
want to sit back in his own house here in America, with
his wife and his kids around him. No sir. He wanted to go
back to the little neighborhood where he was born and be
a big shot, and go down to the *trattoria* every day and buy
a liter of wine. All for himself. His wife—my mother—she
lives right here with my sister, in Englewood Cliffs, New
Jersey, and all his kids are here. I don't think he's positive
whether his kids are alive or dead.

I remember three or four months after I started carrying the icepick, one day I forgot it and I got into a jam
with some kid, and I reached for it and I didn't have it.
The only thing I could do was fight with my fists. I didn't
know anything about fighting, all I knew was that I had to
hit this kid as hard as I could as fast as I could. I was
probably more surprised than he was when I realized I
was winning, that he was the one taking the beating. Like
I said, I didn't know anything about fighting and there
wasn't anything fancy about it, I was just fighting as hard
as I could—maybe because I was scared. I didn't care how
many punches he threw, I didn't even figure the worst he
could do would be to kill me. I didn't think about that
until later.

That's how I fought later, even though by then I knew
more about fighting. The first thing you got to do if you
want to be a fighter is to fight. I figured out once that by
the time I got into the amateurs, I'd already had a thou-

sand fights. Some of the kids I grew up with, they were good kids, their fathers were something respectable, these kids went to school and wore clean clothes. With them it was a big deal if they got into a fight. That's no way to learn how to fight. That's the way to make sure you get your block knocked off. The thing is, if you're fighting all the time, besides learning how to do it, you get so a fight doesn't make any difference one way or the other. And the fact of the matter is you get to like fighting. At least I did.

Along with learning how to fight, I also learned how to steal. In fact, about the only things I didn't learn was what they teach you in school. For me and the guys I knew, school was for the birds, the thing was to get the money. The guys who had the big cars and the broads, they weren't the ones going to school nights. They were the ones who started out stealing, then mugging guys or knocking off candystores and maybe doing a little time in reform school and getting a rep with the mob, and finally maybe getting a piece of the action. Provided they didn't get knocked off along the way, of course.

Maybe I'm not giving my family enough credit, especially my mother and sisters. God knows they were after me enough to do better in school and not get into so much trouble all the time. My mother was a good woman, always working hard, never getting much fun out of life. I always felt good that I was able to make it a little easy for her later on. But it wasn't such a big deal in my family, being a model boy. You can see that with my old man giving me an icepick.

Besides being a slum kid with no great education in anything except how to fight and stay alive and steal, I also had this temper. Everybody has a temper, but mine was set on a hair trigger—something would set me off, the temper would go and I just wouldn't give a good goddamn what happened—you could kill me, you could literally kill me, you could blow up the world and I wouldn't give a good goddamn, I'd kill you first. Ever since I can remember, people were nagging me about my temper. I don't know where it came from. And what made it worse was that I had mastoiditis when I was eight, from the cold in the tenements, and one of my ears was bad. I would see a kid talking but I couldn't hear him, and half the time I'd get the idea he was kidding me and I'd belt him. That's also part of the reason I never got past the tenth grade in school, not that I'm making excuses, I was not exactly a scholar anyway.

All this is getting me back to me and Harry Gordon.

Everybody knew that Harry Gordon used to go home carrying a few hundred bucks every night around midnight, and that was very big money in those days, like a couple of thousand now. It sure was enough money for me. I was sick of mugging a guy and finding he had eight bucks on him, or holding up a store and finding the whole take was twelve. I decided that what Harry had, I was going to get. I knew where he lived and I knew how he got home, the route he walked. I knew when he went home— generally late at night—which was all right with me. One bop, I figured, and Harry would go down, and there I'd be with his take for the day. So I got me a foot and a half of lead pipe and a newspaper to roll it up in and about one o'clock one morning I was in the entry of a tenement I knew Harry would pass on his way home. Most people living in tenements don't stay out late at night, especially by themselves. You don't have a lot of coming and going and if you do meet anybody it's not going to be someone who wants to stick around and start up a conversation.

I had a reason for that particular place, too. It was the last one in a long line of tenements, and between it and the corner of the street there was nothing but a vacant lot where there had once been a building that had burned down, and the owners had fenced it off so they couldn't be sued if someone fell into the cellar. There was nothing there but a lot of trash, and a fence about eight feet high and made of boards with a lot of gaps in it where kids had pulled the boards out to start fires or something. When I saw Harry go by I started after him.

I'd never done anything like this before and I was sweating and nervous. I moved as quick and quiet as I could. I looked both ways and there was no one I could see on the street in either direction. There were only a few lights on in the houses, and none of them were near where I was, and they were high up on the fourth or fifth floors.

I never was so nervous before in all my life. I came up behind Harry in the dark between the street lamps so quick and so quiet that he never even had a chance to turn, and I hit him with the pipe over the back of the head and pushed him through one of the gaps in the fence into the vacant lot. But he didn't go down. He was bent over and moaning and I thought I'd hit him hard enough to flatten him, but, no, he started to turn.

And then I got so mad at him because he was still on his feet, I lost my head. I wanted to kill him I was so mad that he was still up, and I began to hit him again and again. And finally he collapsed.

TWO

I was so much in a panic that all I wanted to do was get out of there. I could feel my pulse pounding in my throat. That's why I had hit him so much, I was so crazy with fear. Somebody—anybody—could be looking at me. But now I'd gone this far and I couldn't pull back. I felt inside his coat and I got his wallet and I ran. The minute I got out on the sidewalk I got a little control back. I knew I'd be in real trouble if anybody saw me running. I made myself slow down to a walk and I realized here I was at two o'clock in the morning walking down a street with a guy's wallet in one hand and a pipe wrapped up in a newspaper in the other. How crazy can you get? I put the wallet in my pocket. I saw a sewer opening cut into the curb, and I went over and tossed the pipe and paper down it.

I'll tell you how close I came to getting it. I was still bent over the curb, under a street light, when an auto turned the corner, its headlights picking me up like a searchlight. A police car. For the first time that night I used my head. I had my foot out in front of me and I reached down and pulled my shoelace loose. By the time the cops got there I was bent over retying my shoelace. My heart was pounding so loud I was surprised they couldn't hear it. I was in a cold sweat. I could feel the sweat inside my legs. The cops went by real slow, looking me over hard, but they didn't stop. To my dying day I'll never know why. If I'd been a cop and saw me bending over a sewer, I'd have stopped. And that would have been the end. A stolen wallet in my pocket, and a guy with his head beat in lying less than a hundred yards away, the guy the wallet belonged to. And then they'd search the sewer and find a lead pipe in a newspaper with two things on it, blood and my fingerprints. I figure I would have gotten life and served at least twenty years, provided I didn't get the chair, even if I was only sixteen. Especially with my record.

Anyway, the patrol car went on by, and now what was I going to do? Gordon was dead, that I knew, or dying, and never before in my life had I felt like I did then. I didn't know where to go or what to do. I was lost. For sure I couldn't go home, and I couldn't stay out on the street, equally for sure.

There was one guy I knew. I don't know why, but somehow we got along, we knocked around together, we'd been on a couple of muggings together, and now I had to see him. I had to start getting this curse off me. Pete Petrella was this guy's name. He was a year or so older than me, he'd already even been in on some big jobs. And the mob guys seemed to like him.

I knew where he'd be at this hour of the night—in the back room of the candy store, playing cards with the saps. I mean guys who thought they could play cards with Pete were saps to start with. I hadn't looked in the wallet but it was fat and, what the hell, Harry might even have six or seven hundred bucks if he'd had a big day, or two or three hundred even if it was an ordinary day. You can see what a future I had as a thief. If you're going to make a living holding up bookies, you have to know when their big days are.

I went into the candy store and it looked like any candy store at two o'clock in the morning that keeps open all night. There weren't many people in it, and the ones that were there looked you over pretty close. If they'd seen you before, that was okay, and if they hadn't, they'd know you the next time. I went through to the back, and Pete was in the middle of a hand. The room was like the rooms they have in the back of candystores in the Bronx for guys to play cards in—crummy. It was I don't know how big because it was used as a kind of supply room and it had cardboard cartons of all kinds of stuff stacked up all around the walls. It had a couple of windows that nobody ever saw because the guy who owned it, knowing the kind of neighborhood he was in, had put quarter-inch-thick steel doors over the outside and then, just to make double sure, he stacked the heaviest crates he had on the inside. But the room had a back door that was a way out in case there was trouble, and in case the cops knew about the back door, as they probably did, there was also a place where you could get down into the cellar and get into the building next door. The main thing about the room, though, was a big round table that was set up for cardplaying with a bright light hanging down over it so you could see your cards without any trouble. None of this meant anything to me.

I had this excitement boiling inside me so much that I felt the only way to stop it was to have my head burst, and what I wanted to do was just crack up the hand Pete was playing, but I knew that would blow the whole thing out. Kids who hang around in places like that, they can smell, they got a sense that picks out when something has happened. That's how they get to keep alive. They're sharks, they can smell blood a mile away. I held on till I could get Pete's eye. I guess I said hello to a couple of the guys I knew. I got Pete to look at me and I nodded my head, and after a couple of minutes he threw in and he stood up.

"That's it for me," he told the guys as he came over to me. I think he could see that I was starting to shake. The reaction was setting in. He looked over at the door to the sideroom and we went in there. It was another kind of storage room except that it had no heat. It wasn't cold storage, it was a room with a potbellied stove in the middle set up on some concrete blocks, and in one corner another round table. Pete turned on the light, which was one bulb, and I couldn't keep bottled up anymore.

"I just killed a guy," I told him.

His face changed. God, how his face changed! You know, unless you're a nut or a junkie or something, you come up against it, a guy has been killed, and it's not for kick anymore.

"You goddamned nut," he said, and I could see him getting mad at me. "You goddamned stupid son of a bitch, now whaddaya done?"

"Don't gimme a hard time," I said. I was getting mad,

too, and shaking with fear at the same time. "It was Harry. Harry the book. I figured to stick him up."

Pete got even madder.

"You goddamned crazy guinea!" he said as hard as he could, but low. "Harry! You know he has an okay to work, he has protection, so you decide to knock him off. And on top of all that, Harry's a nice guy. He never gave nobody a bum rap, he don't break your fingers when you come up short. Why Harry?"

I couldn't take this. "Because I gotta bring somethin' home!" I said. "We got nothin' at home! It's cold and we got nothin' to eat! And my old man does nothin' except beat up my old lady! I'm goin' crazy! I got to make a hit!"

Both of us were talking as hard as we could, and keeping our voices down so the guys in the other room couldn't hear. Pete's face was getting red and he was beginning to sweat. I don't know what I looked like, but I was getting so much out of control that I guess Pete could see it. What he was afraid of most was that the guys would hear me. It began to penetrate on him that I was so close to the edge that he'd better stop pushing. And besides, he was always a guy that could use his head a little.

"Okay," he said, "let's see what you got."

I handed him the wallet and he looked in it. And he kept looking. And then, without a word, he held it wide open so I could see. There was no money inside the wallet.

"Slips," Pete said. "Action. Tomorrow's bets. Nothin'. No dough." He threw the wallet in my face and began that quiet shouting again. "You stupid bastard! You kill a guy and whaddaya get? Nothin'!"

He stopped. I guess we both began to figure then there was no sense going on this way. Money or no money I was going to need an alibi when they found Harry. And the longer we stayed in that room the more those guys outside were going to wonder what was up.

"Look," I said, "say whatever ya wanna say and I'll take it. I blew it, I blew it. Now what do I do?"

He began to relax, too. He sat down in one of the chairs and lit a cigarette. He even gave me a smile. "Okay," he said. "You blew it. We go back out there before those wise guys start gettin' too wise. Then I got somethin' goin' on tomorrow night that I'll tell you about."

"What?"

He was still giving me that half-smile of his, and he shook his head. "Tomorrow," he said. "You're too blown up for me to tell you about it tonight. Also, it might not work out."

I would have given him a lot bigger argument about telling me except that he was right about getting back before some of those guys began figuring things out. We went back out and I don't know how long I stayed there, long enough so that there wasn't any talk when I left. Pete was still there, playing cards and winning, when I went home. On the way home at first all I could think of was what a jerk I'd been working Harry over, working him over and all for what, finally? For nothing. And then I got to thinking about Pete. About him and his deal. Why was I being cut in on it? Pete was a great friend and all, but who cuts you in on a deal unless he needs you for something?

Later I found out that Pete got me in on the deal because the job needed three men, though at first Pete and another guy named Salvy were going to try to swing it themselves. Later I also found out it was the first big job either of them had been on, too—the first real job for any one of the three of us. The first job that somebody had really planned out in advance and done some figuring on, as compared to just mugging a drunk, or, like me, hitting a book and then getting nothing for it. This job had been planned by the mob, and Pete and Salvy were trying to get into the mob. This was a kind of tryout for them.

The next day started out great for me. I got out of the sack about eleven—you got nothing to do, there's not much point to getting up at seven—and I went down to the corner store and got a paper and went through it. It was there, all right. Not a big item, but there.

Harry Gordon, forty-five, with a record of bookmaking arrests, was found beaten to death in an alley off Brook Avenue in the Bronx at four o'clock this morning by Theodore Dreizer, a milkman, who cuts through the alley daily on his route. In his breast pocket, overlooked by the thieves, police found $1,700 in cash.

Have you ever been belted, hard, right in the throat? It paralyzes you. You can't do anything, even breathe. That was me, standing there in that little store.

I don't know whether I'd slept a wink all the night before. I guess I must have because suddenly I'd be sitting up in bed, wide awake, sweating. Then after a while I'd lie back down again and try to think of something, anything, that would make me forget clubbing Harry Gordon. I'd try to dream about me being a big shot, having plenty of dough, plenty of broads and a big Cadillac, living in a big apartment and going down to Miami for the winter, and giving the old lady a nice big house with all the fixings for her own, and—but the dream wouldn't work. I'd think about Harry Gordon and I'd know that somehow I'd pay for that. I never went to church, the priests couldn't scare me with all that crap about hell, but somehow I knew, inside of me somehow I knew that I'd pay for it. Sometime, just when everything was going right and the whole world was perfect, I knew that that would be the time it would blow up right in my face and I'd have nothing left. I'd be on top of the world one day, the next I'd be a bum flat on my ass. That's what I knew that night.

And now this. After all that, all through the night, going through hell, listening to my own heart pounding so it seemed it would shake the whole house, now I found it was worse than being all for nothing. It would have been bad enough if I'd had seventeen hundred bucks in my kick, but I'd been that close to it and I'd blown it.

I didn't know whether to drive my fist through the side of the wall or go back and jump off a roof.

What I did do was go over to the store, where I knew Pete would be. He was in the back, teasing a little broad named Viola who worked for her old man. Pete was always a great hand for teasing broads, and all the rest of it. He's the kind they go for. One thing, he's never too serious about them. He kids along with them and then he makes a move, and if that goes over, or if he doesn't get slugged for it, he goes on to the next move and so on. My trouble was that I really didn't know how to sort of kid along. I only had one thing on my mind and that was it.

Right now I wanted to talk to Pete and I didn't want any broad around no matter how good a figure she had. This one had a good figure even for a little broad, good legs. "You, beat it!" I told her.

She looked at me, then back at Pete to see what he'd say, I guess, and then back at me. "With you around, it's a pleasure," she said, lifting up her head and stepping out of the room.

Pete watched her ass, grinning, and even after she went out the door he stood looking after her and finally, when I was sitting down at the table, he turned around and nodded at me, still grinning. A great guy for grinning, Pete. I didn't say anything. I just pulled the paper out of my pocket and pointed to the item. He looked at maybe the first three lines and the grin went away. He put down the paper and sat down across from me and shook his head. "I been thinkin', Jake," he said. "You know, he wasn't a bad guy, Harry. Whenever I was really hard up for a buck, he never let me down." I could feel the muscle in my jaw jumping and I banged my fist down on the table, but Pete kept right on going. "How do you feel, Jake?" he asked. "I mean, inside yourself, knowin' you killed a guy?"

That was all I needed, this kind of talk at a time like this from a guy who was my pal. For a second I felt like murdering him. "I don't give a goddamn!" I yelled-whispered. "I had to make a score, it was him or me so it was him. I don't give a goddamn!"

Pete didn't say anything at all, and I could feel my heart pounding. "Okay," I said, letting my breath come out. "I had one helluva night. I don't know how I feel. I feel funny. I feel"—I took a breath—"like something's going to get me. I don't mean now, today. I mean something's going to get me, someday, someplace . . ." I waited a minute. "I think I'm gettin' afraid," I said. "I never been afraid before."

I looked at Pete and he looked away from me like he didn't want to look at me. He lit a cigarette, and after a while he picked up the paper again and started reading the item again, and this time he read it through. I could hear him whistle a little under his breath. "I missed this the first time," he kind of half-whispered. "Seventeen hundred bucks. Jesus Christ. It didn't register before. Seventeen hundred bucks. What a ball we could have had with that!" His voice began to pick up a little and I could see a little of that grin begin to come back. "Why, you bum!" he said. "Couldn't even frisk a sucker right, just like a goddamned amateur."

I began to get mad at him again. "How long could I hang around that alley after croakin' a guy?" I snarled at him. "I was hittin' him, two, three minutes. For all I knew somebody's lookin' out a window right at me. When I got the wallet it was so thick I thought that's where he kept his money anyway."

"Didn't have the time?" By now Pete was really grinning. "Baloney! If you got time to follow a guy, set him up, chill him, you got time to frisk him. Right?"

I figured now he was trying to kid me out of the way I felt, and I began to get madder at him. "Whadda *you* so big about?" I snarled at him. "You so goddamned bright you never made a mistake in your whole life?"

"Not like that," Pete said.

"Oh, balls, for Christsake!"

"And what's more," Pete went on, "you better start gettin' smart fast because you ain't goin' to make but one mistake like that if you go out on jobs with me. The guys I'm workin' for, they don't think things like that are a bit funny. There's nothin' a hood likes less than bein' laughed at."

I began to cool down a little.

"We'll see tonight," he said. "I'll be there just to make sure that you don't goof it up again. And no more of this afraid stuff. . . . Once we move in, there's no turnin' yellow, no backin' out."

I grabbed hold of his arm, hard. "You wise son of a bitch," I said, "you try this yellow bit again and I'll break your arm! I'll show you how I back out. Now, what's it about?"

He told me.

It was easy. Just stick up a dice game. Very easy. You know the guys who run dice games? They have a thing about giving their money to heist guys. And while we were at it we were supposed to "take care of"—meaning rough up—Curly, the guy who ran the crap games and was the owner of the poolroom where the crap game was going on.

So we arranged to meet that night at the candy store. It was as good a place to meet as any, and better than most. A lot of the teenage kids hung out there, it was basically not a tough place, though not all of the kids who showed up there were what you'd call angels. I don't know why I talk about them as if they were so much younger than me and Pete—hell, some of them were probably older—but they were still going to school and after they got through drinking Cokes at the store and listening to the records on the jukebox, they'd be off home. Their idea of a big night was to stay out till two in the morning.

When I got to the store, Pete was there outside, walking up and down, smoking a cigarette and waiting. And wasn't a bit nervous. That's why he was taking a drag on the cigarette about every seven seconds, and flicking off the ash every time he took a drag.

"I'm here," I said to him as I walked up. He didn't say anything, just looked at me. We looked at the store. The soda fountain along the right-hand wall was two and three deep with kids, and the booths on the left toward the back held six kids where there were supposed to be four, and in the open space to the front a couple were doing a real fancy version of the lindy while the other kids were clapping. And both of the jukeboxes were on, full blast.

Pete and I walked in and there was this dim-witted broad who got me into the right mood for the evening. I wanted to belt her silly. We're walking to the back, minding our own business and being polite sliding past people, and she's in this booth with three other dames, one of them being this Viola kid. As we're coming up to their booth, this other broad slides out into the aisle so that she's blocking it. She's stacked, and she knows it. She's got her chest up high, and as Pete moves to one side to get past, she moves over to block him. He moves back and so does she. Even Pete isn't impressed with her at a time like this. He's edgy enough as it is without playing games.

"Look, would you mind?" he asked.

She was going for the title of Miss Teenage Wiseass. To this day I haven't figured out what the hell she thought she was doing.

"Mind what, Mr. Big Shot?" she asked, jiggling her hips and looking at her fingernails—too many Mae West movies.

I was too edgy for it, too. I snarled something and reached over Pete's shoulder to belt her one but he caught my arm. From where I was I could see Viola, and she was watching all this with a smile on her face. I didn't dig her, either, but by now Pete had decided to play it his way.

He grinned. "Okay, sugar," he said, cupping his hands and bringing them up to her breasts. She gave a little squeal and started back and took one look at his face and saw that he wasn't fooling. In a flash she covered her breasts with her forearms and made a dash back into the booth. All of a sudden all the broads in the booth were staring at us as if we were something out of a zoo. Viola, too. She wasn't smiling now. Pete, still with that cold smile, started up again toward the back room, and as I passed the broad pushing back into the booth her rump was sticking up and I couldn't resist it. I slapped it as hard as I could. She squealed, and there was a big laugh from the booth. Four stupid broads if I ever saw them.

We got into the inner back room and Pete flicked on the light. There was nobody else there. Just me and Pete.

"Where's Salvy?" I asked.

Pete smiled. "He ain't here."

"I can see that. Where is he?"

"Someplace else. Waitin' for us."

"Then why ain't we there. What are we doin' here?"

Pete's smile widened. "I want you to meet a couple of friends," he says.

He went over to the potbellied stove and patted it on the belly. The stove was standing on a big steel plate laid across four cement-foundation construction blocks. Pete tipped the stove off and slid the plate away, and inside one of the holes of one of the cement blocks were three .38 pistols and three boxes of ammunition. I looked at them, fascinated. I'd never been next to a real loaded gun before and I began to get this strange feeling. All you had to do was look at those guns—and I kept staring at them all the time Pete was loading them—to know you had power in your hands. With one of those, if you told a guy to do something, he'd do it. Pete handed me one and I kept looking at it till he said, "Okay, okay, let's go. Give me a hand." I stuck the gun in my belt the way he did and we put the plate back and put the stove on top of it. Then he went over to the closet next to the refrigerator and showed me two very dark blue summer jackets that were on hangers to keep their press, and two pairs of dark glasses and two black slouch hats.

I was beginning to grin with excitement—me, the poker-face who never grinned at anything. We took the coats and hats and Pete said, "Okay, out the back way"— and out we went.

We took a cab to the garage, one of those big double-door taxpayer commercial garages that you can still see out in places like the upper Bronx or Brooklyn or Queens. We stopped a half block away and Pete paid off the hackie with a couple of bills, and from the tone of the thanks he got, I guess he was starting out to build his reputation as a big spender. The cab pulled away and we walked down the sidewalk toward the garage, then Salvy stepped out of a doorway. He had this nervous grin on his face, and Pete threw his head up in a question.

"We're set," Salvy says. "A nice new black LaSalle."

Both the big double doors of the garage were open, and under the night lights inside you could see these double rows of parked cars, and we walked down toward the end and got into this sleek car and heard the night attendant's voice: "That you, fellers? Now, don't forget. Don't let me down, fellers. Have it back here before seven, and no holes in it."

Salvy yelled back at him, "You know you don't have to worry with us, Terry. We never let a pal down."

"Okay, just don't get me in the middle."

Salvy started the engine and gunned it, and we rolled out of the garage. We were on our way.

THREE

Finally we turned into a long street with five- and six-story commercial buildings. The street was dark except for the street lights every eighty yards or so, and Salvy cut the LaSalle lights to the dimmers and after a while we slid past this long five-story brick building with signs on the ground floor so faded you couldn't read them. The ground-floor windows all had steel shutters on them. On the second floor the word BILLIARDS was spelled out in big letters, one letter on each window. At one end, there was dim light behind three of the windows. The upper floors of the building were completely dark. Salvy stopped the car and shut off the lights. He and Pete, who was in the front seat with him, sat there a couple of minutes, looking up and down the street, and especially at as many windows as they could see. Finally Pete said, "Looks clean to me."

"Yeah," Salvy said.

Pete got out the front and I got out the back. We were carrying the jackets and hats. Salvy was slumped down under the steering wheel.

"Let's go," Pete said, and we started walking toward the entrance to the billiard-parlor stairs of the building, not too fast but not slow either, and looking around as much as we could without making a production of it.

We got inside and there was a wide stairway curving up to the second floor. We put on the jacket and the hat and the dark glasses, then we went up the stairs and down the hallway and came to the door with the words CURLY'S BIL-LIARD PARLOR painted on it. The door was steel. We listened, and through the door we could hear voices:

"Okay, your dice."

"I'm shooting a hundred."

"You're faded."

"Four . . . four's the number."

"A thousand to five hundred."

"It's a bet."

"Anybody else?"

"Four hundred to two."

"You got it."

"All right, comin' out!"

Pete turned and grinned at me. "Sounds like one hell of a game," he said. He reached and took out his two guns, one from his belt, one from his hip pocket. "Ready?" he asked.

I got my gun out and nodded. He rapped on the door what sounded like a code—two, three, then two. We both crouched down. A voice behind the door said, "Yeah?"

"I'm a friend of Fats," Pete said, as cool as he could, his face tense. "I'm here to see Curly."

"Sorry," said the voice, "he's not here."

Pete looked at me. Then he said to the door, "How about letting us in anyway? We want to roll a few."

"Nope," said the voice, "no good. No strangers in here. Besides, it's almost over."

"So then what's the difference?" Pete asked. "For cryin' out loud, I'm here already. C'mon, lemme in."

"I said no good!" said the voice, real hard. "Now beat it!"

We could hear footsteps walking away.

Pete started to put his gun away. "We better blow," he whispered.

I couldn't believe him. I began to boil. "Blow?" I whispered back hard. "Are you crazy? Did you hear how much cash they're playin' around with in there?"

Pete whispered, "I'm not supposed to move in if Curly isn't there. That's the contract—"

I cut in on him. I'd be damned if I was going to blow two in a row, not with dough like this thirty feet away from me. "Contract?" I whispered, "the hell with the goddamned contract! What the hell do I care about Curly and the goddamned contract?" I reached over and took one of the guns away from him. "I'm staying here till they open up," I said. "The only contract I got is with me! The other, that's your problem!"

Pete was staring at me. He let me take the gun and he didn't say anything.

"You wanna go?" I asked him. "You go! Me, I'm staying right here till they open up this door. Then I'm gonna get that dough no matter what!"

Pete stayed.

I began to get that feeling again, like with Harry Gordon. I was going to get that dough, I didn't care what. Like I said, it boils up inside you. I forget now exactly what time of year this was except it wasn't winter, there wasn't snow on the ground, but inside that building it felt like it was the height of summer. We couldn't be careless. We couldn't get too far away from that door, but we couldn't sit right outside it all the time, either. For example, suppose some guy came along to go upstairs to one of the offices on the upper floors? Unlikely at this time of night, but there was no law against it, and that's what you think about at a time like that—what might happen. And every time you hear a click or a noise you jump at it. Suppose some guy came along who knew all about the game, what would he think if he saw a couple of punk kids with blue coats and black hats and dark glasses hanging around right outside?

God knows how long we waited. Thinking back now, it couldn't have been as much as an hour. I don't know what eternity is but it must be pacing around listening to sounds and keeping your eye on a way out and waiting and waiting and waiting, and lighting a cigarette for a couple of puffs and throwing it down and stepping on it and then cursing yourself for being a fool because you need a cigarette and digging out another one and smoking only a couple of puffs of that.

The sweat was pouring off me and the palms of my hands were so wet I began to think I couldn't hold a gun. I kept wiping them off on my pants. And all the time the tension was building in me. I was getting jumpier by the minute, I was getting madder and madder and hotter and hotter, it was the Gordon thing all over again. I was getting so sore at these guys for holding us up from robbing them I began to think about just plain shooting our way in through the steel door. Then we heard the kind of talk that means they're breaking off.

"Christ, he hit it!"

"Horseshit luck if I ever saw it."

"That's me for the night. The hell with it!"

"Hey, wait, fellers, don't break it up now!"

"Great for you, you got all the dough, I gotta get on the hustle again."

"I'm blowin'. Not enough action left."

"Okay, okay, okay."

Now I was on trigger balance. I got out the guns. I was balanced on the balls of my feet. I could barely wait for the door to open, I had so much saliva I had to keep swallowing, and even then I had so much I had to wipe my mouth with the back of my hand. I looked at Pete and all of a sudden he looked worried more than anything else.

We could hear all these guys yattering coming closer to the door, and it opened, and suddenly I couldn't hold myself anymore, I was in the middle of them with two guns in my hands. If they'd been fast enough, a couple of them, they might have taken me, but they weren't and I was yelling at them, "Freeze, freeze, you sons of bitches, I said freeze. Don't move one little bit, the first guy moves I shoot. That's nice. Now turn around." My heart was pumping, and like the diceplayer said, it was plain horseshit luck that ever got us through this, because trying to hold up fifteen or twenty guys, especially diceplayers, is crazy, because there can be a couple of tough guys among them or a couple of guys who know what to do. I knew this, and I was getting frightened and mad and vicious all at the same time, and I was yelling, "Back in, now, right back in where you came from! Turn around, I said, turn around!"

They started back but a couple of them kept sort of half-turning back to look at me and I couldn't stand it. I hit them across their heads with the gun as hard as I could and they went down. I kept yelling, "You believe me now? Now you believe me? Any other wise guy want a busted head? In the back, in the back, in the fuckin' back!"

All of a sudden they broke and rushed for it, into the back room, stumbling and bumping into one another and trying to get away from this madman with the gun.

That's what it's about, a gun. With a gun, you're the man.

Pete was beside me but wasn't saying a word. I looked at him and I couldn't even guess what he was thinking. His face was set and he was sweating and not looking at me.

Some of these guys were looking back at me and I screamed, "You, what you lookin' at, turn around, turn around, everybody face the wall!" By now I was screaming as loud as I could. "Everybody face that stinkin' wall!" Then I screamed, "Everybody down on his knees, you mothers, down on your fuckin' mother knees!" As one man they fell down on their knees.

Pete was beside me, and now I know because he told me afterward that I was screaming so you could hear me clear down in the street. He put his hand on my arm to get me quieted down, and I snarled at him, "Yellow, huh? Okay, wise guy, you watch me." I yelled at the guys who were kneeling down, "Okay, move, take a chance, go ahead, turn around, rush me," but they didn't move, and I turned back to Pete and said, "You're the guy who knows how to get everything. You won't miss anything in the breast pocket, right? Okay, you clean 'em. Clean 'em good so we don't read in the paper tomorrow morning about how much the guy had stashed away, okay? Go ahead, clean 'em good, they're all yours."

I was beginning to feel better and tenser at the same time. It was like I was balanced on the edge of a razor blade. I was walking back and forth behind these guys watching them while Pete went down the line back of them with the hat, cleaning them out. Then I see this fat guy after Pete goes by taking a real good fast, hard look and I jump over and slap him hard across the head with the gun barrel "You wanna see what we look like, is that right? You wanna finger us later. I'll fix you."

Pete came back and without saying a word pushed me away hard. I could see he was mad at me again. His lips were tight and he was saying something under his breath. I didn't know what it was but I could guess—probably

something like, "You nutty stupid bastard." But I knew he
was worried that I'd get carried away like with Harry Gordon. But it wouldn't be that way this time, because I could
see we were getting the loot, so I said to him, "Okay, finish what you're doing, all I wanted to do was belt the guy
down, he was looking at you. If I wanted to chill him I'da
done something more than hit him across the head." The
fat guy was on all fours, not just kneeling, but you could
see he wasn't really hurt.

"You gotta hit 'em first," I said to Pete real loud so all
of those guys could hear. "You gotta hit 'em hard."

Pete pushed me away again and brought his finger
across his throat. Then he went back down the line, and
when he came back the hat was full of dough and rings
and watches and stickpins. He gave me a nod and whispered, "We don't got all night, if they got anything more
it's hid away so we'll have to strip them to find it, let's
blow this place."

With the getaway so close, I suddenly got a brainstorm.
I figured I'd show the mob boys they weren't dealing with
a couple of fairies in me and Pete, so I yelled, "Okay, now
I want Curly. Who's Curly? Don't gimme any crap now, I
want Curly."

I don't know whether it was good or bad, but there
was a couple of the mob guys there, taking this all in,
which Pete and me didn't find out about it till a little while
afterward because even Pete didn't know it at the time.

"Okay, where's Curly? C'mon, you crumbs, which one
is Curly?"

Of course, none of them said a word. Who the hell
would with a maniac teenager behind him with two guns?
I was getting madder, and I ran up behind another one of
these fat guys and snatched off his hat. He was nearly
bald, but that gave me an idea, so I shouted, "Okay, if you
won't talk, off with the hats, everybody off with the hats
before you get a permanent crease."

It shakes me now, today, suppose one of those guys had
a gun? Sure, Pete had shaken them down, but he hadn't
gone over them inch by inch. If one of those guys had a
gun he hadn't been able to get to earlier, all he would have

wanted was a chance to reach up and take his hat off. But that's how it goes. None of them had a gun, but two of them had curly hair, so I put my gun in the back of their necks.

"Okay, you guys, on your feet."

Christ, were they scared. The guy closest to me turned to me and started pleading. "Please," he said, "please, look, I'm not Curly, I'm not Curly. I admit I got curly hair but nobody calls me Curly, I'm not the Curly you want!"

The other guy was practically in shock and was screaming, "Me, too, I'm not Curly. I'm not the Curly you want. . . ."

And all of a sudden I blew my stack again. I didn't know whether these guys were lying. I didn't know what it was. I didn't even know why the hell we should be looking for Curly so hard, or what difference it made, and I started belting those guys from the back and they fell over, and then Pete came up to me again and said, "Knock it off, you stupid son of a bitch. We gotta get outta here."

I kept saying we had to find Curly, and he said the hell with it, and then my eye fell on the toilet door. So I figured that was where we'd put these jokers. That was something that Pete hadn't thought about, and he was supposed to be the brains of this operation. Some brains. These guys shooting craps weren't exactly your friendly neighborhood ribbon clerks. There were at least two windows that I could see that opened onto a fire escape and all Pete and I had to do was go out the front door of this joint and about six of these guys would be going out the back, picking up fire axes as they went.

"Okay, all of you guys!" I screamed. "On your feet! on your feet! In the john! All of you, and drag these slobs along! Move! Move! Move!"

They moved. I think back on it now, I must have been outta my mind. You know, you got that many guys, about three of them start thinking the same way at the same time and Pete and I are dead. But like I said, who wants to get shot first? And they began to act like it was a relief. They piled into the john like it was a way station to paradise. I kept shoving them in, and finally I nodded to Pete. They

were all in, and there was this big ice box where they kept
soda and beer cool, and Pete and I just barely tipped it
over and slid it up against the door. I could hear all the
talk and muttering and growling inside, and I yelled,
"We're still here and we're gonna stay here five minutes!
Now everybody shut up. In five minutes we break outta
here!"

I didn't figure that was going to fool them for much
more than a minute, so when Pete and I got as far as the
door I reached over and got a folding chair that was standing there and threw it against the ice box just to make a
noise before Pete and I charged out and down the stairs
and into the back seat of the LaSalle and Salvy took off
like he was qualifying for Indianapolis.

"Okay, awright, already," I yell at him, "you wanna get
us pinched for speeding? Slow down, goddamn it, slow
down!"

Goddamned fool. Three o'clock in the morning and we
were going down side streets in the Bronx like it was fire
time. Actually, as God is my judge, we almost got hung up
with a patrol car on the way back, and I got to admit that
it was Pete who cooled it. We heard the siren and Salvy
reacted out of sheer nerves and the car leaped ahead. Pete
leaned over into the front seat and said, "You stupid bastard, that ain't for us!" And he slapped him over the side
of the face as hard as he could. "If that's the way you're
gonna drive why don't you stick to holdin' up candy stores?
Take it easy and turn off quiet onto the first lighted street.
Where lights are, get it, no dark streets."

Then Pete looked at me and saw that I was beginning to
hit the panic button, that I was on the edge of the seat
with the gun in my hand waiting for them to come alongside. "Take it easy," Pete said. "Take it easy, buddy, relax. . . ."

I snarled at him, "Nothing is going to screw up this
deal, see, nothing, nothing!"

Pete grabbed my wrist with both hands, pointing the
gun down at the floor, and said, "Let go, you maniac, let
go!"

All of a sudden the sound of the siren began to fade and

we relaxed. Pete flopped back against the side of the car
and let his breath out so you could hear it.

"Two maniacs," he said. "The first big job and I get
stuck with two maniacs. A driver so nervous he can't steer
and a buddy so crazy he's going to fight it out with the
New York City Police Department." Suddenly he asked
me, "You ever even shot a gun?"

I shook my head, feeling silly.

"So you're goin' to start with a shoot-out with the cops.
Nothing like startin' at the top."

I looked at the hatful of loot that he'd put on the floor
when we got into the car. "Let's just hope we don't read in
the paper tomorrow about how we missed another seventeen hundred bucks," I said—like a dummy, it turned out,
because Salvy asked, "What seventeen hundred bucks?"

Pete said, "A gag. We was pricin' a car and the guy
wanted seventeen hundred bucks. Why don't you watch
the drivin'?"

"Where to?"

"Around behind the candy store. Then you can take this
heap back."

Salvy kind of chuckled. "You find Curly?"

I could hear the suspicion in Pete's voice. "Jake found a
couple of Curlys," he said. "Why?"

"You deal 'em?" he asked.

I remembered that Salvy was always the wise guy hanging around trying to get in with the mob.

"Jake dealt 'em," Pete said. "Why?"

"I didn't want to tell you before," Salvy says, "but there
were a couple of the boys there tonight to see the come-
off."

Pete looked at me and I looked at him. I remembered a
couple of the guys there who I guessed came from the
mob. And the look I saw in Pete's eyes—he was so ready
to tear up Salvy that if Pete had been me, Salvy would
have been lucky to get out of that car alive. But Pete
didn't even say anything. That's the kind of guy he was.
Except if I was Salvy, I wouldn't want Pete looking at my
back that way.

Finally, we wheeled in behind the candy store, which by

now was pretty dead, and we went into the back room, and then came the real good part of the day. The fear and tenseness were gone, now we could relax. Pete sat down at the table and divided the money into three piles. Over two thousand bucks apiece we got. Two thousand dollars! I couldn't believe it. Two thousand bucks in my own hands. The rings and watches and jewelry Pete put in his coat.

"We go through this tomorrow," he said. "Anything with name or identification on it, we ditch. It ain't worth the risk. The rest of it, I got a pal goin' to St. Louis next week, he'll get rid of it for us." He waited a couple of seconds. "Unless you two masterminds got any better ideas?"

Salvy and I both shook our heads.

"Then that's it for the day, kids," Pete says, "except for one little detail, Jake. I'll take them pieces back."

I got the guns out from my waistband and kissed them. Then I handed them back.

"Sure thing, kid," I said.

Salvy picked up his dough and stuffed it in his pockets. Then he gave us both a big grin. "I got someone waitin' that I'm gonna spend a little o' this on," he said, "and if she ain't there I'll take the next one. See ya around." He opened the back door, looked out, waved his hand back at us and disappeared, closing the door behind him.

Pete and I went through the stove bit, getting the guns back down into the hollow core of one of the concrete blocks, then we sat down.

"I don't like him," I told Pete.

"Who?"

"Salvy."

Pete looked at me, surprised, and laughed. "Forget it," he said. "Nobody's askin' you to marry him. What brought that on?"

"I just decided I don't like him."

"All right, don't like him. He's got his way and you got yours." He looked at me and shook his head. "And what a way," he said, with a grin.

"Knock it off," I told him.

He stood up all of a sudden. "I'm thirsty," he said. "I'm

going out in the store and get somethin'. You want somethin' to drink?"

"Yeah," I says. "Coke. Soda water. Anything."

It was right there that the night went from pure delight to sheer hell. Pete opened the door and past him I could see the store. Like I said, it was mostly empty and most of the lights were out. There was the night man behind the counter and four, five of those stay-up-all-night-type kids. Then the front door opened and in came these two guys.

You can never miss them, not where I come from—the neat, cheap dark suits and the white shirts and the dark ties, the snap-brim hats and the black raincoats. Cops. Detectives, both in their late thirties, maybe first grade. And wise guys, of course.

"Anybody happen to know where Jakey and Petey are this lovely night?" one of them asked the store at large.

The night guy just shrugged and Pete shut the door, quick and quiet. He picked up the dough and the rest of the loot and dumped it into the old stove. I pushed him back.

"Whaddaya think you're doin'?" he whispered.

I whispered right back at him, "Gedouta the way! They ain't gonna get me without no trouble."

I thought he was gonna scream at me. His whisper could pierce your eardrums.

"You goddamn nut!" he said. "You crazy or something?" All of a sudden his whole mood changed. He took my arm and gave me the soft-soap bit. "Listen, Jake," he said very softly. "C'mon, don't be silly, we can talk our way out of it."

I didn't pay the slightest bit of attention to him. "Get away from that stove," I said, "I want them guns. If it's for Harry Gordon, if it's for that murder, I'm dead."

He shook his head. "It can't be for that," he whispered. "You heard them. They asked for me, too."

I thought it over. Maybe he was right. God knows he and I had done enough jobs so that the cops could be after us for any one of ten things. Maybe I had a piece of good luck that night. If I'd been a little older and more experienced I'd have figured, once the cops haul you in, with a delinquency record like mine, they question you about every crime except did you kill Judge Crater, and I might have got the guns anyway, and that might have been the end of that. Or Pete and I might have got into a fight and the cops would have charged in and it would have taken them about thirty seconds to decide to go through that old stove.

Anyhow, finally I nodded and Pete smiled. "Okay," he said, taking me by the arm and leading me to the door, "now let's go out there smilin'. And keep that goddamned temper of yours under control no matter what they say. Remember they're cops and that makes them automatically right. And *think* before you say anything, before you answer anything. . . ."

I nodded again. "Okay," I said. "I just hope you're right."

We went out the door and started down to the front and I saw the two cops look at us and then turn and look at the kids.

"Never heard of these guys, huh? No idea where they might be, huh? Jerks! Gutter rats, all o' yuh!"

The kids just shrugged and looked away, and suddenly I began to feel good. Now I was smiling, the way Pete wanted, but it was a real smile. I was almost laughing at the way these kids were showing what they thought of the cops, and I walked up to the cops pretty cocky.

"You dicks lookin' for us?"

The first cop looked at me pretty cold. He looked as if he might be tough, and he sighed and nodded. "Yeah, tough guy," he said. "We'd like to have a little talk with you down at the precinct house."

I put on the innocent surprised bit. "Me?" I asked. "What would you want me for?"

Pete thinks I bring trouble on myself by that way of acting. You know, getting a cop even sourer than he is by playing the wiseguy bit.

The second detective looked just as tough as the first. "Can the chatter," he told me in a flat, hard voice. "We'll do all the talking and we'll do it down at the precinct house. Let's go."

I turned to the kids.

"Hey, guys," I said. "Haven't Pete and I been here all night? And as far as that goes, wasn't we here all last night, too?"

The kids looked at me and nodded, then they looked at the cops and turned away again.

The cops looked at each other and shook their heads.

The first one said, "Like I said, jerks. Every one of 'em. Christ, whaddaya do?" And he turned to me and Pete and said, "Okay, you two, on out. Go on, make a run for it, there's nothing I'd like more than a chance to put one in your head."

I began to get sore. Who were these guys anyway—just because they had guns legal I'm supposed to get one in the head, and without thinking, I did the very thing Pete had told me not to do. I said, "What kind of shit is this?"

The cop didn't look one little bit unhappy. "What's that?" he asked.

I was getting madder, so I said it again, louder.

The cop laughed a little. "You got a complaint?" he asked. "Make it."

I admit now that I'm over forty that taking on one cop is stupid enough, much less two, but I started shuffling in on them, fists ready and down low, and they waited till I was close enough so that I started my move, and one of them sidestepped, and as I went for him the other stepped in and I got a fist at the back of the neck as hard as he could throw it and I went staggering out the door and onto the sidewalk, sprawling on all fours. The next thing, Pete was out the door and on top of me so that neither one of us could get up. He had started to move in but these two cops knew better than to give us a chance to start anything, especially with those other kids there in the candy store—if anything started, they'd be outnumbered right from the start, and it doesn't look good on a cop's record that he was jumped by a half-a-dozen teenagers. So out came Pete on top of me and by the time we got untangled and started on our feet again both the cops were outside the store, one on each side of the door, and they had their guns out. That chilled it. Nothing could be started without a lot of bloodshed.

The first dick said, smiling again, "Now do we go to the precinct or are there more games to play?"

I looked at Pete and he didn't even move.

For all the tough stuff I got more and more worried in the drive to the precinct house. There's one advantage the cop always has over you. Leaving aside his gun, it's the *big* advantage the cop has over you. He knows what's coming. You don't. As far as you're concerned, it could be anything. I was pretty sure it wasn't the dice-game thing. It was too quick. And Pete said it wasn't the Harry Gordon thing. But of course he could have been saying that just to keep me from blowing off again. It could have been anything.

The precinct house was like all precinct houses—old, run-down, with the smell of linseed oil they treat the floors with, and stale vomit where some old drunk had thrown up. And there's that strange feeling like it's deserted, except that there's life there somewhere, always behind the closed doors, and plenty of lights on inside the desk room, but nobody there. Empty. Off in the distance, behind a closed door, was the clatter of a teletype machine, every now and then the ring of a telephone and the sound of someone talking. Then the desk sergeant came in and Pete and I got tied up again with the machinery of the law.

Nearly the first thing they do is run a lineup—me and Pete and a couple of bums they dredged out of the drunk tank, and one guy who looked as if he had a regular job, which meant that he was probably another cop.

The way they run a lineup, with the bright lights on you from the top and front and sides, it's almost impossible to see anything in front of you. And I still say lineups like that are a phony because what do you have—a couple of teenage kids, a cop and a couple of middle-aged drunks— how can you get an identification out of that? But, anyway, as I was saying, even with all that light blazing at me I finally could make out our two friends the dicks sitting out in front, and a couple of other guys without coats on, which meant they were cops, since the temperature in police stations is always about ninety degrees, and then a couple of other people, a man and a woman. And after a while the woman raised her hand and pointed at me.

"That's him," she said, and the cops leaned over to her and said something. Then she said, "Yes, it's him, I'm sure of it, I'll swear to it."

And the man went along with her.

The cop pointed to Pete and said something to her, and I heard her say, "No, I'm only sure of that one. I only think there was one anyway."

So they had me. They threw Pete out into the night and took me in for booking.

FOUR

I was so relieved when they got to the booking I almost broke out laughing. I'd almost forgotten about it myself. It wasn't the Harry Gordon thing. It wasn't the crap game. A week or ten days before I'd decided to take a crack at a friendly neighborhood jewelry store because I'd happened to look down on it from the top floor of a tenement and I'd seen this open skylight. So I waited till I got a good dark night, and I got up on the roof and spent about five minutes taking out a pane of glass with a knife so there wouldn't be any sound of breaking glass, and the minute I reached in to open the window—what happened? I hit a burglar alarm. You could hear the goddamned thing from the roof clean out to Montauk. I nearly broke my ass getting down off that roof and I plowed out of that alley as fast as I could go and ran into this couple coming along the sidewalk. And they're the couple that identified me.

I was arraigned the next day and Pete got up the bail for me, and when I got out of the Bronx detention prison I was so happy that I was practically skipping. Pete was waiting for me with a cab, and as I came down the stairs to the sidewalk, beaming all over, he had this sour look on his puss.

"What the Christ are you so happy about?" he said. "What license you got to be lookin' like little merry sunshine?"

I had it figured out. I was so happy I could have kissed him. "Look." I said, "it's the greatest thing that could have happened to me." I happened to notice that at this moment the cabdriver, little mister big ears like most New York hackies, was all but falling out of the cab trying to hear, so I pulled Pete a little way off. "You know what they identified me for?" He shook his head. "Remember the jewelry store I told you I tried to knock off, and I set the burglar alarm going?" He nodded. "So that's what they got me for," I told him, punching him in the arm. "Now you get it?"

"I got the idea that with your record this could send you away for a while," he said sourly. "What's so great about going to the can?"

"That's just it," I said. "Don't you see? This is my first rap. And what is it? At the very most, attempted burglary. And if I'm convicted, what is it at most? Three or four months."

"That's good?" Pete asks.

"You still don't get it. When I come out, the heats off. The crap game, the Harry Gordon bit."

Pete wouldn't go along. He just shook his head again.

"The crap-game thing, the cops ain't the ones you got to worry about," he said. "And the murder thing, nobody knows anything about that except you and me. And I wouldn't have known if you hadn't told me. So how can anyone tie you up with that? I just don't get it, what you're so happy about."

I wouldn't let him get me down.

"Believe me," I said, steering him to the cab, "I got this all figured out."

For the third time he shook his head. "What you got," he said, "is a very peculiar way of looking at things. I personally think that on this you're out of your goddamned mind."

Well, maybe he was right. I don't know. It wouldn't have made any difference anyway how I felt about it, I was being sent away whether I liked it or not. But I think what made me feel so good was that I wasn't getting away completely with what I had done to Harry Gordon. That was eating at me, and I figured that maybe this evened up the score a little. It shows you how much I knew in those days.

Apart from the Harry Gordon thing, let's face it, I had it coming for a lot of other jobs I'd pulled. I remember one of them that was really funny, it was like a scene from

one of those spoof cops-and-robbers movies that come out
every so often.

It happened a few months before I got sent up. Pete and
me knew this guy whose father was a mover and owned
this tremendous moving van. Well, the mover's son, Cliff,
was a bitch. He had larceny in every inch of his soul. He
lived only to steal—it had to be psychological with him.
He was always coming around with the moving van, and
always when we least expected him. Sometimes, around
four or five in the morning, just for kicks, we would hit a
lot of grocery stores and delicatessens after the cases of
milk and large bags of bread and cake were delivered and
left at the front door. We would hit those places on the run
and load up on everything we could grab. Sometimes it
was a tremendous amount, and then we would cruise
down into "Spuyten Duyvil," which is where the famous
Diamond Jim Brady started his career in railroading,
which made him a multimillionaire. But at that time this
was a real poverty-stricken area in the asshole of upper
Manhattan. People, whole families, were living in abandoned freight cars.

You should've seen some of those refurbished freight
cars. Some of them looked cleaner and more comfortable
than what I lived in. Anyway, Pete, me and Cliff would
always, real quiet, leave cases of milk and a square count
of bread and cakes in front of all those freight cars, and
then run off, like Robin Hood's Merrymen. But don't get
the idea we didn't get any appreciation for what we did.
The kids of those poor families knew we were the sup-
pliers and there were a lot of girls our age who were always anxious to show their gratitude. There was a lot of
humping going on in the back of that moving van, a lot of
times while it was going through traffic. With all those
blankets and comforters handy, which the movers need to
protect furniture, that truck became a whorehouse on
wheels.

One day, when Pete and I had the shorts bad, Cliff
showed up in the truck and we were sitting around trying
to come up with a bright idea on how to make some dough
when Pete, out of left field, shouted, "I know, and I just

figured how—let's hit the cigarette wholesaler stock-house!"

I said, "You're nuts! It's wired to its ass."

"The wall," Pete said. "It's right up against a butcher shop. We go through the wall!"

It was three in the morning and there we were, in a butcher shop chopping away with cleavers at a wall that busted open into cigarettes and cigars. Everything seemed to be going for us that night—a pouring rain to cover all the noise, and the streets were dead. We were able to work with a lot of freedom, but since the place was wired we took our time moving around the place.

First, we stepped in very gently to make sure that we didn't trip a colorless wiretrap. Every time I see movie soldiers walking very carefully over some terrain, afraid of stepping on land mines, I think of that night—only we didn't do it with suspense music as a background. It was our hearts galloping around in our rib cages.

Well, when we were satisfied that we could work safely in the area, we started to toss the boxes of cigarette cartons into the butcher shop. Pete handed Cliff a box that Cliff handed me, and I in turn tossed it through the hole in the butcher shop. Every time one of those boxes went through my hands, I giggled like a kid with a new toy. What a score! I was already spending it. Then came the *psst,* loud and sharp—from me. That was the way we had set it up. Every second motion of our eyes was to glance at the huge plate-glass window that opened wide into the street, and the first one of us to spot somebody or something coming was to spit out a *pssst* and the other two guys would freeze like statues until the second *pssst* sounded the all-clear.

Well, the first *pssst* exploded like a rifle shot and we froze. I could see the police radio car pull up right in front of the entrance. How long do you think a person can stay frozen without even batting an eyelash? Especially Pete, who was holding a large box and was about to hand it over to Cliff. You should've heard the curse words he was hissing through his teeth. And I'll never forget the trouble I had trying to keep this crazy nervous laughter that was inside me from busting out.

I never realized how long it took to smoke a cigarette. That's all those two of New York's Finest were doing, taking a ten from their patrol and enjoying a cigarette on a rainy night.

"How the fuck long are we gonna stay this way?" Pete asked. He was as nervous as we. The question was answered by the light bulb. There was a night light in the back of the butcher shop, and, when we had come through from the butcher shop into the cigarette distributor's store, I had taken a hand towel and wrapped it around the bulb so we could operate with a little light. And, wouldn't you know it, at that moment, with cops sitting ten feet from us, I smelled something burning. I glanced through the hole and, sure enough, I saw a small hole burning in the towel. My gut started to do flip-flops. I figured, if it burst into flames like I knew it had to, the cops couldn't help but see the flash and we were dead.

I don't know how I did it. I was never a graceful guy. I leaped through the hole in the wall like a cat, snatched the towel from the bulb and smothered it under my body just as it burst into flames. Pete later said that it was amazing how little noise I'd made while doing all that. But actually, even if I'd made some noise, it probably wouldn't have mattered, because at the moment I was springing through that hole, the cops gunned their motor and pulled away. Talk about split-second timing.

That sort of timing can also make you split a gut, because after the cops pulled away and the pressure was off, that's what happened to us. We all got a sudden siege of the runs and we all played musical chairs with the two toilets between the butcher shop and the cigarette joint.

Then Pete got the bright idea that we should break open the boxes and get the cartons of cigarettes ready for the candy stores that were always ready to buy a swag if it had the right discount. We all climbed into the back of the truck and tore open the boxes—about a hundred, which gave us over fourteen hundred cartons of cigarettes, which later gave us about twenty-five hundred bucks in cash. While we were waiting for daylight to break, we lined the cartons of cigarettes on the floor of the truck like so many tightly packed tiles or a parquet floor and covered them with the padding mats, blankets and comforters. Then we took off.

We were going down the Grand Concourse in the Bronx, feeling pretty high because of the size of our score but mostly because we'd come so close to getting caught and had outsmarted the cops, when all of a sudden a siren blared and a radio car pulled alongside with a grim-looking pair of cops signaling us to pull over. Boy, could we have used those toilets again! The charge—driving a commercial vehicle on a restricted road. Of course, Cliff hadn't gotten the truck registration from his old man, and, of course, the cops were going to haul in three dirty, sweaty teenagers driving an unregistered truck on a non-commercial street down to the precinct.

There we were, parked outside the Ryer Avenue Police Station, scared out of our heads and probably acting it because the two cops decided to climb into the truck to look into the deep peak of the van over the cab of the truck. To do this they had to walk over the whole fourteen hundred cartons of cigarettes. They tossed out everything in the peak, didn't find anything they could rap us with and jumped out of the truck. They gave Cliff a ticket for driving an improperly registered vehicle on the Concourse and told us to beat it till Cliff came back with the registration.

It took Cliff most of that day to steal the registration from his old man's wallet, and that truck, loaded with swag, just lay there, right at the entrance to the police station, most of the day. Pete and I hung around outside the station till Cliff finally got back. We could hear all the reports coming in and investigators streaming out to try and get a lead on the great cigarette robbery that took place that morning.

So, like I said, it wasn't exactly a miscarriage of justice that I got nailed for the attempted jewelry store job. Though I got to admit that when I got in front of the judge and listened to what he had to say, I didn't feel quite as cocky as I had when I was talking to Pete. It didn't seem to me that the lawyer that the judge assigned to me really broke his ass over the case, but maybe he looked at the clothes I was wearing and figured out that here was no short cut to Easy Street. Anyway, the thing I remember first about the sentencing was the lecture I got to go along with it.

"Wrong," the judge was saying to me as I stood there in front of him, looking down at the tips of my shoes. When a kid like me is looking down at his shoes, you can bet that everything you're saying is going in one ear and out the other. "Wrong in your attitude, wrong in the company you keep, wrong in your whole approach to life." Then he started shuffling through the papers he had up there on the bench. You may think it's funny I can remember things like that this much time later, but there are a lot of scenes in my life that I can see in front of me whenever I want just as clear as if I was looking at a photograph; I can even remember that my crummy lawyer that day was wearing a white- and blue-striped tie. Anyhow, the judge went on about how the probation report that he had showed that the cops had nailed me three times in one month for hitting teachers or for stealing things off pushcarts and how now that I was older I'd moved up to bigger things in the crime department—to wit, in this case, attempted burglary. And he ended up:

"Further leniency in your case is useless. You've already had three chances to prove that you wanted to reform, and each time you've gone out to commit another offense. I hereby sentence you to an indeterminate term of one to three years in the State Reform School at Coxsackie, New York. . . ."

This was tougher than I expected, and I looked up at the judge and started to say something, but the lawyer put his hand on my arm and the bailiff came over, so I just shook the arm off. "Lay off, crumb," I snarled at him as I turned away with the bailiff.

In the back of the courtroom there was my mother and father, and Pete, and some of the kids from the candy store. I didn't like looking at my mother. Maybe it was seeing her in a strange setting, away from the dump we lived in, away from the kitchen where she was always working, there in the courtroom dressed in her best clothes, the shabby black that she never wore anywhere except to go to church, but she looked older all of a sudden. I could see she was older, older than I thought, and kids hate to notice people getting older. At least their mother. My old man had one of these I-could-have-told-you-so looks on his face mixed with hate and his-son-going-to-reform-school feelings.

The kids had that kind of fascinated look they have for things like that—a sort of wondering if maybe it wouldn't be worth spending some time in reform school to be the hero of the hour, or at least the minute—the fascination that the not really bad kid finds in the kid who's really done something that's got him in a jam. I don't know exactly how to explain it, but I know what it is. The whole bit you go through from the time you're born till you're grown up—whatever that is—is devoted to the world, your parents, the schools, the cop on the corner, all telling you what you can't do. You're not supposed to go around knocking down every broad that looks good to you, or drinking all the booze you want, or belting every guy who gives you a hard time, or stealing stuff from jewelry stores. The kids who are the good kids, the ones without the nerve to say the hell with all that, fuck it, they got a sneaking admiration for the kids who do.

That was the way the kids in the back of the room looked at me. All except Pete, and that was because he was as bad as me, if not worse. The look he had on his puss meant he thought I was pretty goddamned stupid going up for an indeterminate one to three, which meant at least seven, eight months, even if I behaved like the second coming.

There was one thing that took part of the bite off my going up for me. I had told Pete to take my share of the dice-game loot and make sure it got to my old lady—and to make up a story to cover it. The story part was up to him, but I could just see my mother, somebody coming in and giving her a grand or more and saying Jake sent it. I could see her putting it in the fire, that's what I could see, she wasn't going to touch any stolen money that sent her boy up to reform school. But I thought that figuring out a story was just what Pete would be good at.

I learned all about it afterward. When the family got home from court, my old man acted just as big as he ever did. They all went into the kitchen—where else do you go in a cold-water flat but the kitchen?—and the old man lit up one of them stinking little Italian cheroots—all you got to do is smell one of them and the stink is in your nose till your dying day—and he started yammering about me.

"What the hell are you bawling about anyway?" he asked my mother, who was crying, naturally, like she frequently did for one reason or another. That's why peasant women everywhere have the kind of faces they do. They spend a third of their lives crying, the way other women spend a third sleeping. "The kid's a bum, I keep telling ya," my old man went on, "so stop bawling about him before I belt ya and give ya something to really bawl about. What the hell, he ate like a horse around here and he never brought in a nickel. Now he's off our hands. Now at least we know where he is, and they gotta feed him enough to keep him alive and he's got a place to sleep and clothes. . . ."

"He tried," my mother said through her tears. "Whenever he did earn money he gave us some of it. He worked on the cart."

"Ha! He worked on the cart when I could catch him, when he wasn't running off to the candy store with that friend of his, Pete—some bargain he is. And he always cost more than he brought in—clothes, food, shoes, coats. . . ."

"He tried," my mother insisted, and Joey and Albert thought he was going to bust her—bust her again. He was always doing it.

The old man roared, "Cut it out, goddamn it. He's a bum, he always was and he always will be! Always giving me a lot of his goddamn lip, me, his father, who he's supposed to respect!" He hit himself on the chest. "Who's he supposed to respect if he don't respect his own father? I try to teach him the right way, the right things, and he acts like he wanted to kill me. He can't stay in school, he hits the teachers, he steals things outta school. The cops always comin' here, where's Jake? Is that any way to have a family? The other boys, the girls, whadda they think when they see the cops comin' here all the time? All the neighbors know, too—'There go the cops after that La Motta boy,' they're saying. He drags our whole name down in the gutter." He stopped shouting to take a breath. "Respect, that's what they teach you in reform school! Respect! Respect for the law! Maybe when he comes home he'll have a little respect for his family! For his father!"

Joey and Albert told me that a couple of days afterward they were at home after school in the afternoon and the old man was in a foul temper as usual and my mother was crying about something as usual and that they made the mistake of asking her when I was coming home. They were just a couple of little kids then, remember, so to them two days seemed like two weeks.

"And Jake said he'd take us to the movies," Joey said.

"Movies!" the old man yelled. "Movies! I'll give you movies! G'wan, get oudda here, g'wan!"

The boys noticed that their mother had a black-and-blue mark on her face and they turned on the old man.

"Whaddaya looking at," he yelled to them. "You should go look at your stupid brother! Stupid, that's what he is! He wants to steal, he gets caught when he didn't even get anything, that's how stupid he is! Why don't he go to work and bring some money in the house? Eh? Why?"

The boys were glaring at him, and at this point there was a knock on the door. Still glowering at him, Joey went over to the door and opened it, and there was Pete standing out in the hall.

"Hi, Joey," Pete said, patting him on the shoulder. "How's the boy today?"

Pete remembers to this day that Joey looked up at him worried and said, "Pete, when is Jake coming home? Do you know?" And Pete only shook his head and said, "Hi, Mamma La Motta. Hello, Mr. La Motta." And they both tried to smile at him a little and Pete walked into the room and took a huge wad of bills out of his pocket and put them down on the table in front of my mother.

"For you, Mamma La Motta, while Jake is away. . . ."

You can imagine how surprised and confused she was. She didn't even reach for the money. She just looked at it. Then she looked up at Pete, and her face was one big worried question mark. "How?" she asked. "But how? Where is this from?"

Pete gave her an uneasy smile and sort of shifted around a little. He got to be a better liar later.

"A collection, Mamma," he said. "We all got together, all of Jake's friends, and we made up a collection to sort of tide you over. You know how it is. We made up this collection. . . ."

Then things got a little nervous because both my mother and father had this peasant thing about money and they knew by instinct that this money was not what the friends of Jake La Motta had ever put into a collection.

Pete decided this was a great time to change the subject, so he reached into his pocket and brought out a couple of more bucks and grinned at the boys and said, "Hey, I nearly forgot, Jake said to make sure that Joey and Albert got some money so they could go to the movies." He stuffed the money in their hands and moved toward the door. "So long, folks," he said, still trying to smile. "I gotta rush now, I got an appointment. I'll see you soon. Jake oughta be out in a couple months."

The boys, of course, were going crazy over the money they got. A couple of bucks in a house like ours in times like that was a fortune. Pete said the faces of my mother and father were a helluva study: she not knowing what to make of it, not liking it, not trusting it, but there was all that money that God knew the family could use; and my father, there was no doubt or qualm there, nothing but sheer, straight, unadulterated greed. Then he sort of felt that everyone was looking at him, so without taking his eyes off the money he began to rub his hands up and down his thighs.

"Hey, arr," he said, "that's pretty good, eh? Never thought anything like this would ever happen. Even from up there he can help his family, eh? I guess his pals must respect him a lot."

"Yeah," Pete said. "Yeah."

This time Pete really made a break for it, and as he slid out the door he heard my old man say, "I never said he was all bad, Jake. . . . Now if they only can teach him a little respect up at that place."

FIVE

Well, that's what they were trying to do all right—teach me a little respect. When I got to the warden's office at Coxsackie, he started to give me the whole bit you get the first time you show up at a place where they don't know you, about how if you behave yourself and keep your nose clean you won't have too hard a time of it, but if you want to be a wise guy they can give you all the trouble you can handle, and here's a chance to rehabilitate yourself and learn something so that when you get out you can reform and make something of yourself and stay away from the troublemakers because that's a sure way to get yourself into even more trouble.

All this time I'm looking at my shoes and minding my own business and not saying anything and I guess that began to get to the warden because suddenly he stopped and said, "You. Yeah, you. Look at me when I'm talking to you!"

So I looked at him. As I said, even back then when I was still a kid, I never smiled at no one practically ever, and so I just looked at him, and this seemed to make him even madder.

He nodded his head. "Another tough guy?" he asked with the soft voice of a guy who knows he has you by the short hairs, that it's your neck if you decide to make trouble. "Another tough guy?" He looked down at the papers on his desk to get my name. "I want to let you in on a little secret, La Motta. There's only one tough guy up here, and that's me. And I'm undefeated. I've had a lot of young punks in here who thought they were tough, and I'm undefeated."

I kind of shrugged, so his voice got harder.

"You can learn it the hard way, if you want, like a lot of others," he said, "but just keep one little fact in mind. You're in here on an indeterminate one to three. I don't care how long you stay here, minimum or maximum, it's up to you." He pushed a buzzer on his desk and a guard came in. "Take our friend here and put him into some clothes and give him a shovel."

The guard kind of grinned at the way the warden said "friend," then took me by the arm and turned me around and kind of gave me a little shove toward the door. "Let's go, you," he said.

I turned back to him, but all I got was another push.

Like anyplace else, they start making up their minds about you in reform school from the first time you open your mouth, and right away they had me pegged as a guy who needed pushing around. But I knew about my temper, the way Pete kept needling me about it all the time, and I was turning around in my mind at the same time how hard it would be to bust out of this place, and whether it would be bright to try.

I went through all the bull you have to go through when they enter you in reform school, the records office and the physical and the shower and haircut job and the prison clothes, those beautiful handmade shoes they give you, all the time with this guard on my back, and finally I got a shovel issued to me and the guard took me outside the prison, down a paved road where there was a work gang of the kids cleaning out a ditch alongside the road. This gang had another guard watching it, standing on a little sort of knoll about twenty yards away, a rifle in the crook of his arm. My guard yelled up to him, "Hey, Tully, I got another prize package for you."

The second guard looked down at me as if I was a hundred and sixty pounds of garbage and said, "Just what I needed. The day isn't complete without another of these bums." He nodded his head at me. "All right, you," he says, "down in the ditch with the rest of them. Get started." I stared at him and he grinned and took the rifle out of the crook of his arm. "Look, scum!" he said, "when I say jump, you jump, or a rifle butt in the back! Get it? Down in the ditch!"

I got into the ditch and started shoveling with the rest of them. I could hear the other screw say to my guard, "Warden thinks this guy thinks he's a tough guy. Watch him. Get plenty a work outta him."

He was standing there above me, his legs apart, picking his teeth and watching me. The guard with the rifle says, "Don't worry. Full treatment for him."

The other guard walked away and I kept on shoveling.

The trouble with work like that is it keeps your body busy but your mind goes on working, too. What I was thinking was that eight months of this and I'd be off my rocker. And I also was thinking that none of these guys I was with, in the first look I got at them, was going to turn out to be the kind of guys you'd pal around with. I was never a great one for making real pals, anyway. Pete was probably the only friend I had.

I really missed the son of a bitch. I don't know exactly how Pete and I became such good friends. How is it, some people you meet and right off you know they're the kind of person you'll get along with, and some you meet and right off you say to yourself, now here's one fine bastard I'm never gonna let get behind me.

Maybe one thing about Pete was that he was so much the opposite of me. Me, I kept what I felt to myself— except when I blew my stack, just blew up like a volcano erupting. Everybody that knew me then thought I was a sullen kid who never laughed or smiled and who never talked unless he had to, and I guess they were right. What the hell was there to laugh or smile about? I was fighting the whole goddamned world except for my family—and even in the family I was fighting my old man—practically ever since I was born. I never trusted anybody, and anybody that trusted me was a goddamned fool.

But Pete had a million friends. He always had a laugh or a smile, he could kid the dames and the guys alike. When we first met, he already had a rep—you know, toughest guy in the neighborhood, afraid of nothing. I never figured out why he paid any attention to me, except that he told me once that the very first time he met me he sensed that quality that I kept to myself—that somehow I was going to make it in the world or die trying. Nothing was going to beat me except getting killed. And he liked that. And over the years we got to become real good friends, though I will admit that it took a lot of doing.

Anyway, after a few days I began to get used to the routine at Coxsackie. Not used to it really, but got so I knew what it was. The first thing wrong with it, outside of everything else, was that bit about getting up at six o'clock in the morning. Brother! If there's one reason at all for a guy like me to stay out of the can, it's getting up at that hour. I figure around eleven is early enough. And, of course, there's no drinking, no smoking, no nothing, or there isn't supposed to be. No staying out, hanging around with the kids. It's early to bed and early to rise, like the saying goes, the same goddamned lousy show at the same time every day, and the work, and the exercise.

One afternoon after the first few days, I was out in the exercise yard, where we're supposed to move around, though actually all we did was gather up in little groups and yak—even in a place like that the guys break up into gangs, most of which hate each other's guts, and they talk about breaking out or lie about the number of broads they've laid or other things they haven't done. I was already pegged as a loner and I was off against the wall looking up at the other side and watching these two screws on the top with their rifles looking down at us. There was this gang of kids and they were smoking. They gathered in a knot so the screw couldn't see the kid in the middle, who was doing the smoking, and he took a drag or two and handed the butt on to somebody else, then he went to the outside of the circle, letting the smoke out in little puffs that didn't show up much to the screw on top of the wall. Suddenly one of the kids broke out of the group and took a look at me, then a closer look, then he came charging over.

"Jake!" he yelled. "Hey, Jake! It's you! Bullhead! I didn't know you was here? How long you been here? Whajja do? How long you in for?"

It was Rocky Graziano, the kid I used to fight with when we weren't off stealing together down on the Lower East Side. When things would get slow in the Bronx I'd come down to Rocky's neighborhood, and we'd go off on a job together. We used to have a running gag: we only stole things that began with an *a*—a car, a radio, a watch. Rocky came charging over and threw his arms around me and belted me on the shoulder, yelling at me all the time. Finally he stopped long enough for me to answer him.

"Rocky! How are ya, boy? Hold off now, hold off, goddamn it, stop punching me. How the hell are ya? God, it's good to see a friendly face around here! But what the hell are you here for? Before I came up, everybody said your time was up, you was comin' home any day now."

Rocky made a face. He sobered up and backed off from me and shrugged his shoulders. "Because I'm a kook, that's why I'm still here, and going to stay. I can't just walk away from some loudmouth, that's why. I got to belt somebody. I got into a beef with a coupla these clowns and I belted them around a little." He shook his head. "I got away with it all right the first time, they just put me in the hole for a coupla days, but then these guys come back at me and it was the same old thing all over again, and after that happened a coupla times, they took all my good time away from me and now I gotta serve out the whole goddamn sentence."

By the time he finished talking, all the laughing was gone out of him and he sounded harsh and bitter.

I said, "That's what I'm afraid of, Rock. . . . It's the same thing with me. I got a temper and I can't stay three years in this cage. Christ, I been here about three days now and I'm beginning to go stir crazy already. I'm already beginning to figure out how to bust outta this place."

Rocky looked at me and shook his head. Then he put his hand on my shoulder. "Look," he said, "I know what I'm talkin' about. Forget it. They can get awful tough with you up here. They can put you in that hole and throw away the key and forget all about you. They got all the aces and you got nothin'. I seen 'em handle some pretty tough guys. Give it up."

"I can't give it up, Rock," I said. "Maybe you, you got used to it, but I don't think I can get used to it. It takes me hours to get to sleep at night and I wake up in the morning and it takes me a couple of seconds to remember where I am and I think to myself, Jesus, another day in this goddamned cage. And then I get to thinking about all the days I still got to do before I get out."

Rocky tried again. "Forget it, Jake, I tell ya. Forget it. I'll say it again and again. They not only got all the aces, they got all the cards. You don't even have a hand. I know how ya feel. I felt the same way myself. I still feel it. But look at it this way. Time passes. They can't keep you in here forever. For a long time I was gonna take a shot at bustin' out but then I figured what the hell, I'd have to keep runnin' forever. What good is bein' out gonna do you if you have to spend all your time hidin' in cellars and every guy you meet you gotta figure he's a stoolie?"

I said, "Look, Rock, I'm built different than you. I can't stay in here, I'll go nuts! I'm not kiddin'! Nuts! I'm half nuts right now." I took his arm and lowered my voice. "Okay," I said, "I know you're right and maybe I'll be able to talk myself out of it. But do me one favor. You ever figure how to get out of here if you wanted to?"

Rocky shook his head slow. "You always was nuts," he said, "now you're setting a new record." He dropped his voice and looked around to make sure no one was close enough to hear us. With stool pigeons, you got to worry before, during and after the fact. And half of them learn their trade in reform school, anyway. "Well," said Rocky, very low, "there's this truck . . ."

What he told me about was a delivery truck that came in every so often to bring in all sorts of junk, or carry furniture from one building to another, or cart out stuff that was no good anymore—like, say, broken chairs—and how two guys could probably work it if the truck was taking something out. One of them could talk to the driver and distract his attention long enough for the other to get in and hide. Every now and then the guards would search the back of the truck as it went out, but what the hell, you got to take chances in this life and the guards only did this spot-check bit every fifth or sixth trip, so the odds looked pretty good.

I had only myself to blame for what happened but you

know how kids are. And criminals, too, I figure. Neither one of them can ever get it through his head that things are a lot more likely to go bad than good. They somehow figure that everything always goes bad for the other guy but somehow it's going to go good for them. A guy once told me that in fatal professions like soldiering or auto racing, that's what keeps those guys from either quitting or committing suicide.

Anyway, Rock said that if I wanted to go on being as stupid as everybody said I was, he'd help because it seemed like a pity for some other guy to be able to say that he was stupider than Jake La Motta, and sure enough a week or so later I was at my usual daytime occupation, working on Tully's road gang, when one of the prison station wagons came along and stopped near the guard. The prison chaplain was driving, and alongside him was Rocky. The chaplain, for a priest, looked as if he could go a few rounds himself without getting too winded. He grinned and said, "Good morning, Tully. I have need for one of your strongmen to give us a hand in moving a few pieces of heavy furniture."

Tully grinned back at him. "Take your pick of the lot, Father, and let's hope you can take a minute or two to instill the fear of God into whichever of these heathens you choose."

The priest laughed heartily and turned around to Rocky. "You know them, Rocky? Which one of them would you pick?"

Rocky shook his head and gave him the wide-eyed innocence look. "I don't know them, Father. They're mostly new ones just come along, not an old-timer like myself. Take your own pick is what I'd say." Then he stopped and sort of nodded his head toward me. "That sour-lookin' one there, he's got a pretty strong-looking build, for all of what his face looks like."

So the priest said, "Okay. Tully, we'll take that one there."

Tully looked at me with his usual sour mush and said, "Okay. At least he's strong." Then he told me to hop into the station wagon.

I shrugged my shoulders and dropped the shovel and walked around the station wagon. Rocky and I exchanged looks as I climbed in. The father turned the station wagon around and we started back toward the prison.

As we drove along the chaplain started giving me the same old treatment you learn to expect from the Establishment. He craned around so he could half see me, then he said, "What's your name, son?"

What difference did it make? And how could I have been his son? Him a priest and all that? But you couldn't spend every minute of your waking hours fighting, so again I just shrugged and answered, "Jake."

He turned for a second so he could get a better look. "Just Jake?"

"Jake La Motta."

There was a little pause because I wasn't making an effort to keep the conversation going.

"How's it going?" he asked in a final effort.

"Okay."

He looked at me again, then he turned and looked at Rocky. I could see from the way he was sitting that Rocky didn't think much of my performance, but what the hell—I get that way. Who the hell wants to be sociable all the time? Every time everyone meets you and asks you how you feel, you say great. You know he doesn't care and neither do you. What's wrong with just saying balls to get a little truth into the conversation for a change?

Anyway, the conversation came to an end and the priest drove on back in through the gate and way around the yard, which must have been a half a mile at least, and to the chapel, which was a small brick building with stained-glass windows set off in one corner of the yard. In a reformatory, you don't really need a big building for the chapel.

There was a truck backed up to the side door of the chapel and there was this civilian truck driver leaning on the front mudguard, smoking a cigarette and waiting for us. The chaplain pulled up to the side and we all got out and went inside and the chaplain showed us the furniture that was to go. Rocky and I were the muscle for this deal. The chaplain just told us what to do, and all the truck driver did was show us how you loaded the furniture in so that you used all the space and didn't have it rattling around.

When we were just about finished the chaplain came out, and he was looking at his wristwatch.

"I want to thank both of you boys for your help," he said. "It's almost lunchtime. In fact, it's so close to noon that why don't you just stay here in the recreation yard and wait for your gang to come. There's no sense in me driving you all the way back again now."

I nodded. For the moment, it was all the same to me. Rocky came up with that big grin of his and some more of the soft soap. "Sure, Father Joseph," he said, "whatever you say."

The priest just looked at the both of us and then turned around without saying anything and went back into the chapel.

The truck driver had finished checking his load and roping it up and he slid out the back of the truck. I looked at Rocky and lifted my eyebrows, and all he did was give me that little shrug of his that meant if I wanted to try it it was okay with him, no skin off his nose no matter what happened. Well, I wanted to try it.

So Rocky and me gave the truck driver a hand putting up the tailgate of the truck and locking it, then he went to the truck cab and climbed in, and Rock followed him up. I stayed in back, my back to the back of the truck looking at the chapel in case the good father decided to come back out. I heard the cab door slam and I heard Rocky's voice talking to the driver: "How about asking me to throw away that cigarette pack for you? The one with three or four butts left in it?"

The truck driver looked out. In a way he was apologetic, because he was a little sorry for teenage kids in a reform school. On the other hand . . .

"Jesus, kid, I'd like to, but I don't dare. We get caught, and they'd tell my boss and I'd be out a job, with three kids to support." He laughed a little. "In case you don't know, there's a Depression outside. What's more, you'd be in trouble, too."

I took one final fast look around. I didn't see anyone

watching from the towers or the chapel. I swung myself up over the tailgate and down onto the floor of the truck and started getting myself under the heavy matting the truck driver used to protect the furniture. Later I found out that's what gave me away—swinging myself in. The truck driver happened to be looking in the rear-view mirror at the time and he saw the shift of the truck body as my weight made it move. But he pretended he didn't notice anything and Rock kept on trying to hold his attention.

"Aw, I can't get in no trouble around here," Rock told him. "I blew the parole but I'll have my full sentence finished out in a coupla months. What can they do to me? Give me five years for a couple of lousy cigarettes?"

The driver started the motor and said, "Jesus, I can't, kid. I'd like to, but it's too much of a risk. You never know when one of them screws will be looking down from the tower, and if he sees me give you something . . . This lousy job ain't much but at least it pays the bills so we can eat."

Rocky nodded his head.

"Okay, yeah, no harm in trying. Well, take it easy, you got quite a load in back there."

"I know," the driver said, starting up.

He stopped at the gate, where there was one guard up in the tower on top and another in the booth at the side. The gates worked by electricity, and the guard gave the driver a wave and he had his hand on the control that opened the gate, but the driver shook his head and waved his hand no. So the guard came over and the driver leaned out and whispered that he was pretty sure he had an extra passenger in the back.

I knew all this because after the truck stopped for the gate I heard this muttering up front and then about four seconds later I heard the guard's steps alongside the truck and from the tailgate I heard his voice: "Okay, Dillinger, out!"

For a couple of seconds I didn't move, wondering what to do, then the voice said, "Look, wise guy, if I have to go in after you it's goin' to be that much worse for you. Out!"

What the hell. I got out.

SIX

A prison guard is not a Mister Nice. I got a couple of belts in the gut stumbling between the back of the truck and the guardhouse at the gate. They sent a car for me and I got a couple of belts between the guardhouse and the car, just so he wouldn't get out of practice.

When I got into the warden's office, there was nothing I could do except play it cool. I'd been stupid, I'd been caught. Like Rocky told me, they not only had the aces but all the cards, and all I could do was take it.

I could see that underneath his calm, the warden was boiling. That's all a warden in a place needs is another troublemaker like me.

"What are you out for?" the warden asked, "a new track record of some sort? You just got here and you'll be pleased to know you've already tried one of the stupidest breakouts I ever seen. What's the matter, tough guy, you gonna try to see how much we'll stand for?"

What was there to say? Everybody in the room, me, the warden, the screws, we all knew what it was about. So I just looked up at the ceiling, which I knew would make him madder than anything else, and it did.

He suddenly roared, "Get this goddamn moron out of my sight. Throw him in the hole for a month. Let's see how goddamn tough he is when he comes outta there!"

I wouldn't fool you, the hold in any prison is a place you should stay out of—but a month! *A month!* I think even the screws were a little surprised, because I saw one of them look up at the warden, but all the warden did was yell again, "Get him outta here!"

Whatever the guard felt, he certainly wasn't going to let me see it. So he just spun me around and said, "You heard

57

what the warden said, Mac, let's go, let's not hold up the rest of the parade," and he gave me a shove.

I spun back. I crouched on the balls of my feet, my fists balled up ready to take him, but now there were two guards and they were just laughing at me. They both pushed me backward and when I lost my balance they took me by the shoulders and slammed me around again and gave me a jab on each shoulder about every half-second so that I never could get my balance, and I stumbled out of the office and into the corridor with these two clowns behind me laughing.

The hole at Coxsackie is a block of the toughest and nastiest cells in the whole joint. At Coxsackie at this time the cellblock was below ground level, so there weren't any outside windows or bars to worry about. It was cut off from the rest of the prison and there was only one way in, and out. There was one corridor, maybe a hundred and fifty feet long with a line of light bulbs overhead and a string of cells on each side.

I got sort of half-pushed and half-jostled down the stairs to the little sort of platform where there was a guard sitting outside, reading a newspaper, then a double set of gates with a desk and chair inside where there was another guard with the controls for the gates, and then inside to the cellblock.

Like all the rest of them, the guard on the outside platform was a born comic. As I stumbled down there he looked at the two screws behind me and laughed and said, "What are ya bringing me this time? He sure looks like a real sour one."

"A real tough one," one of the screws said. "A real Al Capone. Already tried to bust out. He needs something to bring him down to size. Something to cool him off a little."

The gate guard got up and put down his paper and opened the gates, and I got another push through.

Here I knew I was going to get a going-over. Every new place you go there's always a gang waiting to size you up, and if it was bad enough in the regular place, down here it was going to be that much worse.

All these jerks in the cells had their faces plastered to

the bars to see who the new boy was. What the hell else did they have to do? And I heard all the comments:

"Hey, look at this new fish."

"Boy, is he a beauty."

One of them sang: *Hey, there, my man,*
Don't walk with your head held so high,
For soon they're gonna bang it as low as your thigh.

And another said:

"Hey, boy, they're gonna soften you up good, then you'll be a nice little girl for somebody here."

Finally a sour, surly type:

"Yeah, she's ugly enough to be my type. Boy, you gonna be my girl, you hear?"

I knew enough to know that this kind of talk could be habit-forming and the thing to do was nip it in the bud.

I figured the guy to go for was this last one, Mister Loudmouth, and before the guards behind me could figure what I was doing I jumped over to his cell and belted him through the bars hard as I could. It wasn't my best punch—the easiest way to set a punch is not through the bars of a cell—but it put another dent in his ugly puss. Then the guards grabbed hold of me and hustled me along three or four more doors to an empty cell where they threw me in. When I got back on my feet I was raging with fury again. It didn't make any sense, but I was past making sense—if I could have I would have killed them all, I didn't care how many of them there were. I was throwing punches just as hard and as fast as I could, and I saw one of the guards go down to his knees, another one grunted as I landed a fist in his gut. The third one had his hard rubber club and he got in a couple of licks but I kept on fighting, but the bit about one guy taking on three guards and licking them happens only in Hollywood.

All the other inmates were on my side now, of course, and I could hear them yelling:

"Keep hittin', keep punchin'! Hit 'em low, low, that's where they can't take it. Keep hittin' 'em low, that's where they're soft. Keep bangin'!"

I remember one colored boy in the cell across the corridor shaking his head and saying, "Man, if that stud is a girl, I'm giving up romance."

And then I got a clout over the head from that rubber club again.

Well, I remember I took a pretty fair beating. The trouble is when guys are afraid maybe they're going down they start fighting for their lives, and then when they've got it won, they got so much adrenaline running that they can't stop, they just keep on beating.

A couple of days later I was getting over it—anyway, I wasn't still bleeding, and the worst of the throbbing had gone away—when I heard steps coming down the corridor and the cell gate opened and in came Father Joseph. I was lying flat on my back on my cot looking up at the ceiling, still black and blue all over, and for a few seconds he didn't say anything at all. Then he said, "Hello, Jake. Can I come in?"

He was already halfway in, you understand. I looked over at him, then back at the ceiling. "Get lost," I said.

He took this as an invitation to come in and walked the whole way into the cell.

"What are you sore at me for?" he asked. "I want to be your friend."

I sat up suddenly, which did me no good because my gut was still sore and the move caught me right in the side.

"Jesus!" I said. "Look, beat it, willya? Like I said, get lost!"

Father Joseph shook his head. "Look, Jake," he said, "maybe I shouldn't say it, but I'm ashamed for those men. Beating up a kid like you, and they told me there were three of them. And I know you won't understand it now, but I have to say it to you and hope that sometime you'll remember it. You can't hate all men just because of the ignorance and brutality of a few."

"If this is the brotherhood-of-man sermon, you can skip it," I said. "I've heard all the bullshit before and I'll believe it when I see it."

"There's no sense in talking to me that way, Jake," he said. "I've heard all that kind of language before, too. What I want to do is to help you, to be your friend. There are all kinds of different people in the world, you know. There are some who believe in helping. . . ."

I didn't feel like listening. Yeah, maybe he meant what

he said, but it was for himself he was doing it, not me, so he'd have a great record he could show the monsignor or whoever his boss was. What I knew then was that there was nobody, but nobody, who would help you except yourself. Old number one, that was the only one you could trust. I got myself up off the cot without his help and walked to the back of the cell.

"If you want to know what I think," I said with my back to him, "I think people like you are stupid. The only way you get anywhere in the world is to take what you want. And I don't want to waste my time talking to stupid people. So why don't you beat it back to somebody you can con, huh?"

I heard him move as if he was going to go, but then he stopped and after a while, as if he was trying to control his temper, he went on talking to me in an even voice, the voice of a guy who's trying not to blow his stack.

"Okay, Jake," he said. "I guess I can't blame you for being bitter. I get bitter myself at some of the things I see around here, grown men who are supposed to be civilized human beings with immortal souls, the way they behave. But you've got to have some friends in this world. If you want to think I'm stupid, all right. But it doesn't change the fact that I want to be your friend. If only because it's my duty to God, if it's no more than that. Won't you let me be your friend?"

I could feel myself getting to the point where I was going to break, and I didn't want to. What the hell, I was a teenage kid in a reformatory, and I'd just lost a fight with three grown men and taken a solid beating, and I was in the hole for God knows how long.

The father came up behind me.

"I got a friend," I said, still being sour.

He put his hand on my shoulder and I could feel myself getting even closer to breaking. "Don't you have room for another?" he asked me, putting his arm around my shoulders and turning me around.

All of a sudden I was sobbing, but what made it worse was that I was trying to hold it down and it was making my whole body shake and tears kept coming out of my eyes no matter how hard I held them shut.

I jerked myself away from him, and stumbled over to the corner of the cell and sat down with my face inside my arms, partly hating him for making me cry.

He went on talking: "Don't be ashamed of tears, Jake," he said. "I've seen grown men cry, and I've respected them all the more for it. Tears come out of good emotions, Jake. Sorrow. The need for love. Wonderful human emotions. And tears can help wash away a lot of confusion."

All the time I was just trying to stop crying and wishing he'd go away, and then all of a sudden in a different tone he said, "I wouldn't want you mad at me, Jake. I knew you were strong when I saw you and Rocky moving that furniture, but I didn't realize you were as strong as you are." He sort of half-laughed. "I know you lost the fight with those guards, boy, but you ought to see the shape they're in. They look as if they'd been fighting a grizzly bear."

I looked up at him and he had this half-grin on his face. "Yeah?" I asked him. "You're not kidding me, are ya?"

He shook his head, still smiling. "Of course not. Why would I do that? Maybe I ought not even to be telling you. But they deserved what they got." And he laughed again a little. "You know, they were so ashamed that they didn't even make out a report on you? They were too ashamed to admit that a kid barely more than sixteen years old was able to take on three grown men and put them in a shape where all the other guards are laughing at them."

"Yeah?" I said. "Is that so?" Then I began to wonder. By now I was able to stop crying and I wiped my face with my sleeve. I shook my head at Father Joseph and said, "I don't get you, Father. Are you supposed to be takin' the side of one of the guys in here against the guards?"

"I told you how I felt about them," he said.

I still didn't get him. "Yeah," I said, "but figuring that you're a priest, are you supposed to be standing up for fighting at all in the first place? I thought you was supposed to turn the other cheek if somebody slugged you."

He laughed again.

"Not necessarily," he said. "Do you remember in the Bible where Jesus blew up at the moneylenders and went after them with a whip, driving them out of the temple?

Does that sound like a man who was afraid of getting into a fight?"

I shook my head. "Naw," I said. "I heard about it, I guess, about driving the moneychangers from the temple, but I don't know exactly what happened. I'm not too good when it comes to the Bible. But if you say so . . ." I began to think that maybe this priest did know a little bit about what went on. "Maybe you're not so square after all," I told him.

"I've been around a little bit," he said. "When you get around, you get hep." He saw that I was looking at him and he began to get serious on me. "If you're wondering why a guy like me ever became a priest," he said, "it's because I got the feeling that Jesus was the greatest man who ever lived. The son of God, and he died to save us poor sinners, Jake. But he was hep, too, you know. Believe me."

I began to get the feeling that this was leading up to another little sermon about saving my soul and I guessed it must have showed on my face because he changed his tune again.

"What I really came down here to say, Jake, is this," he went on. "I can make an argument for you and it could do you some good, seeing that this is the first trouble you've been in here. But what you've got to make up your mind to is—okay, you got sent up here and it's no vacation home, but you aren't going to get yourself anything except trouble by trying to bust out or getting into fights with the guards. I don't expect to change you into an angel overnight or even to change you into the model prisoner, but if you think at least you can stay out of real trouble, I'll go to bat for you. There isn't much point in my doing it if you're to be right back in here the day after tomorrow, but if you'll go along with what I'm saying, I'll try to see if I can square this beef a little bit."

"Yeah?" I asked him. "What else do I have to promise? What's it really going to cost me?"

"Nothing else," he said, shaking his head. "I'd like to talk to you a little. See if I can find out why you're the kind of a guy you are. What makes you tick. Why don't you have any friends except this one? Most kids have a gang they hang around with, they have a dozen friends."

I shook my head, trying to think. "I don't know," I said, "except the family I came from. All I can remember ever since I was a little kid was fighting and yelling and working and stealing and more fighting. And getting beat up by my old man. We're five kids at home and we never have a goddamned nickel. My old man never had a steady job. For one thing, he's an Italian from the other side and he ain't the type to go to night school. He ain't no expert with the English language and, I don't know, everything that goes wrong—which is everything—he takes it out on the family. It's always somebody else's fault, not his. He's always beating someone, my mother or us kids. Not me anymore. He knows now, he tries to lay a finger on me, I'll throw him out the window."

Then I remembered something. "You want to know how it was around our house? You know what we got for Christmas once? Coal. *Coal.* We hung up our stockings the way all kids do and when we came in the next morning, that's what we found in our stockings. Coal. We knew there wasn't enough money for a lot of fancy presents, but what kid was ever bad enough so that the whole thing he got for Christmas was nothing but one lump of coal? But that's what the old man told us—we'd been bad, he said, and that was the way Santa Claus punished us."

I got to talking, the way you do when somebody asks you something about the past and you think of one thing and that reminds you of something else and the whole of that part of your life begins to come into your mind.

I laughed. "One Thanksgiving we had nothing much to eat, no Thanksgiving stuff at all, so I went out and stole a whole turkey, all cooked and stuffed and a lot of stuff to go with it, from out of the back of one of those fancy delicatessens. I brought it home and told them that I'd won it at a raffle, but they knew I stole it. Nobody said anything. My mother just heated it up and we sat down and ate every bit of it. . . .

"You know something? I been fighting for money ever since I was eight years old. Not fights with your pals like all little kids do, but fights to make money. Not much, I'll grant you, but there are these clubs around the Bronx, social clubs where these guys go to play cards and booze if they have the money and they bring in these kids to fight and they throw them pennies and dimes and nickels and the kids fight over who gets the money. My old man used to bring me down to these places every time he heard there was going to be a kids' fight, which was at least every week and sometimes more, two or three times, then when we got home he'd take the money off me that I won. Great guy, my old man."

Thinking about it was making me so sore that I wanted someone around to punch, so I stopped talking and went over to the cot and sat down. I was still good and sore from the beating I'd taken, but I wasn't crying anymore.

Father Joseph didn't say anything for a while. He was looking down at the cell floor, thinking, then he said, "Jake, I think I have an idea that may help to keep you out of trouble. I'll see how much I can get your time in isolation shortened and then I'll have you assigned to the work detail in the gymnasium. Do you think that would work? Having you in the gym instead of out working on the ditch details?"

It was okay with me. Even back then, practically as long as I can remember, I was thinking about being a fighter, and maybe I could learn something. Like I said, I liked fighting, and I knew it would always be either steal or fight for me. I nodded. "Yeah," I said. "Sure."

SEVEN

And that is how I got into the reformatory fight program at Coxsackie, with Father Joseph, after I finished my time in the hole, which the father managed to get cut down to a total of two weeks.

I'll say one thing for Coxsackie—one, that's all. The gym there wasn't too bad in my day. It was a real, full-size gym, with polished hardwood floors, a regulation ring set up in the middle, a whole series of punching bags down at one end, plenty of weights and barbells and dumbbells and those pulley weight systems all along one wall and even a row of rowing machines. In other words, the whole works.

I know that hardwood floor was polished because I was the guy that did it. That was one of my jobs on the gym detail—they were all jobs keeping the place clean. But it also meant that I could get myself in shape because between jobs I was always using the weights or the punching bags. I guess the gym was one of the favorite spots for the guys because you almost always found someone there and a few of them were pretty good at fighting. That's how I learned to punch the bag—there's a trick to it, you know, especially the small bag, the way you keep it going with that *rat-a-tat-tat*. You have to learn the rhythm of that. I won't say it's the greatest feat of coordination in the world, but you do have to learn it. And how to skip rope, which again is not the biggest deal in the world, but there it is.

Maybe in a way Coxsackie did reform me, because if I hadn't been sent up there, I doubt now that I ever would have really learned boxing bumming around the Bronx the way I was. I might have, but knowing me I doubt it. I would have been much more likely to stop a slug from some cop's gun before I learned anything. So maybe Coxsackie was a good thing, not that I'd really recommend it as a way to get started in life.

Anyway, I got better and better, though I still was just a punk kid, mind you, not up to any real professional fighting, or even top amateur fighting like the Diamond Belt. And I was getting along better because I could work myself till I got so tired that all I wanted to do was go to sleep. And Father Joseph kept his eye on me, and it seemed to me that even the screws were easier to get along with. Anyway, they didn't seem to have such a hard look on their faces anymore—after all, if a kid is punching a heavy bag he obviously can't be making a dagger out of a mess-hall spoon.

One day I was horsing around in the gym and I heard someone say, "Hey, Willie Sutton, how's the big breakout artist?"

I turned around and there was the Rock. He gave me a big grin and waved his fist under my nose. "I told you you couldn't bust outta this place," he said, "but I didn't figure you had to go to all that trouble to prove it to me." He opened his hand and offered it to me to shake. "I just came around to say so long," he said. "I'll see you on the outside, provided you ever get out with a head as thick as the one you got."

I shook his hand. "You made it," I said.

"Like a breeze," he answered, laughing. The Rock is a great guy for laughing, and always was. "Standing on my head. I'm finished with this dump finally. Tomorrow's my last day, then back to the old stamping grounds." He stopped and looked at me. "Say, I was watching you for a little. You move pretty good, and from the muscle you was puttin' on that bag, you might have a punch. You gotten into any of the fights here?"

I shook my head. "Not yet. I been thinking about it."

The Rock laughed again. "You know, I did pretty good here," he said. "I went undefeated on all the cards they held. If you hadn't been such a sap and gotten yourself thrown into the hole, you coulda seen me flatten a couple of guys. But not you . . ." His voice sort of trailed off. "I been thinking," he said, "that when I go back I might take a crack at finding out how you go about getting into the pros."

That was right down my alley. "Why not?" I said. "I been thinking that way, too. I figure I get enough experience around here, I might know enough to win at least a few in the amateurs and show enough maybe to get some manager interested in me."

We were standing there still talking and there was a crash from the ring. Some kid had been decked. I looked over and recognized the kid who was still on his feet. I mean I didn't really recognize him like I knew him, but I'd seen him around the gym a lot—one of those real tough-guy types, always trying to flatten someone.

I punched Rocky on the arm. "Who's that bum up there?" I asked him. "He always seems to be knocking some kid down."

Rocky looked at him and then back at me. "Now I'll give you another piece of advice," he said. "Leave him alone. He's a big, tough, nasty guy. He's the light-heavyweight champ around here. Even I never fought him because he outweighs me by so much. But don't get any ideas. He's not only big, he's tough. A lot of guys have tried to take him because he's a real shit. Even if he knows that a kid is inexperienced and is just sparring with him as a favor, he never holds back. He tries to flatten the kid just as if it was a real match that he wanted to win."

Even back then Rocky was a great guy for telling other people what they should do in their lives. I could feel myself beginning to boil a little inside, so I said, "Why don't somebody tell him to lay off the kids? The guards or somebody? Are they afraid of him?"

The Rock put his hand on my arm. "They have told him," he said. "Especially Father Joseph. But they can't follow him around every minute of the day. He's got a kind of a special dispensation at the moment. He's training for the CYO fights next week and he's in here practically all the time training. Sometimes those CYO kids are pretty rough themselves, you know."

I knew. We all knew that the Catholic Youth Organization in New York was sending up a team of its fighters—

and it's funny, the guy's at Coxsackie were all for their guys winning, even the guards and maybe Father Joseph for all I knew, all rooting for this collection of bums against the good clean-cut kids like the CYO said that it turned out.

At this moment the bum in the ring leaned out over the ropes and yelled out, "Okay, you guys! Who's next? C'mon, one of ya, I need the work!"

I thought to myself inside, oh, shit. Without stopping myself I yelled up to him, "Okay, big shot! Wait a minute, I'll go some with you!"

The big guy gave me one of those shit-eating grins and said, "Okay, hurry it up, I don't want to get cooled off."

Without looking at me and barely moving his lips, Rock said, "You're out of your bloody skull. I'm glad you can learn by taking somebody else's advice."

"Never mind that," I said, "help me into a set of gloves."

The gloves were hung by their laces off a row of hooks screwed into the wall, and I went over and got a pair and the Rock helped me into them and laced them for me, all the time muttering, "Jesus Christ, maybe I won't see you when you get out, maybe you won't live to get outta here, you're too nuts for me, whaddaya got in your head, rocks? Like I told ya, he's too good for ya, wait till ya got a few fights under your belt, why do you always have to learn the hard way?"

I told him, "Aw, he got my goat. He's a big-mouth wise guy. All I wanna do is get one good crack at him, then we'll see how good he is."

Rock wasn't impressed. "I already told ya how good he is," he said, "but you want to prove it again for yourself, so go ahead."

"Even if you're right, it's too late now," I said. "I ain't gonna back down in front of the whole gym."

By now the guy in the ring was yelling, "Come on, come on, either come on or forget it, I'm gettin' cold."

So I crossed over and climbed up into the ring, and Rock was right. Up in Heaven, credit another right for him. The bell rang and I came out of my corner figuring I was fast, so I'd rush him, and I did. I *was* fast, but he was just as fast, and he was fast in the right way. He let me get almost to him, then he sideslipped a little, not much, just enough to let my punch miss him, and I got a left in the mouth. I turned, and I got another left in the mouth. I slowed up just long enough to try to get set, which he didn't bother to do, and this time I got a left-right combination in the face.

It won't prove anything to try to describe what happened in that ring. All it proved was that for all the fights I'd been in over the last eight years, I didn't know anything about fighting. All I knew was to bore and bull and fight my way in, taking five to land one, but this guy knew so much more than I did that I wasn't getting in, no way at all. He wasn't even bothering to try to feint me, he was just letting me get almost to him, then he'd slide his head maybe three inches, no more, and my punch would go by and *bam!* there I was with a fist in my mouth again.

Another thing I found out was that you can't go on fighting that way forever, no matter what condition you're in, or think you're in, and after a while I began to find I was running out of gas. The bell rang and I walked over and down out of the ring, so mad at myself that I could hardly see, and I held out the gloves so that Rocky could get them off, and the guy in the ring yelled out, "Hey, big nose, learn something before you try to get into a ring again!"

I started to jerk around but Rocky had me by the wrists and he jerked me right back.

"Watsa matter with ya?" he snarled. "That guy was cutting you apart. You wanna go back and get cut into hamburger? Didn't I tell you you needed more experience? What gave you the idea this guy was gonna let you bull in there and hit him first? You know any fighter gonna let you do that?"

Suddenly I lost all the hot I had and all I felt was the hard determination that I knew what I was going to do.

I leaned over to Rocky as he was pulling the gloves off and I said, "Okay, I'll tell you what I'm gonna do. I promise it to you, I swear it to you on my mother's grave, I'm gonna take that guy before I get outta here, I'm gonna take him."

"Yeah, yeah," Rocky said. Then he looked at me again and shook his head slowly. "You know something? I believe you."

The weeks went by.

It's not only the time that gets you in a prison, it's the whole filthy atmosphere. I guess what people think about prisons—people who haven't been in them—they get from writers who haven't served any time themselves either, and they go ahead and write stories about what they think happens there and it turns out mostly to be crap. In the first place a minimum of ninety-nine percent of the guys in prison belong there. My own personal opinion is it's a strain to call them human beings. They're animals and they act like animals. They have gangs and cliques because that's how they exist. You talk about segregation, prison is the place to find it because that's how you stay alive. I remember I almost triggered off a riot because there was this white kid that used to hang around the gym, one of those kids that the world is always picking on because he doesn't fight back enough and he looks like he's dying in front of your eyes, and I found out that one of these black kids is forcing him to be his girl. I dug up the black kid and told him, "If a guy wants to do it, that's okay by me, but any of this forcing and I'll personally take you apart bone by bone, you understand that?" He had a couple of his friends with him, and I could see what was going through their heads—jump me or not jump me? I guess they remembered the three guards and decided no, and for weeks after that I kept hearing how there was going to be this riot that was going to find me dead, and for weeks I kept watching that I was never off unprotected by myself.

I guess the only thing that kept me going, really, was the gym. The rest of it was all such an endless eternal drag that no one who's never done time can imagine what it's like. It's waking up in the morning and knowing this is another day that you gotta do, that you gotta get through, waiting, waiting, waiting—waiting for chowtime, waiting for work, waiting for exercise, waiting to try to get to sleep. Of course, none of my family was any good at writing, but then what the hell could they tell me anyway, that they were still on relief? So I heard damned little from home. But what I did do was spend all the time I could at the gym learning every move I could and always getting a kid as a sparing partner who was either bigger or better than I was.

One day, just as I was finishing a sparring session, I heard Father Joseph call me.

"Hiya, Dad!" I said.

He made the same face he always did when I called him that and said, "If I've told you once I've told you a thousand times that you don't call a priest 'Dad.' You call me 'Father Joseph.'"

I gave him the innocent look I always did. "Yeah, and I've asked you a thousand times what's the difference and you ain't come up with a real good answer yet."

He gave me a little laugh like he always did. "You look pretty good in there," he said, nodding toward the ring. "Maybe you're not ready to go out and win the championship, but you look pretty good."

I knew I did and nodded my head. "Every week I get a little bit better," I said.

He lifted up one of my gloves and started unlacing it. "That isn't what I came to talk to you about," he said. "What I came to talk to you about is that maybe I have some good news for you. Your first parole hearing is scheduled to come up this month, and yesterday I had a long talk with the commissioner. When it came to your case and I told him what I had to say, I got the feeling that he's inclined to give you a break."

I could feel the excitement bubble up in me. He had the gloves off by that time and I took him by both arms. "What does that mean?" I asked him, excited.

He smiled. "It means maybe you're going to get out of here pretty soon—within a few weeks."

I spun around three times. "No kiddin'! Wow!"

He waited till I quieted down a little, then he said, "When you do get out of here, Jake—well, I feel I still have a responsibility to you. Obviously I can't follow you down to the Bronx and make sure that you don't go out nights mugging drunks and trying to break into jewelry stores. But what are you going to do? What plans do you have? I'd be easier in my own mind if I knew that you had something that you were really serious about."

I clasped his arms again. "You know what I'm serious about," I told him. "I'm serious about fighting. I'm gonna be a fighter. I always wanted to be one and up here now I've found out I can be one!"

I began to dance around the gym, shadowboxing. Then I thought of something. This was early in November, and I said, "There's one thing. There's no chance of me being thrown outta here before Thanksgiving, is there?"

Father Joseph looked at me strangely, then asked, "Now what are you up to? Why wouldn't you want to get out of here before Thanksgiving, of all times?"

"You forgot," I told him. "You know I'm matched to meet the champ here. On Thanksgiving. You know for six months I done nothin' except get ready to fight this bum. And you know I'm gonna flatten him."

That reminded me that I'd just finished sparring and I picked up the skipping rope. "Excuse me, Father," I told him, "I'm beginning to cool off too much, I gotta skip rope for a coupla rounds, okay? But thanks a lot, don't think I don't appreciate it. I think you're a real doll."

He grinned at me and nodded and started off. A long time later he told me that what he was saying to himself as he walked away was a small prayer to the Heavenly Father. He was saying, he told me, "Father of us all, forgive me, but this is one fight I've just got to see."

EIGHT

Actually it never turned out to be all that good of a fight, and I think it was mostly this other bum's fault. What he was counting on was the fact that he had at least ten or fifteen pounds on me, and he was the champ and he remembered what a slob I had been the time I sparred with him. Never underestimate anybody, is my thinking.

Anytime he fought, of course, it was a big fight, and the gymnasium was full that night. Besides all the prisoners there were all the guards who weren't on duty, and a whole lot of civilian personnel, and right down at ringside was Father Joseph and the warden.

I was as tense as a strung wire, the way I always used to be when I was a kid before the start of a fight, bouncing up and down in my corner, and when the referee called us out into the center of the ring for the instructions, I swear I didn't hear a word he said. I was looking out over everybody there who had come to watch me fight, and I was so tense and excited you could have fired a cannon and I wouldn't have heard it. I wouldn't even touch gloves with that son of a bitch I was so wound up, and I never gave a good goddamn for that ceremony anyway.

The bell rang and I came charging out of my corner like I always did and I saw this guy sort of grin, because it was like when I offered to get in the ring with him the first time and looked like such a goddamned fool. I could see things like a grin when I was fighting, even back then. There are fighters who tell you they never see anything in the ring, except maybe the other guy's gloves, or just a body moving around that they're trying to kill maybe the way a bullfighter doesn't see anything except the figure of the bull he's trying to kill. Some fighters say they wouldn't

74

even recognize an opponent the day after a fight if they saw him walking down the street, and maybe I wouldn't either, but in the ring I could see this grin.

This time I wasn't the slob I was before. This time I knew that the guy was going to sidestep and I was watching for it, watching which way he was going, and I went with him and held the punch just long enough so that instead of throwing it away I got it in his mush—not a solid punch, not a good punch, but enough of a one so that he knew he'd been hit. I'd also slowed up enough so that I didn't charge on past him. I went maybe an extra step and swung back, and when he threw a punch at me, I was ready and expecting it.

I slid in under it and I got in maybe four or five cuts at his gut before he was able to back off and dance a little to show that he hadn't been hurt at all. By now there was no grin on his face. This time he was looking at me a little surprised and a little wary. He was too good for something like this to throw him off stride, but I don't think he realized how far along I'd come.

A fight is all of a piece, you get moving in a certain rhythm, you can't stop, it's all got to go along. It's true that you have to stop at the end of every round, but once you've started you have to keep going, you don't stop till you get to the end.

Anyway, after I turned around, I just kept bobbing and weaving and, after a second or two, he saw I wasn't coming charging in, and he felt he was still the champ of the place. He knew he was heavier than me and had the confidence to go with it, so he flicked out the left, but I moved my head and it fell short.

Yeah, I had improved tremendously, and it might have gone on to be a very interesting fight—but then it happened. He feinted me and hit me with a powerful right hand. It stunned me, and suddenly this fear gripped me, deep in my gut. I couldn't understand it, he hadn't hurt me that bad. He kept pouring it on, but I don't think I felt any more punches.

I remember pushing him away hard and that he went skittering away from me. I remember him grinning again, a real cocky grin, because he was professional enough to know that if an opponent pushes you rather than returns with punches, he's either hurt or dazed or confused. Well, the grin must have done it, because that fear turned into a blinding rage. "Fuck it," I said, "I'm not gonna let him get me. Fuck everybody. I'll get it some day, but not now, you rat bastard, not if I get you first. . . ."

He came at me, still grinning, skipping in and side to side gracefully, and jabbed once, twice. I slipped under the jab and then I went after him.

I still don't know how to explain it, but I felt that if I didn't destroy him, he would destroy me, and that for some reason he had a right to destroy me. And that enraged me more—the fact that somehow I felt he had that right. And that's what I went out to fight, to kill.

He tried an uppercut after his second jab, but I blocked it and countered with a shot into his gut. He gasped and tried to slither away, but I wouldn't let him. I bulled him against the ropes and I must have got in eight or ten punches. All I was thinking was, I've got to get this guy first! I've got to get this son of a bitch! I'll get him! I'll kill him! And even while all that was going through my head in a wild swirl—and if you'd have been inside my head, you'd have thought I was crazy—even then I saw that the punching was getting to him and that his guard dropped a little, and I saw an opening and I let go the gut-punching and went for his head—and he was at my feet.

He was lying there, and the referee was crowding me, and it had all happened so fast that for a second or two I couldn't realize that I really had won—that I'd really flattened this guy. I was giving the referee some muscle but he was big enough so that I wasn't really worrying him, and he just stayed in front of me and kept saying, "Okay, okay, okay! The fight is over. Ease it off, kid, ease it off. Over to a neutral corner." And he got me there and moved back over to this other kid so he could count him out, but he stood so that he could look at me at the same time, and finally I began to quiet down and get so that I wasn't all out of control. I could feel my own heart beating.

I looked down at ringside and saw Father Joseph, and he wasn't smiling at me. He wasn't smiling at all. Well, the hell with that. It wasn't up to me to figure out what was eating at him. The rest of the gym was roaring over the knockout—not that I was the favorite, mind you, I mean even in the way they felt I wasn't what you'd call a lovable figure. But the crowd is always great when it sees a knockout. That's a thing about a crowd, they're crazy to see some guy get his brains knocked out.

Anyhow, that was the second-last time I saw Father Joseph at Coxsackie. The last time was the day they let me out.

That day they always bring you in to say good-bye to the warden, and of course he always has to give the little talk about being a good, clean-cut American boy and keeping your nose out of trouble. The guard who brought me into the office gave me the "Good-bye, champ, lots of luck" bit, and the warden—well, at least he tried to be nice.

"Well, Jake, you're going home," he said, and when I didn't say anything he went on: "Jake, you know the way you dead-pan it all, I can't tell anything you're thinking, but I just want to say one thing. I saw that last fight of yours, you know, and you've got gold in your fists. I'm no expert on the fight game, but if you can cut down a man that much bigger than yourself when you're only sixteen, I'd be willing to bet that one day you can become a real top fighter. But I want to give you a couple of words of advice, and I hope that you'll listen to them. If you go back to the city and take up where you left off, you'll be back here in three months with a lot tougher rap."

I didn't say anything, and after a while the warden got up from his desk and walked around and stuck out his hand. "Well," he said, "good-bye and good luck anyway."

I never knew how to act at times like that, so I just nodded and shook his hand.

"Can I say good-bye to Father Joseph?" I asked him.

"Yeah, sure," he said. "Of course."

At this time of day, Father Joseph would be in the little chapel, so I went there and there he was, kneeling in the front pew. I was standing at the back, but there's some sense that you have when another person comes into a place where you are, and after a minute Father Joseph turned around and saw me. He crossed himself and motioned me to come up and sit down in the pew beside him.

Church or chapel is strictly not my beat, but I went up, sweating, and sat down, and the good padre sort of smiled at me and reached under his habit and brought out a handkerchief and handed it to me. For a second I didn't get it, then he pointed to my forehead and I mopped it away.

"Sweating quite a bit," Father Joseph said.

"Pretty hot in here," I said.

He knew better than that. He said, "So you're leaving us."

Like I said, I'm not used to being nice, or even honest. So it took me a while.

"Yeah," I said. I looked away from him and mopped my face again. Still looking away I said, "Actually, I just came over here to say good-bye. It's kind of silly but now that I'm here I don't know what to say—except good-bye. And I wanted to tell you that I think everything you did for me is great, and I'm sorry I didn't do more for you. You're the only guy I ever knew that did something for me that didn't want a cut of the take." I stopped for a second or so and then I said, "I'm gonna miss talking to you."

Father Joseph kept looking at me, and after a time he said, "Well, maybe it won't be the same thing, Jake, but if you ever get the feeling you'd like to be talking to me and you can't, just go into a church and have a chat with Him."

He nodded toward the altar, where there was a crucifix maybe five feet tall.

This time I really didn't know what to say. I couldn't tell him about all the things that were bothering me—for example, knocking off Harry Gordon. I'd thought it was such a break, here while the cops were doing their duty by the Harry Gordon bit, but I'd never been able to get it out of my mind. Some times were worse than others, and now that I was going back it seemed to be the worst of all. This obsession I had was getting worse all the time: the feeling that I'd be walking along the street someday and two plainclothes cops could come along, one on each side of me, and one of them would say, "Jake, did you ever hear of a bookie up in your neighborhood in the Bronx named Harry Gordon?"

But could I say all that to Father Joseph? I could not. I don't know what the ground rules are about confessing a murder to a prison chaplain, but I wasn't about to find out the hard way.

Even so, I came within an ace of giving it away.

I could feel myself sweating again, and Father Joseph looked at me with that curious expression of his like he knew a lot more than I thought he knew, and he said to me, very softly, "Jake, is there something you want to tell me? Something else that I don't know? You know I've never tried to trap you, but don't try to keep things bottled up inside you forever. Guilt is a complex thing, Jake—I think you're too young to realize it, but slowly it begins to make you hate yourself because you know you've done something wrong, no matter whether anyone else knows it, and that forces you to know that you're not the man people think you are, and after a while it makes you begin to hate other people, everyone you meet, because they assume that you're better than you are, which is only more of a reproach to you. Don't try to keep things bottled up forever. If you feel this way, don't let these feelings consume you. Release them, talk them out. It may not be as black as you think it is. I've never probed at you, Jake, but I see that something is troubling you. Trust me. Let me help you. Have faith in me."

He saw how I was standing without moving, then he gestured to the altar again and said, "Or if you can't have faith in me at least have faith in Him. Tell Him what's troubling you, Jake, and ask His forgiveness. Ask Him to set your feet on the right path. Jake, you've got to trust someone."

There it was again. I felt like screaming at him, *You don't know what it is! You don't know how bad it is! You don't understand!* But I knew that would blow it, and sud-

denly I couldn't take it any longer. I said in a low, stran-
gled voice, "You don't understand how it is. I can't trust
anybody, I never learned how. . . ."

And suddenly I was afraid to stay there another second,
so I said good-bye and turned and ran out of the chapel.

NINE

I got my stuff back to the administration building and went out the front door and started down the steps—and who was there, down at the bottom of the steps, waiting for me? Pete, of course. Who else? I rushed down and we threw our arms around each other and started punching each other, yelling at each other, "You old son of a bitch, you haven't changed a bit." "Yes you have. You've got uglier." When we quieted down, Pete grinned and pointed a little way down the street toward a shining ball of a new convertible with two little broads inside who looked about sixteen made up to look like they're twenty-two and said, "And what do you think of that?"

"Brother, oh brother," I said.

Pete looked up at the walls of Coxsackie.

"Boy, let's get outta here. Even being outside this joint gives me the creeps."

"Howja know I was gettin' out today?" I asked him as we walked toward the car.

"Your mother told me," he said. "Boy, is she happy. They wanted to send somebody up from the family but—"

"I know, but they didn't have the money," I said, and Pete sort of laughed.

"Yeah," he said, "so I thought I'd make your day for you." He pointed to the car again.

"You did," I told him. "Complete with broads. You must be doing all right since the last time I saw you."

He gave me that shit-eating grin and said, "Yeah, I'll tell you about it."

He introduced the two dames, and I still remember their names—May was his and Tessie was mine. We get into the car, Pete in front with May and me in back with

Tessie, and we wheeled back to the good old Bronx, going about fifteen miles an hour faster than we should, the way Pete always did, and he started telling me how we'd have a ball for a couple of days to make up for the prison, and then we'd go back to work to get a bankroll started. I didn't much like the way he said "work." I made a sour face at the back of his head.

"You still doing the same old bit?" I asked him.

He turned around and took a quick look at me, then he broke out laughing at my puss. "No, of course not," he said. "I turned sucker and I got a regular job with a lunch pail and everything." Then he turned a little serious. "What regular jobs you know get you all this?" He showed me the lapel of his suit, which I'll grant even back then probably cost a hundred bucks. "And this?" and he patted the steering wheel of the car. "And a beautiful doll like this?" and he patted May on the knee. "And finally this?" he asked, reaching in his pocket and bringing out a wad of dough that he waved at me. "Go on, take it, it's for you," he said. "It's a stake till you can get going. Buy yourself some clothes so you don't look like you just climbed out from under a rock."

He tossed the money back to me and I picked it up and riffled through it. I didn't say anything, then after a while Pete said, "Cat got your tongue?"

I let it go for a minute, then I said, "Pete, maybe I'm stupid, but I don't want this dough. I made up my mind back there. I done all the steppin' out I'm gonna do."

He was so surprised he nearly turned the car into a god-damned ditch.

"Watch it, watch it!" I yelled.

"Watch it?" he asked. "When you spring something like that on me? You go soft in the head back up at that joint?"

Well, I was a little ashamed, but I wasn't going to change my mind, even for Pete. "I ain't goin' back into the can," I said. "I ain't smart enough to be a thief. I can't waste time in jail. It drives you nuts."

"What are you gonna do for eating money?" he asked. "Join your old man in the peddling business?"

"I'm gonna fight," I told him. "I'm gonna be a pro."

The goddamned car swerved again. This time Pete swung it off to the shoulder of the road and stopped. He looked at me, then he put his little finger in his ear and wiggled it like he hadn't heard right. "Something wrong here," he said. "I thought I heard someone in the back seat talking about being a pro fighter, and it can't be Tessie. She's too smart."

"Knock off the wise-guy bit," I told him. "I said it and I mean it. What the hell's wrong with that?"

He shook his head. "You know what's wrong with it as well as I do," he said. "It's a sucker game. It's a mug's game. You know what kind of a beating you take in a pro fight? Those guys ain't in there to look pretty, you know. How many of those guys you seen with their brains beat out? Thirty-five years old and they're sellin' apples or shinin' shoes? Come on, Jake, that's for slobs that can't do nothin' else." He laughed. "I know what it is. You're stir crazy! I never seen an actual case before and here I got one right in the car with me."

"Aw, balls," I said. "I tell you I got it figured out. A guy like me, the only thing I can do for money is either steal or fight. You know what my record is in the stealing department. And I tell you what, I'd rather cut my throat than go through again what I just went through. I knew some creeps before, but you should see some of the guys they got up in that place. The only way they gonna reform them is with a bullet right between the eyes. So that's what I decided. Fightin'." And I added: "Besides, for Christ-sake, I'm pretty good at it and I like it. And not every guy that's ever been a fighter has to end up on stumblebum street, there's some guys made a pretty good thing out of it."

Pete looked at me.

"Okay," he said, "I know better than to try to argue you outta something when you got that look on your face. So keep the dough and go into fightin' and get your brains beat out and then come back and tell me I was right all the time."

He turned around to start the car, but I hit him on the shoulder.

"No, listen," I said. "I know I can make it. I can go

pretty far. It's better than going back and having the cops on my ass every time they need to make a quick pickup."

Pete shrugged his shoulders. "Okay," he said. "You haven't *always* been wrong, though pretty near. Anyway, you got your mind made up, so what do I do except say I hope that you make it?"

I said, "Look, why don't you think about it? Okay, I know you're doin' all right. I can see that. Maybe you're smarter than me, but that don't prove you're the smartest guy in the world. You can get busted in the rackets, you know. And you got a pretty good right hand, you're not too much of a slouch yourself when it comes to fighting."

Pete turned around again. "You have got to be joking," he said.

I was getting all fired up. "No," I said, "why not take a crack at it? What can you lose? You win, you got plenty of dough without having to jump every time those creeps in the mob tell you to." Which shows you how smart I was. "Besides," I said, giving Tessie a little pat, "you know how broads always go for fighters. And if it blows up, you can always go back to holding up bookmakers or whatever it is."

As soon as the sentence was out I could have bit off my tongue, and I guess Pete saw it because right away he said, "Running a little action is what I'm doin', and you wouldn't believe how I got the piece. I think the mob was so surprised at an ignorant kid like me moving in on their operation they couldn't believe it, and finally they said, 'Okay, leave the stupid little bastard alone, he's too dumb to kill.' " He stopped and looked at me and stuck out his hand. "Okay," he said. "Why not? Why not give it a shot. I'm in." Then he looked at the little broad beside him and put on that mock-alarm look of his. "Maybe I spoke too fast, Jake. Maybe I oughtta think it over a little more."

"Why?"

He patted his face. Like I said, he was a pretty good-looking guy, not like me. Then he said, "We never was beauties, Jake. Wait till the real bombers get through with us, there won't be a high-class doll east of the Hudson who'll look at us twice." And he turned around to wink at me. *"Wait* a minute! No staying up late. No smoking. No boozing. No broads. Positively no broads at all."

We were both looking at these dames out of the corner of our eyes—and they looked at each other and then at us as if we'd suddenly turned into a couple of lepers—till we both broke out laughing and reached over for them and pulled them into our arms and began loving them up. And we went to a motel—motor lodges, they called them in those days—and you know what? After all those months in Coxsackie, I didn't make out.

That was a strange thing about me and broads. There were times, sometimes months on end, when I'd be impotent. Sometimes I felt I'd go out of my mind about it because it would happen all of a sudden, without warning, and it seemed like for no reason at all. I couldn't figure any reason for it, physical or psychological, and then after I was about ready to commit suicide, I'd be all right again.

What made it ironic was that the nickname that was hung on me early in my fighting career, and the one that a lot of people can remember even today, was "The Bronx Bull"—"The Bull of the Bronx." That was because of the way I fought—charge out of the corner, punch, punch, punch, never give up, take all the punishment the other guy could hand out but stay in there, slug and slug and slug. But the bull, of course, is also the symbol of sexual prowess, the all-conquering male that can handle a whole herd of cows, that has to have a barn to himself because of his violence when he gets on the prod. And here was me, the raging Bull of the Bronx, not able to make it with a very willing teenage chick.

Like everyone else, there was a period when my big idea was to see how many I could get in a day or a week, or whatever, and if you're the champ or on the way up it's no trick at all. But to be impotent? You know, here you are the world's champ, which means you're supposed to be the symbol of complete masculinity, and man number one with the choice of any broad you wanted, and you can't even get laid.

I don't think it was the training or the fighting—like I say, I don't know what it was, but I've known other fight-

ers that will tell you the same thing. In fact I remember
once we were in this apartment, me and a dame, and Pete
was out in the living room drinking and listening to the
radio, and I couldn't do a goddamned thing good for her,
and finally she got so hot she called Pete in and I got so
goddamned mad that I threw my clothes on and went
storming out of the apartment. I didn't see Pete for two
days. But I didn't blame him. It was my fault, whatever it
was. Once he told me that it was because I didn't know
anything about women. If they were high class, you know,
if they looked like one of those expensive blondes you see
in the movies, not the tramp kind, I'd have some block
about making them even if they wanted it, like they were
too good for me.

And, like I said, I didn't hold this dame in the apartment against Pete, because it was my fault, and anyway we
were often trading dames back and forth. In fact I remember clearly that maybe the first time I got laid there were
five of us in this car and it was snowing and we were driving around the Bronx, not doing anything, just driving. It
was night. There was this guy driving—I've forgotten his
name—and there was this dame in the middle of the front
seat, and me, and Pete was in the back with this other
broad. Pete was trying to make out and he seemed to be
going along pretty good, and I was trying a little of it with
the doll in the front seat, but with her it was strictly *no,
no, no, I'm a virgin,* so I gave up. What the hell was I
gonna do, rape her? Like I said, I didn't know how to go
about it, and suddenly I looked in the back seat—we'd
stopped at a traffic light—and I'll be a son of a bitch, Pete
had it made. He was going at it hot and heavy. After he
finished he looked up and saw me, and my mouth must
have been open so wide you could have put a punching
bag in there. And he sat up, fixing his clothes, and motioned to ask if I wanted to come in back. And the doll
was fixing her pants and muttering, "Oh, Pete, how could
you do a thing like that? I'm not that sort of girl at all. I
didn't know you were going to do anything like that." And
when we stopped for another traffic light Pete slipped out
of the back seat and around to the front and I went to the
back seat. I put my arm out for her and she gave me the

same business that one in the front seat had—*no, no, no*—after I'd just watched her getting laid. *Enough is enough!* I got her in a lock where she could barely move and I shoved my hat in her face so she couldn't talk and pushed her down and got on her. Not what you'd call a real big romantic deal, but most women only got one thing going for them anyway, so why screw around?

Anyhow, that was afterward.

What happened that day coming back from Coxsackie was that when Pete drove me home, Joey was out watching for me, and as Pete's car came down the street Joey went charging into the house, and by the time Pete stopped in front of the place everyone was running down the steps, my mother and my sisters and the boys, and they were all crying and laughing and kissing me and hitting me on the back, welcoming me home. Everybody except the old man, who was off trying to pick up a few nickels somewhere, but even if he'd been there I don't know that he'd have bothered to walk down the stairs.

I hadn't been kidding with Pete about the fighting. As he started up his car to pull away after he'd said hello to the family, I yelled after him, "Remember, two days off! Then I see you in the gym!"

He waved and took off, then Mamma said, "Now what, Jake?"

I put my arm around her shoulders. "I made up my mind, Mamma. I ain't gonna be picked up by the police anymore. I did pretty good up there fighting in the ring and Pete and me are gonna give it a real crack and see if we can make some money that way."

She looked at me sort of shaking her head, and tears were coming from her eyes. She didn't know anything about fighting, but she knew enough to know it wasn't like I was going into the priesthood, but at the same time it was a hell of a step up from trying to break into jewelry stores.

Back in those days there were a lot of gyms for boxers, it was no trick at all to get started. Managers, by and large, were a collection of thieves and almost to a man tied in with the mob, but they were always on the lookout for a promising kid, because even if the kid wasn't destined to become a champ, still if you're taking a third or a half of his purses, besides what you can steal, you can make money out of even a second-rate fighter. And there's plenty of fighters who bring in money even if they're not the champ because they're so colorful that the crowd goes to watch them fight. Fight crowds go to watch fighters for a lot of different reasons. Why the hell would anybody go to see "Two Ton" Tony Galento fight except that he was such a tough bundle of lard that you needed an ax to stop him? Look at the trouble Louis had with him. And later, when I had a name, plenty of people came to see me fight just in the hope of seeing me get my brains knocked out.

Right or wrong, I blame the newspaper guys a lot for that. There was a time when there wasn't more than two or three of them I was on speaking terms with, and why? Because they said all I knew how to do was to get in there and slug. I didn't have any style or what they call finesse, not that any of these writers was ever in a ring themselves. Okay, if you want a Fancy Dan, that I wasn't. What's that got to do with fighting? One of the things I'm proudest of is that Rocky Marciano once said I was the greatest fighter he'd ever seen.

But I'm getting ahead of myself. As I said, Pete and I started going to the gym every day and we did a lot of training with each other, but we'd also spar with any guy we could get, so that slowly we were learning. Like anything else, in boxing you got to figure things out in advance and practice just as long as you can, and the more different guys you spar with the more moves you learn and the less likely you are to get into a ring with a guy who's got a style you can't figure out till you hear the announcer telling the crowd that you blew it.

And I also noticed that around the gym all the time there were the mob guys, for the very simple reason that there's always betting on fights, and betting means money, and wherever there's money there's the mob. If you paste that inside your hat it will explain a lot of things to you and maybe even save you some trouble.

Anyhow, there's the mob guys in their sharp clothes, and a couple of them look like some of the guys that were in the dice game that Pete and me held up, though that doesn't make any difference because these guys always look alike, they have the look or they get it, just the way cops do. Salvy is always around with them, and the way he's sucking around, lighting their cigarettes and running to do errands for them, it's obvious he's an apprentice thug.

There was this incident Pete told me about. He was outside the candy store one day, leaning against the corner post and reading the *Mirror,* when a Cadillac pulled up with Salvy driving and this guy Nick in the front seat. Nick *is* one of the mob guys, he's an older guy, maybe in his thirties, and he calls Pete and waves him over to the car and says, "Pete, you know, I seen you and Jakey banging away down at the gym and it seems to me and a couple of the other guys that you two boys got something. We was thinking that we'd like to manage you."

Pete wasn't surprised, even though we were only a couple of teenage kids. "We're just amateurs," he said.

Nick gave him the big-smile bit. "I know," he said, "but every fighter starts out as an amateur. And smart guys pick up fighters then, they don't wait till the guy starts getting himself a name and then there's a lot of yap in the newspapers about who's paying off to take over his contract. Look, Pete," he went on, "you're a knock-around guy, you know the score, I can level with you. You know me and the other boys are in boxing all the way, no fighter can get anywhere without us. I know how you and Jake feel about each other. That's why I came to you. We can help each other."

"Aw, Nick," Pete told him, "I'm just doing this fighting thing for kicks. It don't matter to me one way or another. Maybe I'll pick up a little change. Anyway, I'll get some action out of it. But Jake, it's his whole life. He's got nothin' else going for him. Give him a break. Leave him be."

Naturally, this is not what you tell a mob guy, especially if you're a kid like Pete and the buddy-buddy thing falls flat.

Nick looked at him hard and said, "You know, you bother me, the way you act sometimes. What's this *leave him alone?* I got leprosy or something? Whatsa matter with you two guys? I seen both of you work, you were great on that crap-game contract. You're part of us, you're like us, you live off the streets, whatsa matter all of a sudden?" He looked at Pete even colder. "And if it comes to that," he went on, "how come you're not in the family in the first place? You're one of us, ain't you got no respect for the way to do things?"

You know, the way we were brought up and the place we were brought up, staying out of the mob wasn't the easiest thing in the world, and besides that, if there was one thing Pete did *not* want, it was to have Nick down on him. You can live an awful short life that way. So he said, "No, no, Nick, it ain't that way at all. You know how it is with kids, you want to find some way to make it on your own so that you don't have to be beholden to nobody. That's the way it is with Jake and me. Christ, we ain't even twenty years old yet. . . ."

But Nick was burned, so he broke in: "Want to make it on your own yet? You know what you can make on your own, don't you, Mister Chump?" He snapped his fingers. "Nothin', that's what!" He motioned to Salvy to move and the car started rolling. "I'll tell you what, friend Pete, and you can pass the message on to that thick-headed bully-boy. You're both knocking your brains out for nothin', boy, and that's the way it's gonna stay until you smarten up! Get me a message when you change your mind!"

When Pete told me all this, I shrugged. I figured all along that this would happen, but I hadn't expected it this quick. "Whaddaya think?" I asked.

He shook his head. "Maybe I ain't the brightest guy in the world," he said, "but one thing I know. One thing I now made up my mind about. The mob is not for me. It's too tough. They got as many creeps as anywhere else, and they get fightin', there's always fightin' where there's either money or broads involved, so sooner or later you end up feet first in the East River. I say stay out."

I agreed with him. But it didn't make me feel any happier. I could see the feud going on forever, with no guarantee at all that the good guys would win.

TEN

Pete and I went on with our training and went into the Diamond Belt, and I began to see my name in the newspapers. The Diamond Belt was sponsored by a newspaper in New York, and while that paper gave the fights the biggest play, it was for charity, so the other papers covered it, too. Back then, fights were one of the big things for sports, like I guess pro football is today. Like I read the old Romans had bread and circuses, we had home relief and boxing. At the Diamond Belt thing, the men used to come in white tie and tails, the women in evening gowns, and the photographers would take as many pictures of them as they took of the fighters. I still have the clippings I saved—or my mother saved—of those old fights,

JAKE LA MOTTA AND STABLEMATE,
PETE PETRELLA, STANDOUTS IN
DIAMOND BELT TOURNAMENT

LA MOTTA WINS FOURTH STRAIGHT,
PETRELLA SCORES 3D KNOCKOUT

LA MOTTA WINS IN SIZZLING
FIGHT WITH ZEKE BROWN

LA MOTTA WINS DIAMOND BELT
LIGHT-HEAVYWEIGHT TITLE IN FINALS

I remember one thing from those days that still gives Pete and me a laugh. We'd each fought the same opponent, and a couple of days later, in the gym, we were sparring away when suddenly I held up my hands and said, "Look, Pete, hold it a minute, I want you to do me a fa-

91

vor." And he said, "Okay, what is it?" And I said, "I want you to hit me on the jaw."

His mouth dropped open in surprise and he said, "Tell me again. You want me to do what?"

I said, "You heard me. I said hit me on the jaw."

He looked at me for a couple of seconds, then he shrugged his shoulders and hit me a clip with his right. But it barely jolted me.

"For Christsake," I said, "is that as hard as you can hit? I been hit harder than that by my sister. Come on, get yourself set and hit me as hard as you can. Whatsa matter, you afraid? Don't be afraid, I won't hit you back."

The last crack made him mad, of course, which was what I wanted, so he hauled off and handed me a real belt, which turned me around a little, but it didn't knock me down.

Pete looked at me with his gloves on his hips and said, "Now do you mind telling me what the hell that proved?"

I laughed at him. "I was just trying out a little experiment," I said. "You remember that guy you fought the other night that you knocked out? Well, I only decisioned him and I was trying to find out if you really had a punch or something—and you don't, ya bum, ya! How did you ever flatten this guy? You poison him first or somethin'?"

Pete put his hands on the sides of his head like he was trying to figure out what kind of a nut I was and it was too good a chance to miss so I belted him in the ribs as hard as I could and the son of a bitch had to fall into a clinch so that I couldn't hit him again.

Being an amateur is great stuff for the ego—you walk down the street and people you don't even know give you a "Hi, Jake," and when you go to the candy store you know that everybody, guys and broads alike, is saying, "That's Jake La Motta, he won the Diamond Belt." *But!* But it doesn't put dough in the kick.

Back in those Depression days there was a lot of fight clubs where some sharp operator would get a bankrupt warehouse or garage, which was about as hard to find as a guy out of work, and set up a fight club, which was largely a cheap booze joint where on other nights he was putting on dirty movies or animal acts. The standard fight night was Friday, and actually you could see some pretty good action. Some good fighters came out of these clubs. Since it still was called a club and amateur instead of professional—which would have meant all the business of getting certified by the athletic commission and all the rest of that jazz—what you got paid was a gold-plated watch that was presented to the winner in the ring—and which in the dressing room generally turned out to be tin—and however much money you could hold the owners of the joint up for before the fight. Never after, pal! Ask any hooker. What the loser got was a big thank you.

The place I'd been training at up in the Bronx was a gym called the Teasdale Athletic Club, and one of the operators around was a character called Mike, who didn't know much but who did know his way around the fight game, so I took him on as my first and last manager. The regulations say you got to have a manager, so after I got rid of Mike, I had my brother Joey on as manager, but he was only a front. Joey now lives out in Forest Hills and he has a bar in the Bronx and a jukebox route that pays pretty good.

I had my troubles with Mike as a manager, to put it mildly. I was a stupid kid, and he'd put a piece of paper in front of me and say sign, and I'd sign. So by the time I got to where my name was known he gave me a piece of paper that he said he had to have because the contract was running out and he had to have this to cover him through the rest of the year. So I signed. What else? Then I was out in Detroit for a fight and a guy said to me, "I hear you signed with Mike for eight years." And I said, *"What?"* And he said, "That's the grapevine."

When I got back to New York I called up Mike and said I had to see him, but he made a date to meet at his lawyer's office. I got a lawyer, he fixed up a release form, and I met Mike at his lawyer's office. I could have killed him without blinking an eye. Here I was getting my brains beat out fighting, and this cheap son of a bitch without the guts to fight a dead man was robbing me blind. I didn't even say hello to him. I took the release out of my pocket and said, "Sign."

He looked at me without saying anything. Then he took

the release and read it and handed it to his lawyer and said, "Jake, I can't sign that."

I said, "You cheap, chiseling son of a bitch, you sign that right here and you sign it right now or I'll strangle you. You think I'm kidding? Right here and right now, or you go out that door dead!" And I started for him.

He signed it, all right. Then he went for the cops. I found out he really didn't want to call the cops. What he really wanted was to tie up my earnings in the civil courts so that I'd pay him off just so I could eat, but to establish his civil suit he had to swear out the criminal complaint.

Well, I beat the criminal rap. My lawyer told the jury, "Look at this man, Jake La Motta, a professional prize fighter, a man as strong as a bull, he could have beaten this man to within an inch of his life, et cetera, et cetera," and the jury believed him. On the civil thing, though, he won the case, and finally I had to make a four-thousand-dollar payoff out of court to the son of a bitch to get him off my back.

Anyhow, at the start Mike had gotten me fights around the New York area, all four-round prelims, and what you got for them was twenty, thirty, forty bucks, depending on the kind of guy the manager is and how good you fight. You know, with a good fight, the crowd wants you back, they yell and applaud, the manager sees you can bring them back, so you get the fifty bucks. There was one fight when I'd really had the crowd yelling and screaming, and after it was over Pete saw the promoter come over to Mike and say, "I'm sorry, all I could get up was thirty-five bucks for the kid, but here's another ten out of my own pocket for him." Ten bucks in those days was not to be sneezed at, but did I get a smell of it? You guess.

Four-round prelims are a step up from club fights, but they're also no way to get rich, and it began to sink in on me that Mike might know the fight game, but that his connections were lousy.

Nick the mobster had been right. Without the mob I wasn't going to get anywhere in New York. There was a chance, though, to get some action in other fight towns, places like Detroit and Cleveland, where there was a different mob with their own boys who would take strangers on as opponents. As a matter of fact, my name got to be better known out there than it was in the East.

These were the years when I was fighting a lot of guys you never heard of, not even if you're a fight fan—a lot of them I can't even remember myself unless I look at the records. Floyd Lemon. Monroe Crews. Joe Baynes. Joe Fredericks. Jimmy Casa. I remember Johnny Morris because I fought him three times, and Lorenzo Strickland for the same reason, and I don't think all six fights totaled a thousand bucks in prizes.

I remember fighting a guy named Cliff Koerkle because of a funny little thing. Pete was supposed to see that fight and he was bringing a couple of bimbos but he was late, held up in traffic or something, and the fight had started by the time he came in. I wanted to show him I knew he was there and to get a closer look at the dolls, so I maneuvered this Koerkle character so that he had his back to the seats where Pete and the dames were sitting. Koerkle was banging away at me as hard as he could but I ducked under a hard right and gave Pete and the girls a little wave.

"You silly bastard," Pete told me later, "right in the middle of a fight and you're waving to your friends. Don't you know you can get flattened that way? Don't you know you're supposed to be concentrating when you're fighting?"

"Ah, he was a bum," I told him.

"A bum?" he asks. "With twenty-eight knockouts? If he was such a bum how come you only won by a split decision?"

Most of the guys that I fought then were colored and they weren't able to get many bouts. A colored fighter could starve in those days because if a manager had a white kid who seemed to have some potential he would baby him and try to build him up on stumblebums or used-up names who were just looking for a payday.

In those early days, even though Louis and Robinson had broken through, just the fact that they were so great made everyone leery of colored fighters. And some of them were great, believe me. Many of those colored six-round fighters would have chased some high-priced top-notchers right out of the ring. A lot of them would have to fight with handcuffs on just to get a pay night here and there.

Well, with me, there was nobody getting paid to fight with handcuffs on because my manager wasn't afraid of anybody. *We'll* fight them all, he used to say, and fight them all *I* did. When one of those bombers got a chance against a white kid on the square, they sure tried their best to show what they could do, because they all had the dream that maybe they'd get enough of an audience clamoring for them so that someday some promoter would give them the chance they deserved and they'd get a shot at the real money. And I mean they were hungry fighters. You would just about have to kill them before they'd give up. Well, I had something going for me, too, on that score—I was just as hungry as they were.

In those days there wasn't anybody I wouldn't get in the ring with. Not only did I fight the colored bombers, but I took on guys in any weight class. My own weight could go from one fifty-five to one ninety-five in a matter of two, three days. A lot of it was around the gut, I grant that, but in the ring I could fight anywhere from one fifty-five to one seventy-five. I figure that all through my career, I lost four thousand pounds of weight. Two tons.

Welterweights to heavies, I figured I could learn something from all of them. The welterweights, you know, are tricky and fast, so you learn to duck and weave so that when you get into your own weight class you're not a sitting duck. And the heavies—well, against them you learn to take a punch.

In fighting, weight is a big thing. It's the mark of the legendary fighter, the Grebs, the Dempseys—the ability to fight a guy out of your weight class. I'll never forget the night, a long time later, when I was sitting at this bar with Pete, drinking. I don't think I was champ right then, but I was around the top. We were in this bar up in the Bronx somewhere, not one of the fancy places, just a bar you go into to get a couple of drinks. That night Pete had on this real sharp topcoat. By this time he was in the money and that coat must have cost him about seventy-five bucks. Nothing but the best for Pete when it came to clothes—or dames either, for that matter—and seventy-five bucks back then was a lot of loot. It was light-colored camel's hair. Anyway, these two guys down the bar a little way got into this fight and after they threw a couple of punches one guy got in a real belt at the other and a blob of blood flew over and plopped on the sleeve of Pete's snazzy new coat. You should have seen the expression on his face. First he just looked at the blood lying there on his sleeve, then he realized that if blood was hard to get out of any fabric, it was impossible to get out of this coat, so he got madder and madder and madder. Finally he took the coat off and went after these two guys, so they both turned on him. And with the two of them, they started beating him up. And I was laughing so hard at the whole thing that I couldn't do anything about it. Maybe I wouldn't have anyway because Pete was big enough to take care of himself. I couldn't stop laughing. Finally he belted out one of them and the other one backed off. When Pete came over he was so goddamned mad I thought he was going to belt me.

And suddenly I started crying. For no reason. And Pete said, "For Christsake, now what?"

And the minute he asked me, I knew. I said, "I can't fight Louis."

He stopped. He didn't know what the hell I was talking about.

I hadn't either, till he asked me. He said, "Are you nuts? You gone nuts? You can't *what?*"

"No matter how big I get," I said, "I'll never get big enough to fight Louis. Joe Louis. If I get big enough so my weight will be anywhere near his, I'll be so fat and slow, he'd murder me."

Pete looked at me and finally got what I was saying. And he broke out laughing. "For Christsake," he said. "You have to be nuts. Sitting in a lousy barroom in the Bronx and crying because you can't get big enough to fight the world heavyweight champ while I'm your best friend and I could be getting the shit beat out of me."

But I was serious. Because I knew I could beat any man alive, given the weight. I remember when I first knew that. It was in 1941, the year that I began to make it, the year that I stopped being a six-round bum and began to get ten-round fights. It was in this fight out in Cleveland, with

a very tough colored boy named Jimmy Reeves. There I
was, only a six-round middleweight bum, thrown into a
ten-round fight with a big, seasoned light heavyweight who
had already licked Solly Kreiger, the N.B.A. (National
Boxing Association) champion, in an over-the-weight
bout. Reeves was belting me and belting me, outboxing
me, outfoxing me, banging the hell out of me, when all of
a sudden, around the fourth round, I lashed out and
caught him coming in with a hook. The way he fell on me
and clinched tight, I knew I had hurt him badly. The ref
finally separated us and I could see he was on queer street
and wide open. All I had to do was bang him in the belly
and he'd go. But all of a sudden I froze—just like I had
done back in that fight at Coxsackie. I was scared. Not of
Reeves, he didn't even count anymore. This time was different. My opponent hadn't hurt me. I had hurt him, and
badly. But that's what I was there for—to hurt him as
badly as I could. It was like something in me seemed to be
screaming, "Hey, you can't lick this guy! You don't deserve it! You're no good! What you deserve is to get
killed!"

Well, for the next three and a half rounds, that's just
what Reeves did, gave me a pasting I'll always remember.
But even though he kept punching me and punching me,
and hurting me like hell now and then, I stayed on my
feet, and finally I realized he would never hurt me enough
to drop me or knock me out. And all of a sudden I was
saying, "Fuck you, that's enough," and it was like Reeves
suddenly became me or the part of me that I hated and
was always afraid of, the part that I could never control. I
ripped into him like a madman, and for the next three
rounds I destroyed him. I dropped him five or six times,
the last time at the end of the tenth round as the bell rang
at the count of nine. They gave Reeves the decision while
he was still out like a light.

Well, you never heard a roar in your life like the one
that came out of that crowd. The way they booed over the
decision did something to me. They were yelling and
screaming for me. They liked me and were defending me
against a bum decision. It was so bad that they had to call
out the cops. I was in the ring ducking chairs and bottles

and the poor old organist was playing the National Anthem over and over again, full blast and as fast as he could, and even when the cops got there it took them twenty minutes to get things under control. It felt great to know that I could get people stirred up to the point where they would fight like that for me. And yet, while all this was happening, there was that feeling bothering me that if those same people knew what I was really like, they'd all turn on me and boo me with a lot more hate than they felt for the judges that minute.

I had to keep it from them, and I had to prove that I was worth that kind of reaction. All I had to do was become as great a fighter as that crowd seemed to think I was that night, and I would deserve to have everybody like me as much as they did then. I could do it. What the hell, I had just proved that. When I could take all that a top contender like Reeves could dish out and come back to take him apart like I did, I was sure that I could do it. And that nobody or nothing could stop me.

ELEVEN

By going from the four-rounders to the six- and ten-rounders, I began to get out of the agate type in those little summaries newspapers have at the bottom of the story of the big fight of the night. You know: "Jake La Motta, Bronx, 168 pounds, TKO, third round, over Jimmy Miller, Newark, 172."

After the Reeves fight, Frank Gibbons, the Cleveland boxing writer, had written: "He [meaning Reeves] bruised everything in La Motta except his heart. Had the fight been held in an alley there isn't any doubt in my mind which man would have been the winner." I began to get stories, pictures, items in the boxing columns. Dan Parker, one of the sportswriting greats—God rest his soul—had a couple of lines in his "The Broadway Bugle" column in the *Mirror* about how I shadowboxed for three rounds *after* a fight to get cooled off. Not earthshaking, but it was in Dan Parker's column. They walk racehorses after a race to cool them off, don't they? What's so nutty about that? And there was another item by a sportswriter in his column "Jack Tanzer Says," which was about a fight card for Bill Johnston, who used to be a pretty well-known promoter. Pete and I were both on the card and Tanzer wrote that the "young Bronxites save[d] Bill's show. If it were not for these two, Bill Johnston would have had another odiferous performance. . . ." And there were pictures of me with Tony Canzoneri, who was one of the big ones, and the caption read: "He puts 'em on the floor" and called me "one of the country's young and promising middleweights." There were stories about me going for my twenty-fifth straight win, and there was a drawing of me on the front page of *The Ringside,* which is a weekly magazine about boxing.

What's funny was that I got some of my biggest notices over a fight I lost—with a guy named Nate Bolden at Marigold Gardens in Chicago. And whan I say I "lost," I mean, I got *beat!* Jesus Christ, what a pounding. If he'd been stronger he'd have flattened me. I've granted right from the beginning that I never was the world's greatest classic boxer. What gave me the most trouble with Bolden was that he was a straight boxer. He wanted absolutely nothing but points. A guy like Sugar Ray Robinson, for example, he was a real cutie when it came to boxing, but he also liked the knockout on his record, so there came a point in the fight when he figured to take a few on the chance of getting a knockout. I mean, he wasn't exactly a pansy, and I think it still bugs him—I hope it still bugs him—that he was never able to flatten me. And I'm one of the few guys who ever took him.

Well, leaving Robinson aside for the minute, Bolden had no intention of mixing it up at all. What he intended to do—and what he did do—was let me charge, let me swing, and all he did was jab, dance, counterpunch, duck, hit.

Like I said, I lost, and not only did I lose, but he hit me so much that I was as much a mess as I've ever been. Those sliding punches of his weren't intended to knock me out because he knew he couldn't, but the trouble with them is that the leather of the glove, when it hits your face, tends to sort of bunch up the skin and break the tiny blood vessels under it, so that even though you aren't bleeding, you're getting all these little black-and-purple blotches under the skin where the blood vessels have broken.

When I got back to New York, I looked Pete up. He couldn't believe his eyes. "What in the name of Christ happened to you?" he asked me.

Like I say, my face looked like a piece of liver that had been put on a butcher block and beat with a mallet. "Whaddaya mean what happened to me?" I said. "You know where I been. That Bolden is one of these wise guys.

Jab, jab, jab. A coupla more rounds and I would have had him."

Pete looked at me and tears came into his eyes. He put both of his hands on my arms. "Jake," he said, serious, "this is for the birds. This is crazy. Fighting is for bums. It's for nuts. Let's get out the guns and go back to work!"

I shook my head. "Maybe you're right," I said. "Maybe I am nuts. But I like fighting. Hell, I even like training. When I get in the ring, I don't mind taking a few punches if I can get a crack at the guy."

"A few punches?" Pete asks. "You look like this guy was using you for a punching bag for a full three minutes of all ten rounds."

It hurt, but I laughed. "I'll fight him again," I said, "and the next time I'll take him. And there's something you forget, Pete. Deep down, you ain't really a fighter. Oh, you can fight, all right, but to you it's just somethin' to do. If there's an easier way to pick up dough, that's for you. But you know, for me, I'm gettin' pretty good. I'm gettin' so I think there's no guy alive can beat me. You know what that means? It means that someday I'm gonna be the champion. People will have to call me champ. How many men are there in the world you can call champ? There are loads of senators in the country, and dozens of presidents and thousands of big shots of one kind or another, but there's only one guy in the whole world can be middleweight champ and less than ten at any one time that's champs together. That's what I'm gonna be, the champ."

All Pete did was shrug and say, "Yeah."

After that fight people began to talk about me a lot more. Even if I did lose it, it was one helluva fight, the kind that people remember. Now that I was back in New York I could start going after the top guys, guys like Georgie Abrams, Coley Welch, Ken Overlin, Billy Soose, Jimmy Bivins—even Tony Zale, who was the champ then.

Of course, my rep wasn't big enough to get those guys right off—or even big enough to get me into the Garden, to tell the truth. I still was doing most of my fighting at Bobby Gleason's Westchester Avenue gym, and at the

Bronx Coliseum, where Billy Brown was the matchmaker. But there began to be a lot of comments about me: "the Bronx Ripper," "a bundle of boxing energy," the "Bronx one-man gang," "He bobs and weaves and wallops and waves"; and in the columns they began to write: "We wonder why they don't bring Jake La Motta, the hardest hitting of the middleweights, down to the Garden?"

They began to quote odds on my fights, and to have interviews with me before and after the fight—you know, the questions sportswriters have to ask because what the hell else can they do? Like before the fight do I have any plan on how I'm gonna fight him and how much trouble do I think he'll give me. Hell, they know as well as I do that I only know one way to fight. I'm gonna fight this guy the same way I fought the last guy and the guy before him, and as for the amount of trouble he'll give me, they know as much about it as I do, maybe more. They've seen this guy fight and all I know is what I read in the papers. And then afterward they all ask what punch you hit him with. They've been sitting there all through the fight, what've they been doing all this time, reading a magazine?

About that time I got my first big feature article with pictures in *The Ring* and the Italian-language newspaper *Corriere d'America* started printing stuff about me. Outside the fact that every now and then I'd wake up with the screaming meamies about Harry Gordon, things were going good at the time. I was still living at home, but I was making enough dough so that we weren't living in a cold-water tenement anymore. We were living in a pretty good apartment with decent furniture and we weren't fighting all the time like in the old days. For one thing, my old man wasn't always on my mother's back. He knew I wouldn't let him. And more than that, since I was bringing in good dough and we were all eating regular and had decent clothes, there wasn't so much to fight about. Half the fighting in the world is over money. And still another thing, my old man was getting real proud of me. He let everybody know he was Jake La Motta's father, and he'd go down to the gym to see me train, and he'd be at ringside with Joey, who already wanted to be a fighter himself.

Yeah, everything was going great. I was getting to be known, I was getting real dough for fighting.

But somehow I didn't feel right about it. It began to bother me that a guy like me should have it that good. I had a feeling it was too good to last.

TWELVE

One day I went around to the candy store to find Pete. He was in the back and he'd been playing solitaire. At least the cards were all spread out on the table for solitaire, but when I came in he had Viola on his lap, playing with her. I felt a little sore, so I said, "Jesus, if you could only go around winning fights the way you go around winning all these broads . . ."

Naturally that got her ass in a tizzy and she jumped up and ran out of the room, straightening her skirt as she went.

"I knew you'd get to her sooner or later," I said, "for all the 'I'm not that kind of girl' bit she's always handing out."

Pete only shrugged and looked down at my hand, which was in a plaster cast. "What happened to you?" he asked.

"Ahhh, I broke it on that bum's head."

He looked at me sourly. "Broke your hand on his head? What round?"

"The sixth."

"Sixth round. You break your hand in the sixth and fight four more rounds with one hand and end up winning." He shook his head. "You know, you *are* nuts. Only a nut would do something like that. It ever occur to you to tell the ref what happened?"

I said, "Aw, forget it. I been away five days. What's new around this dump?"

He threw his hands up. "Nothing!" he exploded. "Not a goddamned thing! I'm goin' nuts! Sweating my balls off for weeks in that lousy stinkin' gym and now my fight's been postponed because this jackass came down with the clap or somethin' and the doc says he can't fight for ten days." He looked at me and a grin began to work itself over his face. "I got an idea to try and make life worth livin'," he said. "How about you and me bustin' loose? Let's get a coupla chicks and get some drinks and live it up a little! With that mitt of yours you ain't gonna be fightin' for a while, and neither am I. Whaddaya say?"

I like fun as well as the next guy, but like I said, I had this hangup about sex. I shook my head. "They keep tellin' ya how sex and fights don't mix. It kills the legs . . ."

Pete broke into a roar of laughter. "Ah, balls!" he said. "Maybe it'll kill your legs but right now it's killin' all of me!"

I laughed, but Pete went on needling me. "Jesus Christ, and they call you the Bronx Bull! A great bull you are, for Christ's sake. I read this column where Gene Tunney, he's telling about Harry Greb. How he was at this hotel where they have girl elevator operators and he has her run him all the way up to the top and shuts off the elevator and gets a quick piece right there. And on the night before a fight—*before the fight,* mind you—he'd screw not one but two broads! One of the greatest fighters that ever lived, and you're even afraid to take a night on the town."

"You're kiddin' me."

Pete turned serious and shook his head. "No. Honest. Honest to God."

Well, what the hell! What could I lose? One night? "Okay," I said. "You're on."

I don't know how Pete did it or where he got them, but that night he picked me up and we drove in his convertible to this fairly ritzy hotel up in the Bronx and he left me in the car and went in. After a couple of minutes he came back out with a big grin on his kisser and said, "Okay. They'll be right down."

He slid in under the wheel. The "right down" meant about twenty minutes, and I was building up a head of steam when the doorman opened the door and these two dolls come out. Right away I forget the head of steam. Pete looked at me and dug me in the ribs and said, "Get that look off your face. You wanna scare them back into the hotel?"

I laughed. "Man, oh man, what a pair."

Pete jumped out of the car as they came over, always the Sir Galahad.

The front one said, "Pete, I'm so sorry to be late. I had so much trouble with my hair."

Pete patted it gently. "Looks absolutely beautiful to me," he said. "Worth every minute of it."

The doll tittered. "And this is my girlfriend Ginny."

Pete gave doll number two a small amount of his charm and introduced everyone all around and we roared off.

The nightclub we went to was a pretty classy joint—a lot classier than I could have gone to, say, a year earlier, and after a couple of drinks I began to feel pretty good. I guess about half the people there were in evening clothes, which always gives a little tone to a joint, and we had a pretty good table. Girl number one, Fay, was with Pete, which left Ginny for me. A drink or two was making them both giggly, and after a while Ginny said, "Jake, how did you break your hand?"

"On a guy's head," I said.

Pete decided to give me the build-up for them. "In the ring, the prize-fight ring," he said. "Jake fought in Detroit a couple of days ago and he broke his hand like he says hitting this guy on the head about halfway through the fight, but he went on fighting with one hand and he won the fight anyway."

Ginny lapped it all up and looked at her girlfriend and said, "Fay, you didn't tell me . . ." She looked back at me. "I didn't know. Fay didn't tell me you were a prize-fighter. . . . And you won fighting with a broken hand. My, you must be so strong." And she squeezed my arm.

I began to think that this evening was going to be all right, which was a mistake.

"Okay, girls," Pete broke in, "this guy has been eating, drinking and sleeping fights every day and night for nearly two years and I been almost as bad. So let's cool it on the fight bit for tonight, okay? Tonight we're lovers, not fighters." He waved to the waiter and ordered another round of drinks.

After a while there was a little commotion as the band came out from backstage and settled on the bandstand and the house lights went dimmer and the spotlight came on and the MC came out and took the mike and pointed it at the drummer and there was a long roll of sound. Then the MC began:

"Ladies and gentlemen, welcome to the Stardust nightclub. In a moment the band will play for your dancing pleasure, but first I would like to make an announcement.

"It gives me great pleasure to tell you that seated among you tonight is a neighborhood boy whose name is currently on everyone's lips. He is the rough, tough, hardpunching middleweight challenger who is known as the Bronx Bull. Ladies and gentlemen, let's give a round of applause to . . . Jake La Motta!"

It was the first time anything like this had ever happened to me, and, of course, it had all been set up by Pete. The spotlight swung over to our table and the people started applauding and I got up—embarrassed as hell—and after a couple of seconds of waving my hand and bowing around I sat back down, glad it was over. The spotlight went back to the bandstand and the band started playing. Then Pete said to his girl, "C'mon, doll, let's dance!"

After they went off, Ginny got up and hauled me onto the floor. I made no secret of the fact that dancing wasn't my long suit. After a couple of dances we went back to the table and the first hint I got that we were in for trouble came when the band had stopped and all four of us were sitting down and I heard a voice behind me: "Look at them two broads over there. They're not so bad. What do you think they're going out with a couple of punchy clowns like that for?"

I turned around and there was a table with four of these young hoods at it, dressed up so you can't miss them, very, very sharp. They were lookin' straight at us, making sure we know the crack was meant for us, and I started to get up.

Pete grabbed my arm. "Hold it, Jake," he said, low and fast. "Take it easy. Those guys are real bad medicine."

I was surprised at him. "What is this?" I asked him. "From you? Come on, we can take four punks like that between us."

"You don't know who they are," Pete said, just as hard and low, his face all set and tense.

"I don't give a good goddamn," I said. "They want trouble and they've come to the right guy to get it. Who are they?"

"They're Nick's boys," Pete said. "He must have given them an okay because we turned him down. Now listen, you're not in some goddamn gangster movie, so don't act stupid."

"So I'm stupid!" I said. "Screw Nick! And screw you, too, if you feel that way!"

"Jake! They don't fight your way. I tell you lay off!"

"Balls! Then I'll fight their way."

I could hear the hoodlums needling us: "Look at that. The big-name fighter wants to come over here but his friend won't let him. Now, what do you think about that? His friend trying to save big name from gettin' hurt. Isn't that nice?"

"I wish big name would come over here. Then he and his friend both would realize you don't get anywhere alone. You have to have an organization behind you to help you."

Pete was on his feet now and was looking at them, so they started in on him.

"Oh, look, Petey is getting mad at us! Don't he look fierce! But he's too good to kick around with us. He'd rather be alone. Wouldn't you now, Petey?"

Pete said, "Okay, Patsy, you've had your fun. Now knock it off."

Patsy laughed. "Ah, Petey, you sound so tough, but you're not really. Hey, how about sending your girls over to our table?"

By now it was getting loud enough so that people around us were all looking at us, not getting what was happening.

Pete laughed. "Maybe the girls want to be with men," he said.

The girls were getting nervous, too, this wasn't exactly their idea of a fun-filled evening. Ginny said, "Come on, Pete, you're all acting so crazy. Now, stop it."

Patsy said to Pete, "And what are we supposed to be?"

Pete was losing his temper by now. "Fags, maybe?" he asked Patsy. "Four fags out on the town for the night? Or maybe just the four stooges? A new comedy team? The four stooges?"

This was all that was needed to get these four on their feet, and they started toward us. Some of the other people were beginning to duck away from their tables when another voice cut through the whole bit. The voice was deep, rough, and mean: "Hold it."

We all turned around, and it was the owner. And the only one he looked at was Patsy. "Ain't you forgetting something?" he said to Patsy, very pointedly. "Ain't there never supposed to be any trouble in this joint?"

He was wearing a black tie, but he was big and rough-looking. It was obvious that Patsy knew who he was and what he was talking about because he suddenly seemed to lose a little height.

"Okay, Paul," Patsy said. "Yeah. I guess we lost our heads a little on account of something that was said. Give us the check and we'll leave."

And they all turned around and followed Paul out without another word.

We all let out our breaths and sat back down at the table. We didn't say anything. Pete and I took a couple of swallows of our drink. We were still just sitting there when Paul came back to us, leaned over and said, "Look, Jake—and you, too, Pete—you wanna watch those kids. I heard about them. They're trying to make it big, they're trying to prove something, and that means they're dangerous."

I laughed a little and said, "Aw, Paul, there are people around who think Pete and me are pretty dangerous kids ourselves."

Well, I was wrong again.

We left the nightclub after a while and walked through the club's little parking lot to Pete's car. It'd been raining and the air had that damp, clean, washed smell it gets.

We got to Pete's car and one of the girls screamed. There they were, all four, stepping out from behind another car, and a light from the street reflected off the gun that one of them was holding.

I felt all my hate boiling up in me. I pushed the girls around behind the car.

Patsy opened it up.

"We look like stooges now, tough guy?" he said to Pete, and suddenly Pete lost all control of himself.

"Okay!!" he screamed. "You wanna hear it? Yeah, you're a stooge and you know it, and so are the three creeps withya! What was the deal you got? You supposed to be on a job to work us over, right! But you ain't got the guts for it, you gotta go and get yourself a gun. Four against two, and you need a gun! Creeps, every oneaya! Go ahead and shoot, but don't miss! Make it a good job, and you got two witnesses, that's how smart you are! Or are ya gonna hit them, too?"

All this time Pete and me were inching closer to them. "Go ahead, stooges!" Pete screamed, "because I'm callin' your hand!"

"Yeah, and get me, too!" I yelled. "Get me! Don't miss, or I'll take you apart and drink your blood!"

The guy with the gun looked frightened himself now. He looked at Patsy, and Patsy yelled, "Shoot! Shoot! Hit that big-mouth Pete, you crumb! Hit him, hit him, shoot!"

Still the creep didn't shoot, and Patsy reached over and belted him across the face and in one move took the gun away from him and turned around and fired. Pete went over backward like he'd been hit with a steam shovel. The girls were screaming, then they stopped, and in the silence I could hear their heels as they ran across the parking lot. Suddenly I lurched into action. The first hoodlum I got good with the plaster cast on my fist. The others started running and I went after them, trying to hit them, but it was no use, so I turned back to where Pete was.

"Pete, Pete, how bad is it?" I yelled.

He was moving all right, I could see that, kind of spasmodically but all right, and finally he pushed himself up with his left hand so that he was sitting and used his left hand to move up his right arm. "My arm," he said slow, "it feels so funny . . . so heavy."

I threw my arm around his neck. "Thank God it's only your arm," I said. "Come on, I'll get you up. We gotta get you where they can fix you up."

I got my arm around him and got him to his feet and into the car, and all of a sudden I could feel myself shaking.

Pete looked at me and said, "Well, I'll be goddamned. You like me, eh?"

I didn't know what he was talking about. I got him into the seat and drove him to the hospital and to the emergency ward.

It must have been the night for the hospital to be right, because when we got into the emergency ward it was fast and efficient the way it is in the movies, not the way I've seen it in real life, where you sit around with the blood dripping while some flunky with an IQ the size of your hat goes wandering off to get a form to fill out and stops to take a cigarette break on the way. They took a look at Pete and slid his coat off and cut the sleeve of his shirt and got him on a stretcher and into an operating room in the elapsed time of I should say less than five minutes. I was left sitting at the end of a wooden bench with a day-old copy of the *News* that somebody had left there.

I knew it was only a question of time before I'd be seeing some of our old friends from New York's Finest, because how else do you get a hole in you like Pete had except from being shot, and the hospital has to report gunshot wounds to the cops.

Pete still had the slug in him. They dug it out and had him all patched up in less than half an hour. He was walking out of the operating room, all bandaged and his arm in a sling, when our two old friends, the dicks from the candy store, walked in.

"Well, well, if it ain't the Gold-Dust twins again," the older of them said while Pete and I just looked at each other.

It turned out that in New York even the hospitals have little rooms where the cops can have a private chat with whoever. The older dick pointed to the door of a small office and said, "In there."

In we went. There was a desk and some chairs, and the older dick got behind the desk so he could write and motioned us to sit down, and when everybody sat he waited a few seconds and then said to Pete, "So! Who hit you?"

Pete lifted out his left hand and said, "Who knows?"

The other dick said, "We know. We've made a pickup already. All we need is the corroboration and we've got an attempted-murder conviction."

Pete shook his head. "You might have the wrong guy. I don't know how you could know when I can't. It was too dark to see."

The first cop began to get a little burned. "Listen, you wasn't alone at that nightclub, you know," he said. "There was plenty of people there, people who didn't find it too dark to use their eyes. It wasn't one guy, it was four guys, and you know it. There was enough light in that parking lot to read a newspaper."

Pete only shrugged again and made a big production of getting out a cigarette and lighting it. No one offered to help him.

The cop turned to me. "How about you, Jake? You was there."

What the hell could I say? I don't know what I would have done if I'd been alone, but this was Pete's deal and I wasn't going to get into it. I just shook my head.

The cops were sore, but what could they do? The first one said to Pete, "Still the rat in the gutter, eh? I heard that you was straightening yourself out with the fighting, but I see you're still going to stay with the pack."

"You gotta use the word 'rat'?" Pete asked. "It's not nice language."

The dick jumped up. "Listen, you crumb," he said, "any lip from you and you'll find yourself in the can as a material witness. The only reason I don't do it anyway is you'd only be using up a cell. But I know about you. I hear a lot about what you do when you ain't training for a fight, and some day you're gonna slip, and when you do I'll be right there to catch you. Don't think it won't be a pleasure. I seen wise guys like you ever since I been a cop and they's always a day when something blows!" He pushed back suddenly on his chair and said to his partner. "Come on, let's find a sewer where the air is fresh, I can't stand the way it smells in here."

They started out, but the second detective stopped and turned around and said to me, "Jake, I've been reading and hearing a lot of good things about you. A lot of people who should know think that you can make it fighting, and make it big. So you've got my best wishes, go ahead and make it big. But I'll tell you one thing," he said, pointing to Pete, "you keep hanging around with guys who get shot down by small-time mobsters and we'll be picking you up in a parking lot some night. Don't blow a good thing by hanging around a no-good guy."

Both the dicks disappeared, leaving Pete and me with nothing to say. We went home.

It's funny about the mob. It seems like some punk in the organization was always trying to get me for one reason or another. I mean even after I was out of the fight game, long after that run-in in the parking lot, they wouldn't let me alone. Like one night in a whorehouse out on Long Island, I came as close as I ever want to getting killed. One thing you got to understand about the mob—they never lack for recruits. You take any group of young kids hanging out in, say, the Bronx. Maybe some of them are smart enough to know that if they get tied up with the mob they got a very good chance of ending up either in Sing Sing or bleeding to death in the trunk of an abandoned car in a vacant parking lot in Secaucus, N.J. But at the same time, there's also a certain number of these kids who see the money and the Cadillacs and the dames and the booze and they figure, what the hell, they'll go along with the deal, you name it. But getting into the mob is not as easy as you might think. There aren't any ads in *The New York Times* for how to get a job as a gunman so they have to make it in other ways. Like in this whorehouse on Long Island. This dame had set up a place—you may have read about it in the newspapers—using housewives for whores. One night when Pete and I didn't have anything better to do, we decided to go to this party we'd been invited to out there. They had this big downstairs room with a bar and lots of tables and music, and everyone was sitting around drinking and talking and having a good time.

Then I noticed these three guys. One of them was a guy named Tony. I'd been his alibi for a murder rap, so I figured we should be pals, right? It was a straight alibi, I didn't lie for him. He was with me when the cops said this guy was killed. I didn't know it, but what he was doing was setting me up to get knocked off by these other two guys. A real pal. And why would he want me knocked off? Just to show the mob what a tough guy he was, that's why. He wanted in with the mob, really in, and he figured that if he got someone like Jake La Motta knocked off the mob would figure him to be a real tough guy.

What happened was that Pete was telling a story about the time when he and me, when we were just punk kids, held up this whorehouse. Pete knew the three guys I already mentioned. He knew they were small-time thugs, and he knew that one of the first things a small-time thug wants is to make everybody think he's a lot tougher than he is, so Pete figured that probably at least one of these guys had a gun. So he looked at this guy who must have been about six-four and two-twenty and said, "Hey, you, come over!" And the guy came over. And Pete said, "You got a gun?" The guy unbuttoned his coat and there was a .45 in his belt, a big gun to be carrying around. Big and heavy. Pete was laughing and telling these dames about the holdup, and for the point of the story he needed the gun. He was also, I might add, on about his fifth drink and feeling no pain, so he said to the guy, "Look, lemme borrow the gun just for a second," and reached out his hand for the gun, but the guy belted it away.

Right away things started to change. Up to now, it's all been a lot of guys and gals together having a good time, but all of a sudden this guy started making muscle. Hell, if Pete were going to do anything with the gun, would he have started off by asking him for it? Pete didn't get what was happening right off. He's an easy-to-get-along-with drunk. He has a few drinks, he just wants to have a good time, like everybody else—he doesn't want trouble. So when the guy started getting hard, Pete just leaned back, put his hands up, laughed and said, "Forget it, friend, I didn't mean nothin'.'"

"Whaddaya mean you didn't mean nothin'?" the guy says. "Tryna take a gun outta my belt. Whaddaya mean you didn't mean nothin'?"

Pete couldn't have been better. No losing his temper, no offering to belt this guy out. This guy was four inches bigger and thirty pounds heavier, but that wouldn't have made any difference. Pete was like me that way. But no, he smiled and said, "Look, I apologize. If I was out of order, I'm sorry. I don't want no trouble. We're all friends here together. I was just tellin' the girls a story about a holdup and I wanted to show them something."

Well, after a couple of minutes the big guy went back to Tony and his other pal. I was off at one side of the room and didn't get all of it. I just sort of half-saw what happened between Pete and the big guy. Then I noticed that the big guy and Tony and the other guy were off in the corner near the men's room and that they were whispering to each other. Then the big guy went into the men's room. I looked over toward Pete and noticed that he'd also caught this out of the corner of his eye. Pete may have had an extra drink or two, but he realized that there was something not real kosher here. Then Tony was beckoning Pete to come over to him, and after he waved his hand a couple of times, Pete went on over, but instead of stopping to talk to Tony, he went right on into the men's room, and there was the big guy standing there, the .45 in his hand. He was so surprised, Pete moved so fast that when the door slams open before he can do anything Pete has jerked the gun away from him and slapped him across the side of the face with it twice, as hard as he can. By this time he's really blown his temper, he's raging at the top of his voice, it's touch and go if he'll kill the guy.

"Whatsamatta with ya?" he's screaming. "What's goin' on here? I apologize, whaddaya gonna do? You son of a bitch, I'll drink your blood!"

Now I blew my stack. At that moment I didn't know exactly what was going on, but Pete was in trouble with this gang of three guys and one of them had a gun, so I went charging across the room, tearing into them. I was out of my mind and yelled, "And I'll drink your blood, too, you goddamned bastard!"

By this time the whole room was in an uproar, and if there was one thing that could really blow it, it was to have somebody shot in there, but me and Pete were so mad we didn't give a damn. Some of the others did, though, and now about eight other guys were in the act, pulling us apart, and finally one of them got the .45 away from Pete. By now Tony and the third guy had disappeared and we were left with the big guy, who wasn't so tough with his two pals gone and no gun.

It was ten days or so before we found out what had really happened, and it was one of the mob who told Pete about it. As I said, this guy Tony wanted to pick up some mileage with the mob by knocking me off. The whole thing was a setup to get me in a fight so the big guy could bust me, which he might very easily have done if Pete hadn't clipped him for the gun first, and there would have been a dozen people to testify that Jake La Motta had been knocked off in a drunken brawl in a whorehouse. And most people would have said, "It figures."

And incidentally, a couple of years later some of the mob guys were pulled in for trying to muscle their way into an insurance company, I think it was. Tony was one of them, and he blew the whistle on them, getting immunity for spilling his guts, which goes to show what a nice fellow he was all around. He's still around, too, which is the biggest surprise of all.

But all that was later.

A couple of weeks after the night that Pete got shot, during which time I hadn't seen anything of him, I went into this joint called Richie's up in the Bronx. Well, it's not a joint, it's a fairly decent place, actually—it's divided into halves: one is the bar half where they have a big long bar and a couple of dozen tables and booths with red and white-checked tablecloths, and then there's the dining-room half, with the tables covered with white tablecloths, and you could bring your girl or your family there for a meal and not have to worry about some drunk saying "fuck" in a loud voice. Basically it draws a sports crowd and the walls are covered with pictures of athletes, mostly boxers and some ballplayers.

I was very big at Richie's at that time, and everybody gave me the big hello and the "Hi, Jake, boy," and Richie himself came up and said, "For crying out loud, Jake, when do I get that picture of you, remember? An eight-by-ten glossy and I'll have it framed myself. I want it to go on the wall right there," and pointed to a blank space on the wall. "It's a special spot, the best spot on the wall. I always give the best spot to the kids coming up, but Christ, I can't do nothing without the picture."

I said, "Gee, Richie, I'm sorry, honest I am. I appreciate what you're doing and I promise you'll get one tomorrow. I'll make a special trip. I just forgot. . . . Say, look, you seen anything of Pete lately?"

Richie jerked his thumb over his shoulder and said, "You're in luck. He's in the restaurant, having dinner."

I looked over and sure enough there was Pete having dinner. With a dame. Or rather, not having dinner but still with a dame. Naturally. As I looked I saw her laugh and blush and slap Pete in the face. Not hard so it was a federal case, but suddenly I recognized little Viola, and she sure looked different from the way she used to when she was switching her ass around the candy store. Suddenly she was a woman, with curves and a woman's dress instead of a little girl's.

I went into the restaurant and alongside the table without them seeing me and said, "Ya bum, ya, whatcha trying' to sell this girl?"

He looked up and broke into a great big grin and said, "Jake, Baby! Siddown, siddown."

So I pulled up a chair and looked at Viola. "Viola," I said. "Boy, how you've changed. You're grown up."

"Yeah," Pete laughed. "Once the chest comes," and he uses his hands to outline the female chest, "they ain't little kids anymore. They're grown-up broads."

Viola drew in her breath and made a move under the table.

"Jesus," Pete yelled, "if you're gonna keep on kickin' me in the shins, change around, willya? That's twice you've kicked me right in the same shin, right in the same spot."

"Whaddid she kick ya for the first time?" I asked. "And where the hell have you been, anyway? I thought I was gonna see you the next day and I ain't seen you for a coupla weeks. Where you been keeping yourself?"

He put on an expression that I couldn't read at all, as if somehow he was ashamed, as if he didn't want to answer, or as if I hadn't even asked the question. Then he sort of sheepishly half-smiled. "Aah," he said. "The doc says I can't fight anymore." He worked his shoulders. "I got all my strength but he says the bullet hit some nerves in the arm." He raised his right hand and tried to make a fist, but the hand wouldn't close all the way.

"How long is it going to be like that?" I asked.

"How the hell do I know? Forever, for all I know—or the quack. But I should wait so long. What am I gonna do, sit around tryin' exercises and hopin' that some miracle will make it better?"

I shook my head. "It don't mean you shouldn't ever come around the gym or around the house," I said. "At least you could come around the gym and give me some free advice on what I'm doing wrong."

He didn't even smile. "Come off it, Jake," he said. "You're past the point where I can tell you what you're doing wrong. Besides, you know it's better you shouldn't be seen always palling around with me." He looked at my face and said, "You know what I mean. I'm always for you, I'll always be for you. We oughta get together, say, in a place like this"—and he threw out his hands—"for dinner and some drinks and a few laughs with a dish like Viola, but it ain't gonna do you too much good to have me hangin' around the gym. It ain't like the days when I was trainin', too, so it was just two fighters trainin' together."

I got mad at him. "So that's it!" I said. "It's what the cops said, and you believe it! My pal! My real true pal! Since when have I ever listened to anything the cops said?"

He didn't say anything, and he didn't look at me. I began to get another idea, and it didn't make me feel good.

"Or maybe it's somethin' else," I said. "Maybe it's not that, what the cops said. Maybe you're steppin' out again." I lowered my voice. "Look, Pete, don't. You ain't steppin' out?"

Viola said, also quiet like because a tone of voice affects another person, "What are you both talking about? Pete, you're not doing anything bad, are you?"

I said, "Shaddup." Then to Pete I said, "Look, I'm gettin' some good money shots, I'm steppin' up in class. I need a guy like you. Work with me and I'll give you a cut of it. You can do better with me. Don't mess up again. I need a guy like you to keep the thieves away." I made my last pitch to him. "Pete, you know you're the only guy I've ever been able to trust."

I didn't know what was going through him but after a while he said, very low, "Jake, I appreciate that. Thanks. Thanks a lot. But I can't live off you for the rest of my life. We've both seen the big champion fighters, the way they always have a gang of creeps around them, hanging on."

"But that's what I want *you* for," I said. "To keep the creeps off."

He shook his head again. "Thanks again," he said. "Really. But I can't. I got to make it on my own, like I said. You know how it is, Jake." Then he smiled a weak smile.

"Okay," I said. "I think you're a jerk. Have it your own way. When you bust yourself, give me a ring. I'll be there."

I looked over at Viola and leaned over to Pete and pretended to whisper to him. He looked at her and pretended to whisper something to me. She looked at both of us and blushed. Then she jumped up and slapped him in the face, but not too hard.

"Better than a kick in the shins," Pete said, and we all began to laugh.

THIRTEEN

I began to provide myself with wife trouble about this time. My basic trouble was that I got married more than I should, not that I'm saying anything against any of my wives. Why the hell should I? After all, St. Peter ain't ever going to give me his personal regards. I'm no bargain.

My first wife was a Bronx girl. She was barely nineteen and I was only twenty, and to be honest about it, the thing that got us together was plain sex. She had a great body and I was crazy for her. So I married her, and she moved into my room in the apartment. Even if I'd had a regular job like a bank clerk, we were both too young for married life. But with me being a fighter and going off all the time, and no playing around when I was training—no going out and no sex—well, what nineteen-year-old bride is going to put up with that? It was a marriage that was fated to break up, which it did about a year later. One good thing about it, though, was that it produced my first kid—Jacklyn.

I remember one thing about my first wife that will show you how nuts I was back then. I guess I must have just won a big fight, though I forget with who now, because there was this big party we threw in an apartment up in the Bronx with a lot of guys and dames and a lot of noise and booze. I remember coming out of a drunken coma and most of the people had gone except the real boozers, a couple of dames and half-a-dozen guys including my brother Joey. My wife was lying on the floor, not moving. "What's with her?" I asked.

Joey, I guess it was, said, "You don't remember?"

"If I knew would I be asking, for Christsake? What's wrong with her?"

121

"You got into a fight with her because you was makin' a play for some other dame and you belted her."

"What's wrong with her?" I repeated.

Joey said, "If you want my opinion, she's dead. She ain't movin' and I can't see her breathing and we thrown water on her and everything and we can't get her to move or even open her eyes."

This was a helluva thing. Jesus! That's what I needed, a manslaughter rap. I could see the headlines right in front of me:

LA MOTTA KILLS WIFE IN DRUNKEN BRAWL

POLICE ARREST JAKE LA MOTTA FOR
SLAYING WIFE

Beautiful. Absolutely beautiful. A minimum of three years in the can. I felt like killing myself on the spot. And I had a hangover, the hangover to end all hangovers. I got up and took a good slug straight from the bottle and went to the telephone.

"Who you callin'?" Joey asked.

"Pete," I said. "Maybe he'll have some ideas."

After I told Pete where we were and hung up the phone, Joey said, "I got an idea."

"What?"

"Throw her in the river."

"*What?*"

"You heard me. You got everything goin' against you. In the first place, you're a pro fighter and there's a law against you using your fists on *anybody* outside the ring. In the second place, you already got a record. In the third place you don't have so many friends on the cops that they'd be breakin' their backs to cover up for you. In the fourth place, you do about three or four years in the can and come out and you won't be able to fight Shirley Temple. In the fifth place there ain't a promoter in the world who'd book you, a wife-killer, so it's right back to peddlin' fish for you, just like the old man. You want me to give you a couple of more places? I still got some left."

"Never mind."

I know. Right now it sounds like I was a maniac to be even thinking of throwing a woman in the river, but maybe I was a maniac back then. Dead nuts. And desperate to boot.

"Okay," I said, "but you got any further bright ideas? We can't just pick her up and carry her out to the car and drive over to the river and throw her in. Somewhere along the line somebody might comment."

Joey thought a minute, then said, "We could roll her up in the rug. Then if people saw us they'd just think we was carryin' a rug."

It was along about this time in the conversation that Pete got there. He listened to us talking for a couple of minutes, then he threw up his hands and broke out near the top of his voice, "Are you guys nuts? *Nuts?* Throw the dame in the river? Where am I, in a lunatic asylum? You're all doctors, I suppose, so you've written out a death certificate? And, of course, nobody will ever come around and ask you where she is? Like maybe her father and mother? And then what do you do, throw them in the river, too?"

"So what do we do, Mister Wise Guy?" I asked. "Call the cops and tell them I'm sorry I killed her?"

Pete shouted, "Call a doc and tell him the dame was drunk and fell down the stairs, for Christsake! If she was drinking as much as you goddamned clowns she must have enough booze in her to open a liquor store!"

Shows you what clear thinking will do!

We called the doc, and, of course, she wasn't dead, thank God. One dead man is enough to wake you up screaming without having a dead wife just because you got drunk. But it was a marriage that was headed for divorce right from the start. The kind of dame who would marry a guy like me was slated to end up divorced.

To make things even better, it was about this time it turned out that for all that Pete thought he was such a smart guy, he was nailed—on a stickup and assault charge—and sent up. With him gone I was really alone.

I guess I was beginning to grow up. Growing up is having bad things happen to you for no reason. You know, when my old man beat me when I was a kid there was a kind of reason to it, no matter how stupid the reason was, even if it was just him losing his temper. But now all this was—just happening. Like my marriage going on the rocks—there was nothing I could do about that, no matter who was right or wrong. And Pete getting sent up—there was nothing I could do about that, either.

The only thing that was going good was the fighting. I was getting better and better fights, and I was fighting better and better. There was a Negro kid out of Detroit, Jimmy Edgar, who was a protégé of Joe Louis. I fought him twice and beat him both times. There was a real tough Polish guy you oughta remember if you know anything about fighting, Henry Chmielewski. I fought him in a good club up in Boston in the Mechanics Building and came out of it with a decision.

As always, I had my knockers in the daily press, like some guy named Joe Cummiskey in a New York paper that no longer exists called the *PM,* who decided that I was the "bully of the block" because I had a weight edge of anywhere between nine and thirteen pounds over my opponents in seventeen straight fights. But a columnist named Leo MacDonnell called me "Mister Five-by-Five" and said that I fought like Harry Greb and that my career was a "modern ring sensation."

By now I was getting fights in the Garden, and I was getting eight-column headlines on the sports pages— "Kochan vs. La Motta Wednesday."

My biggest fight up to now came the last week of September in 1942: my first fight with Sugar Ray Robinson.

I fought Sugar Ray six times in all, and I should have won three of them, but we'll get to that later. At any rate, as far as our careers are concerned, there's a curious relationship there. In one sense, he was the only guy I was never really able to nail the way I wanted to nail. He was a nemesis to me. But on the other hand a lot of his reputation was built on the fact that he had beaten me. One fighter even said to me, "Jake, I never figured Robinson was that good till after he'd fought you."

It doesn't make any difference now, of course. What the hell, are we gonna make another fight, two middle-aged jokers?

I still have the clippings from that first Robinson fight.
All the writers in New York, and probably everywhere,
had big stories on it: Milton Gross in the *New York Post*,
Hype Igoe in the *Journal*—Hype picked me to win—
Lester Bromberg, also in the *Journal*—"Robinson Foe
Dangerous" was his headline—Joseph C. Nichols in the
Times—"Robinson Favored . . . Bronx Foe Hard
Puncher." The New York *Enquirer* had an eight-column
headline, "Robinson Meets Good Man Friday." They had
color stories about how I was the sole support of a family
of seven, how I ate steak and macaroni—the steak for
strength, the macaroni because I was a poor ignorant Italian who didn't know any better. They didn't say that, of
course, but that was what they meant. Well, there was
some truth in it all. I had got to the point where I could
pay for steak, and even more important, I could get delivery on it, because now America was in World War II and
getting steaks was not easy. My old man had enlisted, he
was able to get in under the age limit, but after maybe
six–seven months they gave me a discharge. As for me
and the army, all the doctor had to do was take one look
at the ear where I had had the mastoid operation and that
was that.

Well, Robinson outpointed me over ten rounds in the
first fight, so I was down one. I went on to flatten guys
like Bob Satterfield and Wild Bill McDowell and Jackie
Wilson, another colored kid from the West who was making his debut in the Garden. He was a sergeant in the
army on leave, and he was supposed to be "better than
Robinson," to quote one newspaper. He came into the ring
a 4–1 favorite, and he went out of it a sadder but a wiser
man.

The third week of January, 1943, out in Detroit—
where they were spending war-munitions money like you
could be fined for having it—I interrupted the career of a
kid named Charley Hayes, who had never been knocked
down in more than a hundred pro fights. I got a TKO over
him in the sixth round and one story called me a "fero-
cious, two-fisted whirlwind, a one-man riot." The gate was
over $21,000, the biggest crowd they'd had in two years.

Two weeks later, still in Detroit, fighting for Nick

Londes—a smart Greek who had got the fight away from New York and Boston into his Olympia Stadium to a gate of better than $40,000—I got my second crack at Robinson.

He came into the ring a 3–1 favorite, and he went out the loser.

It was the first loss in a hundred and thirty pro fights for Robinson, but there was no doubt about the decision when I knocked him through the ropes for a nine count in the eighth round.

"A shot in the arm to boxing everywhere and especially in Detroit," the papers said. I was "the most talked-about fighter in years."

I would have to say that Robinson was the best I fought—a cutie, fast, with all the tricks, but he could also take a punch and he could throw one.

As a result of the Robinson fight, I guess, Billy Stevens in his column in *Boxing* picked me as one of the best fighters of the year; the *Enquirer* had a big, almost full-page drawing of me with the caption "All's Jake Now"; and Nat Fleischer, editor of *Ring,* picked me as the world's number-one middleweight.

There was only one problem.

I may have been the number-one middleweight to practically everybody, but I didn't have the championship. Sure, I got the number-one treatment wherever I went, but there wasn't anyone calling me champ and really meaning it. It was just a sort of a courtesy.

The newspapermen were after me all the time now. I was always giving an interview to somebody, or holding a press conference, because by now the writers were getting a byline story in the papers just describing what happened at the signing for a fight, like when I signed to fight Robinson for the third time. It was a front-page story over eight columns in the Detroit papers, and the question from the reporters was always the same: "Jake, why do you think they're not giving you a shot at the championship?"

The newspaper guys knew the answer as well as I did, at least some of them did—that I wouldn't play ball with the mob, that I wouldn't take on a mobster as a front man for manager, which was the main thing they wanted. What the newspapermen wanted was for me to say that. It doesn't make any news if a newspaperman knows it and says it, but if the world's number-one middleweight says it, then it's surefire for the front pages. But I was afraid that if I shot off my mouth about it I never *would* get a shot at the title, and you can believe me when I say that the only thing I wanted then in the whole world, forever, was to get a crack at the title.

I remember at one of these press conferences, held in the gym, my brother Joey—who was getting to be a pretty fair fighter himself with a string of eighteen KOs—came up to me and said, "I hate to interrupt, but there's some broad on the phone over there for you."

I went over and took the phone, and it was Viola. "I got a letter from Pete," she said.

"Pete?" I asked. "Hey, that's great, what does the old bum say?"

She told me he was getting along as well as you can when you're doing five to fifteen in a state pen and that he wanted me to write him a letter.

"Aw, Viola, I can't do that," I said. "I don't think I ever wrote a letter to anybody in my whole life. I can't write a letter. I don't know how. I tell you what, you write to him."

"You got to tell me what to say," she said. "I can write him about me and what's going on in the neighborhood, but I can't write him all about you. You know, I can tell him about you licking Robinson, but he knows that already. You've got to tell me."

Well, the way it worked out, she had a date for later and was going to write to Pete right away, so I agreed that I'd drop by and tell her what to say, which shouldn't take more than five minutes, and I'd be over as soon as I could.

I got dressed and drove off in my new Cadillac convertible, and it took about twenty minutes to get to Viola's house, which was an old brownstone made over into an apartment house.

I swear to God that as I went up the steps I had nothing more in mind than getting Viola to write three or four sentences for me to Pete and then getting back out. But like I say, Viola had changed, too. When I got inside I saw what a stunner she'd become in her own right. She had an upswept hairdo that showed the line of her neck, which I always thought was the sexiest hairdo a doll can wear, and she had on a low-cut white blouse, not transparent but sheer enough so that you could see the straps of her slip and the outline of her bra. And, like I say, low cut enough so that you could see the start of the rise of her breasts. All in all, very, very sexy.

She invited me in and we went into the kitchen, the room where most business is conducted in homes like this, and off it was a door that I knew from experience must have led to the bedroom.

She picked up the letter and said, "Well, this is what our dear buddy wrote—the letter is really to both of us though he addressed it to me, probably because he knew I was more reliable." Then she laughed. "There's a lot of little stuff here that doesn't really amount to much," she said, reading down the letter. "Oh, here it is—'Tell that big bum Jake why doesn't he write to me. There must be somebody he knows who can write a couple of lines for him. Tell him I want to know more about the Robinson fight. We all heard it on the radio and the way the announcer was talking it was all Robinson until Jake hung that one on him for the nine count. I started a La Motta fan club up here but, of course, all the black boys are for Robinson. They're all going around saying it was a lucky punch, wait till the next time. And tell Jake I'd sort of appreciate it if he'd look after a sweet little chick I know named . . . Viola.'"

Here she sort of blushed and sat down at the kitchen table. I hadn't been able to take my eyes off her the whole time she was reading, and her sitting down made it worse because now I could see down the front of her dress. Finally I realized she was waiting for me to say something.

"Well, yeah, I really miss that bum," I managed to say.

She looked up at me and must have realized how much I could see because she sort of swung around a little and said, a little colder, "Well, what do we say to him? What do you want to tell him about the Robinson fight?"

My palms were sweating, and I was so tensed up I was

shaking a little. My voice didn't sound right. "Tell him: Dear Pete, I miss you like hell and I wish to Christ you'd . . ."

She lowered her head and started to write, and that showed the swell of her breasts again, and without looking up she repeated, "and I wish to Christ you'd . . ."

" . . . you'd get back here," I said, stammering, "and don't worry, I'll look after Viola for you okay."

She looked up at me, and I guess she didn't like what she saw because she jumped up so quick that the chair turned over and I said, "It's okay, Viola, I'm Pete's best friend and we always fix each other up. Don't worry, it's okay, Pete will understand . . ."

She was getting as far away from me as she could and getting more and more frightened. "Jake, you're crazy. Stop it! You're the one who doesn't understand. . . ."

I kept saying, "It's okay, Viola, don't be frightened. Pete will understand. I'm his best friend. . . ."

I caught her by the arms and pulled her to me and began to kiss her anywhere I could, hard and fast, and she began to cry, "Jake, don't! You don't understand. . . ."

I kept covering her with kisses, and she yelled louder, "Don't, don't! Stop it! You don't understand. Pete never did anything. He never did. Don't, I'm a virgin!"

I didn't believe her, and I don't know if I would have stopped even if I did, but I picked her up and carried her into the bedroom and threw her down on the bed. All the time she was crying and sobbing and yelling, you're wrong, you're wrong, stop, stop, let me go, but I got her on her back and reached up and pulled off her pants and pushed her on her back and got on top of her and covered her with kisses and pulled her skirt up and got into her. . . ."

When it was over there was no sound in the bedroom at all except Viola's sobbing, so low that you could just barely hear it, and even the ticking of the clock was louder than her crying, and the blood proved that she hadn't been lying about being a virgin.

This was different. This was wrong. This wasn't like those other dames that after a while I'd get tired of and maybe Pete would take.

I'd just naturally assumed that if Pete had been playing around that even if Viola had been a virgin to start with she wasn't afterward, because there were damned few eighteen-year-old virgins around where we lived. I was wrong. I could hear her moaning and I could hear the ticking of the clock. I can still hear it even now, and I didn't know what to say. There was nothing I could do, but the thought kept going through my mind: Suppose Pete was serious about this dame, this is a great thing to have done.

"I'm sorry," I said. "Jesus, I'm sorry. I just didn't believe you, I didn't think. I'm sorry, Viola. . . ."

She didn't say anything. She kept moaning, and the clock kept ticking.

"Jesus!" I shouted. "Jesus Christ alive!" And I rushed out of the room yelling after me, "I'm sorry. I swear to God I'm sorry. I'm sorry!"

I poured down the front steps, and it hit me in the face like a punch that here was the world. I'd been out of the world. Here was the world, with the sun shining and my fully paid for Cadillac convertible parked at the curb. Across the street were about four guys sitting on a stoop watching it, but in my day and age a Cadillac convertible was its own insurance in a neighborhood like that. They might strip a Plymouth, but these bums knew that anybody who could drive around there in a new Cadillac must have the muscle to back it up. So they just looked at me coming down the steps to the car and they didn't say nothing.

I got in the car and just sat there. Never in my whole goddamned life had I felt so goddamned bad. Never. After about five minutes I started the engine. To this day I don't know where I went. I drove and drove.

When it began to get dark I put on the lights and drove home.

FOURTEEN

I lost the third Robinson fight.

That's not right. I didn't lose it, he got the decision. You can ask anyone who was there, or if it means that much to you, you can read the newspaper stories. I know the date of this fight, it was the last week of February in 1943 and Robinson was going into the army the next day. I'm not knocking him on it. I would have done the same thing in his shoes, but he got every newspaper inch there was about the story of this brave boy off to fight for his country. He didn't fight up to his best in the ring that night, but he got a decision by one miserable vote after I decked him once.

That's when I began to think about Robinson as a nemesis. Well, no, not really, but if you score the only knockdown in a really tough ten-rounder and the judges give the decision to the guy you knocked down, you got to figure that things aren't really going your way.

At the time I figured, what the hell, I flattened this guy once before and I'll get him again when he comes out. I didn't figure he was going to use his army career as one long training camp.

But not everything went bad for me then.

I remember one day around this time I'd just finished training for the day and Joey came up to me leading by the hand the most ravishing blonde you ever saw in your life and said, "Jake, this is Vickie. She's been dyin' to meet you."

I couldn't believe him. She looked like a beauty-contest winner, like the blonde who plays the lead in one of those movies about the queen of the campus. I took her by the arm and walked her away from Joey and the newspaper guys I had been talking to. I don't know what I looked like to her, but I felt stunned.

"Did I hear Joey right?" I asked her. "Did he really say that you wanted to meet *me?*"

She nodded and sort of turned away, as if she was embarrassed at being so bold.

"Wow," I said. "Like they say in the song, when did you leave heaven? I ain't seen anybody as beautiful as you in my whole life. And you wanted to meet me, I can't believe it. . . . Vickie, that's a wonderful name. V for victory, how do you like that?"

She giggled, and it seemed to run right through me. I was standing there, dressed in trunks and boxing shoes, you know, and trying to think of what to say next to show her that I was crazy about her without looking as though I was trying to rush her off her feet.

Well, finally I kind of pulled myself together and asked her out for a date.

I'm not going through all the details of my courtship of Vickie, but I really went nuts for her. Like I said, she was such a looker that I liked to walk behind her when we went into a restaurant or something, just to see the expressions on guys' faces as they turned to watch her go by. And she was a load of fun to be with, gay and laughing and happy, and on top of all that she was crazy about me. That's what she said, anyway, though I told her that any dame who was crazy about me was off her rocker.

At the end of about three months we were married.

Besides marrying Vickie, I was fighting good. There were good fighters everywhere in the middleweights and welterweights, and by now I was fighting the best and winning a lot more than I lost.

I made more than a million dollars in purses, and you don't win that by fighting your Aunt Sadie. A couple of weeks after I fought Robinson I took on Jimmy Reeves again, the tough colored boy who'd beaten me in the ring that night in Cleveland, and I flattened him in the sixth round. The purse was six thousand bucks, which is a thousand dollars a round, and it added up to a total of forty thousand I'd taken out of Detroit in five fights.

Six weeks later I fought Fritzie Zivic in Pittsburgh, and

I don't know whether you remember Fritzie or not, but he was one of the roughest little customers who ever pulled on gloves—and Pittsburgh was his hometown. I won.

Well, civic pride won't let you get away with something like that, but the money was good. I signed to fight Fritzie again six weeks later, again in Pittsburgh.

About that second fight I'll quote only the headline that the *Sun-Telegraph* used. The *Sun-Telegraph* is a daily newspaper that's published in Pittsburgh. The headline read:

LA MOTTA WINS, ZIVIC GETS NOD

I fought Fritzie twice more, getting a split decision in Madison Square Garden and beating him again in Detroit.

That was the year, 1943, that I earned over a hundred thousand dollars, which is not bad for a ninth-grade dropout from the Bronx slums.

Much as I hate to sound like a broken record, I *still* was no nearer a crack at the title. The headlines were reading:

ROCKY AND ZALE IN 3D TITLE GO—
WHY *NOT* LA MOTTA NEXT?

And:

ZALE TO FIGHT CERDAN FOR TITLE:
LA MOTTA NOW NO. 1 CONTENDER 4 YEARS

The months passed, and even the years.

Then one day I was in the gym, working out, and by now I could even charge for people to come in and see me work out and the joint was jammed. I was sort of jogging around in the ring, after the workout, loosening up, and one of the guys yelled, "Hey, Jake, look who just walked in!"

I looked and couldn't believe my eyes. I went out over the top rope and down through the spectators. "Pete! You son of a bitch! Where did you come from? Why didn't you tell a guy?" I threw my arms around him and punched him and gave him a tap on the jaw. I guess it was a little

stronger than I really meant because he fell into a clinch
and held my arms so I couldn't move and shoved me
away, holding his jaw and shaking his head.

"This is because you like me?" he asked, grinning.

"God, am I glad to see you!" I said.

He put his arm around my shoulder and said, "Do me a
favor, don't get mad at me."

I led him to my own private room, which I now rated,
off to the side of the gym, and I heard one spectator say,
"Did you see that? La Motta laughing." And another guy
said, "I don't believe it. Who ever heard of an animal
laughing?" It didn't get under my skin, but I thought,
Okay Mister Wise Guy, so I'm not Mister Nice, but I
made over a hundred thousand dollars last year by not
being Mister Nice.

The reason I wanted Pete in my room first thing was
that Vickie was there, looking like a million bucks. I
mean, she was beautiful enough the first time I saw her,
but now she had all the clothes and jewelry and stuff that
really make a dame shine like a lighthouse. Joey was
there, too, of course, but the thing I wanted to brag about
to Pete was this beautiful doll, and the two kids we had.
So I dragged him in there and introduced him to Vickie,
and to Joey, who he barely remembered, and I told Joey,
"Look, I ain't goin' to work out anymore today. I'm gonna
take Pete home with Vickie and me so he can see the
house and the kids. Fix things up for tomorrow. . . ."

I was proud of this house I was taking him to. By now
I'd started to set my family up a little. My folks were living in an apartment house I gave them, but I'd really let
myself go on this house in a high-type neighborhood. It
was a great house, almost brand-new and very modern
with all the newest type stuff in the kitchen, and landscap-
ing, and nothing but the best for furnishings. We even had
a girl who stayed in the house and took care of the kids,
and a double garage that was under one end of the house
so you could drive in and just get out and walk upstairs
and be in the house—which is nothing nowadays but
twenty-five years ago was pretty hot stuff.

We got into the house and little Jackie Junior came in
to say hello and Vickie went off to make some sandwiches

and tea and I threw my arms out at the fifty-foot living room and said to Pete, "Well, how do you like the castle?"

He walked around a little, looking at the room and shaking his head as if he couldn't believe it. "Boy, Jake," he finally said, "you really got it made. I never been in a place with this class. You really come a long way."

Somehow, seeing him brought me the memory that I might have come a long way but hadn't got to where I wanted. But why the hell start off with that the first thing? I said, "Tell me about you. I hope now you're going to listen to me about staying off jobs. I don't care how smart you think you are. You're not going back to that, are you? You wised up any?"

"Listen," Pete said. "I can tell you this much. You only did eighteen months up at Coxsackie. I did over three years in Sing Sing. Over three years! Nothing to do, but nothing. Nothing to do but think, think about everything you're missing. It's a long time to be able to weigh all the pros and cons. In fact"—and here he grinned—"in fact, you start looking at all the cons who think they're pros . . ."

He stopped and I laughed. It wasn't much, but what the hell, a guy who's been away for three years deserves a little charity.

"Anyhow," he went on, "you don't have to worry about me anymore. Every goddamned jackass up there was a born loser, including me, and the hell with it. I'm not cut out to be a loser. I'm moving over to the winner's side. No more of this shit for me."

I cracked him on the back. "Attaboy," I said. "Let me help you. You remember how you met me at Coxsackie and threw the bankroll at me? Now it's my turn."

He shook his head.

"Don't be a sap," I said. "I'm loaded and you don't know so many people who're loaded that you can afford to be choosy." He was still shaking his head, so I snapped, "For Christsake, it's only a loan, you'll pay me back, what the hell are you being so hard-nosed about? Don't be a schlub."

He was *still* shaking his head and smiling, and he threw his arm around my shoulders. "Thanks, Jake," he said. "I appreciate it, I really appreciate it, and I mean it. But I got it set up. I'm borrowing from my family and my father and I are going into the dress business. It's a real racket, but he knows it, and he's going to teach me. So watch my smoke!"

Then he changed the subject. "So why haven't you got the title shot yet?"

I was about to tell him in a couple of hundred well-chosen words when Vickie came in with the sandwiches and tea and broke in: "Because he thinks he's so smart, that's why. He could have been the champ for the last three years, but he knows more than anybody else. He isn't going to play ball with anybody, he isn't."

That's a wife for you, drilling the old needle into the same old spot in that same sore tooth, even though she knew how goddamned mad it always made me.

"Aw, shaddup!" I told her. "I told you to keep your mouth shut about that. Just like every broad, always shootin' your mouth off. Well, shoot it off about something else besides my business."

She put down the tray and moved back toward the door. "Well, if Pete is your best friend like you always keep telling me, I don't see why I can't say it." Then she turned to Pete. "You see how he is, suspicious of everybody, his brother, his mother, me—you. The most suspicious bastard in the world! That's why he isn't the champ, because he's a chump!"

I snarled at her and started toward her, and she ran out of the room. But she had started me going again and I paced up and down the room, not bothering to eat or drink.

"Aw, she's right, goddamn it," I told Pete. "I *could* have been champ three years ago. Who the hell's around to beat me? You know, Pete, this is the only thing I ever wanted since I grew up. The only thing I'll ever want. Shit."

Pete looked at me. "So?" he asked.

I shook my head. "Ah, you been away," I told him. "You don't know what it's like now."

"Tell me. What's it like now?"

"Worse than it ever was. The mob was always in boxing, you know that. But now they're running it. You know, really running it. Nobody sets up the matches except them. And they set them up on how they can clean up on the betting more than anything else. Our old friend Nick and his pals, they got it organized just the way they got the jukeboxes organized. They told me often enough. All I got to do is do what I'm told and I'll be in. But . . . I don't know. Like everybody says, I'm a stupid, stubborn bastard. I don't know how long I can hold out, but . . . I held out so far. You understand, don't you, Pete?"

"I understand."

"I'd like to win it on my own. Not have these bastards fix it for me."

He nodded again and repeated, "I understand."

I stopped walking around and threw myself down in a chair. "What do you think, Pete?" I asked him. "Am I doin' the right thing? What would you do if you was me? What do you think I should do?"

Pete thought for a little while, then said, "I think you're doing the right thing. Stay away from them as long as you can. You're getting yourself plenty of matches. You can always go to them in the end. Take a little more time."

I jumped up and started pacing again, feeling that old familiar tension rising in me. "Time!" I said, pounding a fist into the palm of my hand. "Jesus, am I glad you're back, Pete. You're the only guy who understands. You're the only one who knows—you know. Nobody else knows, not even—not even Vickie. Not that I'd be enough of a jackass ever to let a woman know. And not Joey. A lot of the time now I get the feeling that I'm running out of time. That I'm coming to the end of something, that all of a sudden all of this is going to end. Something bad will happen, I know. I get the feeling that maybe I'm fated never to be the champ. Maybe there is a God. Maybe I'm being punished for all the wrong things I done all my life. I don't deserve to be champ." I looked around the room. "You come right down to it, I don't deserve any of this," I said, gesturing with my arm and dropping into the chair again.

After a second or two Pete nodded at me and said, "Yeah, I know how you feel, Jake. As a matter of fact, I feel the same way myself plenty of the time."

"Yeah? No kiddin'? I thought I was the only one. Why would you have a feeling like that?"

"The psychiatrist up in Sing Sing tried to explain it to me once when I told him how I felt. It's something to do with knowin' you're guilty of doing somethin' wrong, somethin' that if people found out about it you'd be punished for it. . . . We did some pretty bad things when we were kids, Jake. And the psychiatrist said that sometimes it's worse to get away with doing somethin' bad than it is to get caught and get punished for it. He said that if you get away with it, sometimes you go and do something worse, subconsciously hoping that you'll get caught for the worse thing and get a worse punishment." Suddenly he broke into a little laugh. "Listen to me, talkin' like a psychiatrist. I don't know if I explained it so that you understand it, but that's about what he said." He gave me that smile of his. "Well, I done my three years in the can, so I guess the psychiatrist would say that I'm square with society and myself." He laughed again. "The trouble with you, Jake, is that nothin' but good keeps happenin' to you. This place, Vickie, money . . ."

"Yeah," I said. "I know. I get it." I shook my head. "But sometimes I get the feeling that I don't know what's happenin'. Things are just happenin' to me without me being able to do anything about it."

Pete jumped up from his chair and laughed. "Ah, forget it! Here I am just back out of the can and we're sittin' around talkin' like we was tryin' to solve all the problems of the world. Let's laugh it up a little, for Christsake. Where's your booze? I'm not on the wagon, you know. There's only one thing for you to do."

"What's that?"

"Keep on fightin'. Keep on winnin'. If you beat everybody in sight there'll be such a stink they can't keep you from fightin' for the championship."

FIFTEEN

Some time later, Pete told me about how he went into Richie's one night when I was out in Detroit for a few days for a fight.

My picture had a place of honor in Richie's now, but the shock Pete was in for was meeting Viola. I hadn't seen much of Viola, deliberately, but I had heard about her. I don't know how much responsibility I have to take for her, but I'll take it, though I still swear I didn't know she was a virgin. Anyway, she was no virgin now. She'd gone all the way down to hell, and she looked it—overpainted and overdressed, and, when Pete first saw her in Richie's, drunk. In fact, the very first he saw of her she was slugging a guy with her purse and yelling at the top of her voice, "You're a slob! You're all slobs! That's what you are, every last one of you goddamned good-for-nothing bums!"

She swung at the guy again and he pretended to reel back against the wall. "I want some respect!" she yelled. "That's what I want. I want people to respect me! Who the hell do you think you are?"

"Baby," the guy said, "five minutes ago when I bought you the drink you told me you loved me."

This line got a laugh and Viola slammed her bag against the bar. "Richie!" she yelled. "Where's Richie? I want Richie!"

So Richie came charging out and said, "Oh, Viola. It's you again. Now what is it?"

And he took her by the arm and edged her toward the door.

"Richie," she said, "you know me. You ever have any trouble with me?"

Richie was still trying to ease her out. "Never, Viola. You know better than that. You're always welcome around here. But now don't you think you oughta go home and get a little rest—you know, you've had a little too much to drink."

"Well, you're gonna have a whole lotta trouble if your customers don't show me a little respect," Viola said, beginning to cry. "That's all I want, a little respect. A person is entitled to that. I'm a good girl, I always was a good girl."

"Sure, sure, now you go on home and get a little sleep, I'll straighten these guys out so you don't have any more trouble from them."

"Beasts, that's what they are. Animals. You try to be nice to them and all they think . . ."

By this time she was next to Pete and sees him for the first time. She stops and throws Richie's arm off. "Pete?" she says. "Pete?" She's having trouble focusing on him. "It's you. You're home. . . ."

Pete said later, all he could do was nod and try to force himself to smile, he was so shocked to see Viola like this.

Viola kept looking at him, then she touched his arm. Suddenly she was crying and Pete started to put his arm around her, but she slapped it away. She turned around and stumbled over to where my picture was pasted, close to the bar. She mumbled something, but Pete couldn't hear what it was. Then she started crying hysterically. Pete went over to her, but Viola pulled away from him and ran out the door.

Pete was about to go after her, but Richie put his hand on Pete's arm and shook his head. Pete looked at him, waiting for Richie to say something, but Richie took Pete over to the bar and ordered him a drink. Richie sighed, then said, "She was such a nice kid. I knew her old man. It's tough to figure why some of them turn out like they do."

Pete had a couple more drinks. All the while he was staring into his glass, listening to the guys talking about Viola, and they were saying things like, "She'd love you and lay you one minute, hit you and want to kill you the next."

Pete was standing at the bar maybe twenty minutes, half an hour, when Salvy walked in, chewing a toothpick. This was the time when it was very high style for half-ass tough guys to chew toothpicks. God knows where they got the idea—guys like Salvy never have ideas of their own— probably from some gangster movie where a bit player needed a piece of business, but it was very big then.

Salvy clapped Pete on the back and said, "Pete, you old sonofagun! It's great to see you! I didn't realize you was back! Hey, you look great!"

Pete sort of smiled. "You mean I look great for a guy who's been away for three years. This must be old-home week."

"Why old-home week?"

Pete shrugged. "Viola was here awhile back."

"Ah, her," Salvy said, moving into the bar and ordering a drink.

"Why the 'Ah, her' bit?" Pete asked. "I hardly recognized her. She looks like hell. And bombed, too."

"Ah, she's a whore."

Even after he'd seen her, Pete couldn't believe him. "A whore?"

Salvy took a sip of his drink and shrugged. "Sure. Everybody and his brother's laid her."

Pete still couldn't adjust. "But she was such a nice kid."

"Forget it. All I can tell you is what any guy in this joint could tell you. Then the trouble is she gets a few bombs in her and you can't handle her. If you so much as lay a finger on her she starts blowin' her stack and tellin' the whole world that she's a good girl and men are nothing but a pack of animals."

"Which is not so far from wrong," says Pete.

"Forget it! Look, how about you and me goin' into the restaurant and havin' dinner and cuttin' up a few touches about the good old days. Christ, I ain't seen you in years."

Pete agreed, and they took a table for dinner. Pete is sitting there looking down at the bottom of his drink and not saying anything. Then Salvy hit him on the arm. "C'mon, this is a great way to celebrate," he said. "You look like you lost your last friend. Whatsa matter?"

Pete shook his head. "I was just thinking how things

turn out," he said. "Three years ago I was a young punk who was gonna make it big, and Viola was a nice little chick hangin' around the candy store, just growing up, and Jake was just getting started as a fighter. Nobody knew where he'd end up, whether he was any good as a fighter, and now look at him. Viola's a whore and I'm an ex-con and Jake's the only one who's made it big."

Salvy looked at him with those weasely little eyes of his very bright. "Look, Pete," he said, "why don't you come around and talk to the boys? You stand very high with them. They're always talking about what a great guy you are and how big you could be except for that one little piece of bad luck that sent you up. But there's no sense in letting a little thing like that spoil your whole life. Why don't you come around with me?"

Pete shook his head. "Sometimes one little thing like that can change your whole life. I got a theory, you know. If you're gonna succeed, one thing you positively gotta have is luck. I mean, look at Franklin Roosevelt. If he had had bad luck when he got polio, he would have died. Instead of which he got better and now he's President. Well, I don't mean I'm Roosevelt or anything, but if I had good luck with the boys when I was on that job I never would have got nailed. So I got another deal going, with my old man, legit, and I ain't got nothin' against the boys, you know that, but I just got a hunch I'll do it better my own way."

Salvy gave a little laugh. "You and Jake," he said.

Pete looked at him. "What does that mean?" he asked.

"Nothin', nothin'," Salvy said real fast, putting his hand on Pete's arm again. "We heard you was in the dress business and doin' all right."

"What was the Jake crack?" Pete asked, taking his arm away.

Salvy gave the little laugh again. "Ah, I didn't mean nothin'," he said. "It's just—you know, he wants to do it all his own way. He's gettin' to be more and more of a loner the older he gets." Then he got very confidential with Pete. "You know him the best of anybody, Pete. You know if Jake would just bend a little he could be the champ in no time and all of us would make a bundle.

We'd end up with a ton of dough. Why don't you talk to him?"

"Talk to him, Salvy? Talk to him about what? You know him, Salvy. Could anybody ever talk to him about anything when he had his mind made up? You've known him long enough to know that."

Salvy shook his head. "Okay," he said. "I think he's a sap for not going along with the deal, though. You know these guys, they own the whole show, what they say goes. Christ, they got their hooks in all the champs—you name him, they got him. Jake'll have to come around sometime, and meantime look at all the dough he's missin' out on."

"Okay, okay, awright already," Pete says. "You made your pitch and you got your answer. Now are we gonna spend the whole night talkin' about what La Motta should or shouldn't do?"

"Okay, okay," Salvy said. Then he changed the subject. "Look, Pete," he said, "tomorrow night I got a date with two of the sharpest chicks you ever saw. And the guy I was going out with, he got called out of town this afternoon. So how about you come out with me?"

Well, this kind of threw Pete. I mean, he and Salvy had never been that close that Salvy would try to fix him up with a dame. Also—Pete said to me when he was telling me about it long afterward—he had a feeling that Salvy was setting him up for something, that he really didn't have a double date, that the idea had just come to him that minute.

"No, Salvy," Pete said. "Thanks but no, thanks. I can't."

"Aah, come on, Pete. Please. Do a favor for an old buddy. You must owe me a favor from the old days. Or just do me a favor for the sake of old times, anyway. Look, I can't make out on a date with two of them."

"Why me? What would you have done if you hadn't happened to run into me here?"

"I'd have gotten somebody else, but I'm doin' you a favor. Is this any way to treat somebody who's tryin' to do you a favor, for Christsake?" He looked at Pete kind of sideways. "In fact, one of these dolls is so gorgeous I don't think you can score."

This made Pete even more sure that he was being set up for something. "You think you'll score?"

"I'll bet on it."

Pete decided, what the hell. "Any day you can score, I can," he said.

Salvy laughed. "Says you. You think you can prove it?"

"Okay. You're on."

And he spent the rest of the evening trying to figure out what the hell Salvy was up to.

They agreed to meet on a corner near where Pete lived. Salvy would be doing the driving because he had a brand-new Cadillac convertible that he wanted to show off. Pete was there on the street corner, leaning against a lamp post and reading an advance story in the *Mirror* about me and the fight with Costner that was coming up that night in Detroit and the *Mirror*'s guess about how it would come out, when the car rolled up to stop beside him.

"Hop in," yelled Salvy.

Pete went over to the car. Salvy was sitting behind the steering wheel with his date beside him, and alone in the back seat was Pete's date. Vickie.

That's right. My wife, the mother of my kids.

Pete froze, and Salvy busted up with laughter.

Vickie put her hands up over her face and started crying, panic-stricken. "Oh, Salvy, how could you do this to me? With Pete, his best friend! Salvy, how could you do this? Oh, my God, my God! If he ever tells Jake!"

Salvy was still roaring with laughter. "I just wanted to show this guy how stupid he and his pal can be!"

Pete charged around the car to Salvy's side, pulled open the door, got him by the coat front, jerked him out of the car and swung into him before Salvy even knew what was happening, and after Pete had belted him five or six times, Salvy was crumpled up on the pavement. Then Pete got Vickie by the arm and snarled. "Okay, you, you're coming with me. Get out." He flagged a cab.

By this time Salvy had staggered to his feet and was leaning against the Caddy and pointed a finger at Pete and said, "You stupid son of a bitch. You made the mistake of your life hitting me. You may not know it but I'm one of the boys now and I'll get you for this if it's the last thing I ever do. And that goes for that stupid thick-headed fighter pal of yours and his slut wife. . . ."

For a second Pete thought of going back, but then he figured, what the hell, and he went and got into the cab with Vickie and took her home.

She cried all the way home, and when she got into the house she about collapsed. Pete said he didn't say a thing. What the hell do you do to a woman who's trying to cover up what she's been caught at by having hysterics? Pete just stood in front of the picture window, looking out into the night until finally she began to slow down the sobs long enough to say, "Well, say something. . . . Why don't you say something?"

But Pete didn't know what to say, so he kept quiet.

"I know what you're thinking," Vickie went on. "Well, "I can't help that." Then, with a sudden change of mood: "Go ahead and tell him! Go ahead! I wouldn't be surprised if he killed me, the temper he's got! Go ahead and tell him, but now get out of here!"

Pete shook his head and came back from the window into the room. "No, Vickie," he said. "You tell him, if you want to. What you want to do with yourself is your business. Nobody ever told me I should take over other people's lives for them. I ain't gonna be the guy to blow the whistle. You do what you want. . . . Besides, I think I know the way Jake feels about you, and I'm not sure that if I told him he wouldn't call me a goddamned liar and bust my head open."

She couldn't believe him. Slowly she sat up straight and stopped bawling. She got out a handkerchief and blew her nose and dabbed at her eyes, all streaked with mascara.

"Honest to God?" she asked. "You mean it, really? You're not going to tell him? Aw, Pete, you wouldn't be cruel enough to be just kidding me?"

Pete shook his head. "Not me. I don't kid about things like that."

Then she had another change of mood. She got her purse and got out her compact and began to work on her face. "Well, thanks, Pete," she said. "What it means is I get killed later instead of sooner."

Pete looked around the room and shook his head again.

"All I got is one question, Vickie. Why? In the name of God, with all this, why?"

She laughed, a little hysterical. "You remember the old saying from the Bible about man doesn't live by bread alone? Or is that too high class for you, too much over your head?" Then she got serious again. "Or that cornball old song about only a bird in a gilded cage, remember that?"

Pete nodded.

"Oh, Pete, what do you know about a woman and what she really wants, I mean away from the sex part. Do you think that a big rich house and expensive clothes is what she really wants?"

Pete said nothing.

"And how well do you know Jake?" she asked. "I mean, really how well?"

"Pretty good, I think," Pete said.

She shook her head. "No you don't. You know him as a man, but I know him as a woman. It's a whole different thing. You were telling me once about how he doesn't trust anybody, not even his own brother. Well, he doesn't trust me either, and I'm his wife—what do you think of that?" Her voice started going up. "It's like living in a goddamned jail, I tell you. You can take all this furniture and these clothes and stuff them! I can't even breathe deep without him wanting to know why. If he even thinks I have a wrong thought he uses me for a punching bag! You think you know him so well, ask Joey. He'll tell you what goes on."

During this she had gotten up and was pacing back and forth, tearing her handkerchief into pieces. She started to cry again. Then she took Pete by the hand and pulled him down on the sofa beside her.

"Look at me, Pete," she said. "I don't look so bad, do I? I'm young. I'm not even twenty-two yet. I don't want to be bad, but I want a little out of life. I want to enjoy it, I want to learn about it, I want a little fun, I don't want to be locked up here and have a husband who belts me if he just thinks that I looked the wrong way at some other guy." She looked away from him and let go of his hand. "Pete I want you to believe one thing. At first I didn't care what you thought of me, but now it's important to me that I have your respect. I would never have done anything wrong tonight, honest. I wouldn't care who the man was Salvy brought along. I couldn't *wouldn't*, let myself, no matter how I felt about Jake. Do you believe me?"

"Sure, Vickie. And I don't think bad about you. It's just that Jake—well, if you're kicked around ever since you can remember, since you was a little kid, and you had to fight your way up every inch of the way . . . well, you can see what it can do to a man."

"Then why did he get married?" she asked. "Why did he want to marry me? You've got to have *some* trust, Pete. . . . Oh, I don't know what to do. I want to love him the way I used to. We have two wonderful kids, but he's just *punched* the love out of me and—God, I want to leave him now, but I just don't dare. I'm afraid of him. I'm not joking when I say I'm afraid he'll lose his temper so bad someday that he really will kill me."

Pete didn't really know what to say, but he had to say something. "He's under a lot of pressure, Vickie. He keeps the pressure on himself. He keeps himself in a pressure cooker. I guess that's what you have to do if you want to be the champ, at anything. Drive yourself, not let anything stop you. And you know how determined he is to get to the top, to show them all, to be Jake La Motta, world's champion."

"I know," she said, "and between you and me, I don't think he'll ever be champ. . . . I hear things. He's got too many people against him."

"One thing you forget, Vickie. He'll do *anything* to be champ. *Anything*. It's like those guys that went after the Holy Grail, or whatever it was. It's the only thing that means anything to him—you, me, the kids—even himself! I swear to God if he knew in advance that he'd take such a beating fighting for the championship that it would kill him after he won, he'd still go ahead and make the fight."

"All I know is what I hear," Vickie said.

"Look, Vickie, there are people kicking around this town that you're much better off not knowing, much less talking to. And even more, much less talking to about Jake."

"There's one thing you can say for them," Vickie said. "They're the only ones I know who aren't afraid of him. They're the only ones who dare talk to me without being afraid that Jake will hear about it."

Pete figured there was nothing else he could do, so he said, "Vickie, I still say there are people you ought not even to be seen with, and you know who I mean. I don't know what to say to you about Jake. But this much I do know about him, Vickie. Whether he knows it himself or not, he needs you and needs you bad, so give him as much of a break as you can, okay?"

He got up and started for the door, and Vickie went with him.

"Okay," she said, "I'll do what I can. But you can't know how bad he can be. . . . Pete, can you and I be friends? You know, tonight I only went along because I wanted to get out and have some laughs. . . . I want someone I can talk to. . . ."

"Sure, we can be friends."

"Can I talk to you? If things get too bad can I tell you and ask you what to do? Around here I have nobody to talk to except the maid, and I can't talk to her."

"Sure. You can talk to me anytime, anytime at all. . . ."

SIXTEEN

Vickie was right about the lack-of-trust thing. From as early as I can remember, I didn't want to trust anybody. You trust a guy, pretty soon you find that he's using you to give you a screwing. You trust a dame, pretty soon you find she's giving you a different kind of a screwing. But if you don't trust anybody, or make sure that basically you don't give a good goddamn about anybody, you're safe. If a guy sells you down the river, it's your own goddamn fault, you got only yourself to blame. So what if a dame does go off with someone else, there's always plenty more of what she's got. Just don't trust anybody, anywhere, anytime.

Right after the Salvy-Vickie thing, Pete had another interview with Nick. Pete was coming out of his house one night and just as he got to the sidewalk the black limousine pulled up, and in it was a couple of the hoodlums from the parking-lot shooting, Patsy and some other guy. Patsy smiled at Pete and said, "Hi, Pete, hop in."

"Thanks," Pete said, "I'd rather walk. And all by myself."

"Aah, it's okay," Patsy said to him. "No hard feelings. We ain't lookin' for trouble. Nick just wants to have a talk with you, and he went to all the trouble of sendin' a car for you."

Pete thought it over for a second, and he thought he'd better. He got in the car and they drove for fifteen, twenty minutes and pulled up in front of one of those dreary loft buildings that the Bronx has thousands of and got out.

The building was all dark except for a neon sign out front that read DEBONAIR SOCIAL CLUB. Pete and the two hoods went through the door and up a stairway, then cut through a very expensive-type club room with card tables, billiard tables, an extra-long bar—all very plush, with thick rugs and leather chairs and phony oil paintings on the wall. Finally they came to a door marked PRESIDENT and Patsy rapped on it and a voice said, "Come in."

They went in, and there was Nick behind a big, high-class mahogany desk. This room, too, was furnished as rich as they could—give a hood some money for an office and all the furnishings look like Warner Brothers. There were three other guys, all part of the mob, and one of them was Salvy, who still had two red eyes and a fat mouth. If looks could kill, the one he gave Pete would have stretched him out right there on the rug.

Nick was smiling friendly-like and waved a hand at one of the chairs: "Siddown, Pete," he said, "and make yourself comfortable."

Pete sat down, then Nick got very serious. He leaned forward and looked at Pete. "Pete," he said, "you been around long enough to know . . . you shouldn't lift your fists to one of my boys. After all, you was a pro fighter—not that that's what the main point is."

Pete looked at him like he was something crawling out from under a rock, and Nick put his hand up and said, "I know what the story is, or I think I do, provided Salvy didn't forget anything." Nick looked at Salvy for a minute to show him that he *better* not have forgotten anything. "I'm not sayin' Salvy should or shouldn't have done what he did with the dame, even if he did think it was only a gag. Let's not get into an argument about that, it's all water over the dam. And I know about you and Jake, too. How you're his best friend and all that and you probably lost your head at Salvy. I know, I know. But I want to get to the main point. And the main point, Pete, is that maybe things have changed since you been away. Maybe you don't know the score the way you think you do. Pete, we're a lot better organized than we used to be, and along with the new organization we got new rules. One of the rules is, no fightin' among ourselves. That's the new score around here. We got one big organization here, and anybody takes on one of us takes on all of us—and Pete, you better believe it, we got an army. *Nobody* fools around with us. *Nobody*. You understand that?"

Pete didn't say anything, so Nick went on: "What I want to say, Pete, is you always were a good guy for us and nothin' is goin' to happen this time." He smiled again. "This time, you're getting away with it." He stopped smiling. "But don't you ever do it again, not if you want to stay in one piece. You understand?"

"I guess so."

Nick shook his head and sighed. "How are you, Petey boy?"

Pete shrugged. "Okay."

Nick jumped to his feet and shook his head at Pete.

"You *guess?* That's all, huh? Nothin' else to say? I don't figure you, Pete. You too good for us just because you're in the dress business? I got news for you and the dress business if you ain't already heard it. We can meet you there, too. Whatsa matter with you and the quick answers. You want to get outta here fast?"

"Aw, Nick . . ."

Nick bunched his fingers and waved them back and forth. "I don't get it," he said. "I just don't get it. You was a good man, Petey, a good stand-up man. You proved that when some o' my boys got stupid and lost their heads and fired off a gun at you. You stood up then. You didn't tip your mitt to the cops, you kept your mouth shut. That's what I like, that's what everybody likes. You're like in the family! I respect you. Everybody does, everybody hears about you."

He looked at Pete again and shook his head and moved around the desk. "But now, like I say, I just don't get it. You get out of the can, you're a different guy. You act different. What did they do up there, give you a whole new personality? You don't even come around to see your old pal Nick anymore. That hurt me, Petey, when I heard you'd been out days, even weeks, and you hadn't once come around to see me, and I sincerely mean it. I was hurt. No matter what it was, at least you could come around and say hello. I figure we could do a lot together."

He laughed. "We got some things in common, Petey, you know. After all, we're both ex-cons, ain't we?"

Pete switched in his chair. "Aw, you know how it is, Nick," he said. "You know I'm out on parole. I owe them an awful lot of time, and Christ I don't want to go back to that place for another five, ten years. The time I had up there was enough. And you know about the parole laws. You know that bit about consorting with known criminals—"

"No, no, no! That's got nothin' to do with it, you know what I mean. And what about your buddy Jake? He ain't on parole, is he? How come he forgets his old buddy Nick? There was a time when he had the shorts, when he was lookin' for any piece of dough he could get. I used to see a lot o' him back in those days. But now he's rollin' in it, I don't see so much of him. . . . You remember that heist you guys pulled for us on that crap game, that was one beautiful job." He kissed his fingers and waved them up toward the ceiling. "A beautiful, beautiful job. I knew right then that you boys could go a long, long way. A little guidance from old Nick and a little luck, and both of you guys could be rollin' in it. . . . Look at Jake now. Fightin' around. Three years he's been fightin' around to get to be champ, when he coulda been champ all this time if he'd only come around to me. He disappoints me. Frankly, he disappoints me, and you don't know exactly how much."

Nick turned around to Pete again and an idea hit him, so he waved to his boys. "You guys get outta here. I wanna talk to my old pal Pete in private for a coupla minutes."

After the boys went out, Nick started pacing back and forth. "Look, Pete," he said, "regardless of whether you come back or not, I want you to do me a favor. One favor, for old-times' sake."

"What is it, Nick?"

Nick stopped pacing for a second. "You gotta talk to Jake."

Pete made a sour face. "About what?"

"Aw, come on," Nick said, bending over to shake his finger in Pete's face. "You know what about. You know, privately, just between the two of us, that boy is gettin' to be a real embarrassment to me. A *real* embarrassment."

Pete sort of half-smiled, which didn't make Nick feel any better.

"It ain't funny," Nick said sharply.

"How's he embarrassin' you?" Pete asked. "How the hell can he do that?"

Nick sort of coughed. "Look, Pete," he said, "everybody in the world got a boss, that right? No matter how high up you get, you got a boss, right?"

"I suppose so."

"Well, I got a boss, too," Nick said. "Especially in the matter of this goddamned boxing. Now they're settin' it all up as just one racket and Mister Big wants the whole thing run nice and orderly. He already got most of the boxers with any sort of reputation, he's even got two or three of the champs, and you'd figure if anybody could fight the mob off, it would be them guys." He shook his head. "Except, of course, they're too dumb, they mostly do what they're told. But who's the one dumb slob my guy doesn't have control over? Guess. Mister Jake La Motta."

"Yeah."

"So you see why I'm embarrassed. Mister Big is gettin' awful peeved at me that I can't deliver Jake, especially since I always figured I could after that heist he went on."

Pete began to see an angle. "So that's why you been tryin' to work through his wife?" he asked, as cold as he could.

"In a pig's ass!" Nick snapped back. "Whatsa matter with you, you losin' your mind? Or you think I'm losin' mine? I ain't never worked through a broad in my life and I ain't about to start now. That was the bright idea of that goddamned idiot Salvy. He's all set to carve out a new career for himself as a lover. He thinks just because he's got a Caddy convertible on payments all the broads are gonna fall down in front of him."

Pete had to believe him. He spread out his hands. "Nick," he said, "you know Jake like I do. You know when he gets set on something God himself could come down out of heaven and he couldn't talk him out of it. I have no influence with him in a thing like this. He's absolutely convinced he can buck the system on this and make it on his own. That's how good a fighter he thinks he is."

"Is everybody a nut?" Nick screamed. "Make it on his own? Does he know the kind of dough involved? I don't mean his crummy purses, I mean the real dough in the odds? He thinks he's gonna become champ on his own? You mean the boys are gonna sit by and see some nut come in there and hold one of the two or three most important titles in the world? He's crazy! A nut who don't listen to anybody or respect anybody? Listen, Pete, you understand, you tell him. I don't care how great he is or how colorful, he ain't gonna get a crack at the title without us! I stand before you and swear he'll never get a crack at the title without us! Now do you think you can make him understand that one simple elemental fact of life? I'm not askin' you to do another thing except get that message into that thick head!"

Pete nodded. "I don't know how much good it'll do, Nick," he said, "but I'll tell him. I'll tell him what you said."

Nick smiled. "You do that, Pete. And tell him if he comes in with us how much money he can make. We'll make him richer than he ever dreamed he could be."

"Yeah."

Vickie was right about one thing. I was insanely jealous. I read now that it's a sign that you don't have confidence in yourself, which seems like a pretty silly thing to think about me, but when it came to broads I guess now it was true enough. Like I say, I knew I could take any fighter except maybe the heavyweight champ, and he'd better be in good shape. But expecially with very good-looking dames, and most especially with blondes, I used to wonder what they saw in me. Here I was a bum and they—they could get any guy they wanted just be crooking a finger at him, so why the hell would they waste their time on me? I guess that was it. And Vickie was a real beautiful blonde—she tried acting a couple of times, and I'm still surprised that she didn't make it just on looks alone. I've seen some dames who didn't have half her looks playing the lead in movies. Anyway, I guess the reason I was jealous was that I would think—no, not *think,* it was deeper down than that, an emotion, an instinct—that whenever she looked at a guy longer than I thought she should that maybe she suddenly realized that here was a guy with a little class who could measure up to her a little better and from now on I was going to be strictly second-class.

I remember when Pete came over to tell me about the Nick deal. Vickie was in leotards and sweater, rolling around on the floor with the two boys, Jacky and Joey. It was after their supper, and I was trying to get the damned television tuned right because there was gonna be a fight on later, Robinson and some bum I forget. In those early days, there was always some problem getting the TV to work right.

When the door chimed I said to Vickie, "You get it. I'm tryna get this goddamned set to work. Jesus, all the dough we paid for it and we can't pick up a station ten miles away."

She went to the door and I heard her say, "Pete! How nice!" I turned around and there was Pete, and suddenly Vickie got up on her toes and kissed him on the cheek. Okay. My oldest friend. But was this necessary?

"Come in, come in," she said, and Pete came in and tousled the kids' hair and flopped down on the other end of the couch from me.

"Gonna watch the fight?" he asked, watching me fiddle with the dials.

"Yeah."

It must have sounded harder than I meant it to because Pete said, "What's bitin' you?"

"Nothin'," I said. I looked up at Vickie, who was standing there looking down at us and for no reason that I could think of I felt myself getting mad.

"How about some coffee?" I snapped at her. "Can't we get some coffee or somethin'? Do I have to tell you every little thing?"

She sucked in her breath and swung her head away and walked stiffly out to the kitchen. I was mad at myself for talking to her that way and mad at her for making me, even though I knew she didn't mean it, which just goes to show you how complicated things can get without you wanting them to.

I tried to carry it off with Pete. "Dames," I said. "You gotta tell them every single thing to do."

Pete didn't look at me. "Yeah," he said. He was just looking at nothing at all. There was no expression on his face and he was talking in that flat tone he put on when he didn't want you to know how he felt. "I dropped by to tell you something, Jake. I think I know what you'll say, but don't interrupt me. Lemme tell you what happened. This you should know, anyway. . . ."

And he told me all about what Nick said, without the Vickie part. I didn't hear about that till a long time afterward. While he was talking, Vickie came back in with a tray of coffee and cookies and things like that, and I looked at her and I could tell that she'd been crying in the kitchen. She didn't say anything. She put the stuff down on a table, and when she saw the boys horsing around while me and Pete were trying to talk she gathered them up and walked back out of the room. All without saying a word.

Pete was finishing off, ". . . so I'm just tellin' you like I said I would, Jake, and I ain't goin' to give you a single word of advice on what you ought to do. I don't know how much bullshit I was getting since I'm strictly tryin' to keep my nose clean and I got nothin' to check against, but Nick certainly sounded as if he knew what he was talkin' about. He sounded as if these boys really hold the aces. . . ."

"Fuck him and his aces," I said. "He can drop dead with his aces for all of me. I got a few ideas of my own. We'll see who's right. We'll see who comes out on top."

Pete seemed to relax. For the first time since he came in the house, he laughed. "Attaboy. That's the Jake I know. You stick with it, Jake. For all their talk I don't know how long they can sit on this racket without the lid blowin' off. It was the war that gave them their start, but the war is over now. Sooner or later somebody's goin' to catch up with them."

"Sooner or later they're gonna have to give me a

match," I said. "I beat practically every one of the bums they got."

Pete laughed again. "Okay," he said, "who's gonna win this fight tonight?"

"Aw, you're kiddin'," I said. "Robinson. Who's around who can beat Robinson?"

"Nobody but you, baby," he said.

SEVENTEEN

As it turned out, of course, the mob did have all the aces, plus the muscle, plus the guns. It was bad enough me defying them, but the way I did it, blowing my mouth off, didn't exactly win me any friends. Pete told me that the next time he saw Nick, in Richie's, Nick asked him how it had gone with me, and when Pete said not so good, Nick just said, "Well, it's too bad. It's just too bad," and turned on his heel and walked away.

Well, they got to me—got to me in a way you wouldn't expect.

A week or so after this I was in my room at the gym and Tiny, who was the masseur at the gym, was giving me a rubdown after a workout, and I'm lying there facedown and sort of sleepy-like getting the kinks out when there's a knock on the door. Tiny went over and opened it and there were the four from the night club—Salvy, Patsy and two others I don't know the names of. One of them gave Tiny the thumb toward the door and he beat it. Salvy gave me that big grin that always made me feel like busting him and said, "Hiya, Jackie boy."

I grunted and turned my head around and put it back on my arms. Talking to the back of my head, Patsy said, "Say, Jake, we caught the Kochan fight. Boy, you sure starched a good big guy out there."

I gave him another grunt.

Still pouring it on, one of them said, "Aw, that was nothin'. How about the night he beat Satterfield. Imagine a middleweight knocking over a guy like Satterfield, who's been flattenin' some of the best of the heavyweights."

"Nuts," Salvy said. "The big thing was the win over

158

Robinson. You guys realize Jackie is still the only guy who holds a win over Robinson?"

I gave up. I sat up, pulling a towel around me, looked at them and yawned. Then I laughed. "You guys don't ever give up, do you?" I asked.

Patsy spread out his arms and came on with his big smile again, but with the hard eyes, which means I was due for more of the needle. That's one thing I hate about these guys—I may not be the smartest guy in the world, but with these guys you can always tell what's coming. They always got to telegraph everything.

"Jake!" Patsy said. "Can't you ever relax? Can't you ever be nice? You always gotta be the hard guy? We just dropped around to say, 'Hello, Champ.' " And he stopped so fast that I knew the point. "Ooops!" he said. "Sorry. I called you 'Champ.' A slip of the tongue."

It was hard to keep from throwing up. "Okay," I said. "You delivered the message for whoever you're working for now. So why don't you blow?"

Salvy had his toothpick out and was chewing on it. "Look, Jake," he said.

" 'Champ' to you, crumb!" I said, getting off the table.

"Aw, Jake, listen . . ."

"*Champ,* I said!"

"Okay. Champ. But listen . . ."

"In this room, *I* talk, *you* listen. Blow! Like I said, blow!"

Patsy had a new look on him. He looked nasty and hissed, "Aw, for Christsake, why don't you get wise to yourself?"

But I was getting wilder and wilder. "Get wise to *yourself!*" I yelled. "Get wise to *yourself* and get the hell outta here and leave me alone! When I wanna throw in with creeps like you I'll let ya know! Now get out!"

Patsy still looked nasty. "Never mind the stack-blowin', Jake," he said. "Don't get carried away with how tough you are. In the ring, okay, you're tough. Real tough. Outside the ring you're just another slob. And not too smart, either."

He snapped around and started on out the door, followed by the rest of the crew. But as they were going out, Salvy turned around and came halfway back into the room. "You know, you could do with a coupla friends to wise you up, Jake," he said. "For example, what is your old friend Pete doing over at your house all the time while you're away fightin' outta town?"

I jumped for him, but he saw the look in my face and was out the door and had it slammed before I could get to him.

I don't know what was in me, but that was the key. I got up to the closed door so crazy with rage and jealousy that I slammed my fist on the panel as hard as I could before I could stop myself. And without a shower or anything else I got myself dressed and out into my car. All I knew was that I'd seen Vickie kiss Pete, both of them lovey-dovey, and how the hell could you tell what your wife's doing when you're out of town? But this time, by God and by Christ, I'd find out! I went charging home, driving like a madman, and burst into the living room so mad that I couldn't even talk. Vickie came in from the kitchen, wiping her hands on a dishtowel, her eyes opening wider as she looked at me, not knowing what was wrong. And then I looked down at the cocktail table and in the ashtray there was only one thing—a splintered, chewed-up toothpick.

Christ, not Salvy!

Raging emotion shot through me. Vickie was trembling, huddling in a corner. "Jake," she said, "Jake, what's wrong? What do you look like that for? Jake, say something. . . ."

Finally I got so that I could talk but my voice was so hoarse I could hardly understand myself. "I'll say something," I said finally, slowly. "Who . . . you been seeing . . . when I'm at the gym . . . or outta town? . . ."

She started to talk, the words tumbling out. She was holding her throat with her hands. "What do you mean, Jake? See anyone? I don't see anyone. No one! What do you mean? What are you talking about?"

I shouted, "You mean to tell me Salvy wasn't in this goddamned house today?"

She was terrified and cringed in the corner of the room.

"Yes, yes, he was here. . . ." She began to scream. "I would have told you. He was trying to sell me a mink coat. I told him I'd have to ask you. . . ."

Nothing she could have said would have made any difference, I was in such a rage nothing could calm me. I slapped her, hard, again and again. "You're a damned stinkin' little liar," I yelled. "You got a mink coat, everybody knows you got a mink coat. You got more goddamned clothes than three women could wear. What else did Salvy come here for? What did he really want? Who else comes here? Tell me or I'll kill you, I swear to God I'll kill you!"

Suddenly, from somewhere, she got the strength to push me away just long enough to get out of the corner and slide into the next room, locking the little key on the knob. I came up against the door just as she locked it, hitting it hard. I yelled at her, "Open this door, you goddamned slut! So help me, I'll kill you when I get you! Open this door!" And I meant every word I said. But the door stayed locked, and there was no sound from the next room, and I was so mad with hate that I couldn't see or think straight. I didn't care what happened to me. I was going to take care of her no matter what. I backed off from the door and charged it with my shoulder, not even giving a good goddamn whether I broke my shoulder or not, and the door sprang inward.

She wasn't in the room. The room was empty. But the window was open and I ran over to it. There was a car going down the drive. I jumped out the window and raced over to my own and jumped in and screeched down the drive as fast as I could.

It's a goddamned wonder I wasn't killed. Me and half-a-dozen other people. I wouldn't have cared. I was going to get that slut if it was the last thing I did. We were racing through the streets of Westchester, into the Bronx, doing seventy, eighty, ninety miles an hour. I would have lost her at first except I knew she'd head toward the Bronx, where her family lived, where she knew people, where she could hide, so I just kept my foot down on the accelerator and sure enough after maybe five or six miles I could see her car ahead, not going as fast as I was, so that I was catching up to her, cutting in and out of traffic, passing right or passing left, it made no never mind to me. And suddenly it dawned on me where she was going.

So that was it! She was running for Pete. That was the guy who was going to protect her. My best friend. My pal. I'd read about things like that and I thought they were funny—a guy was a sap to get that worked up over a dame. They're all the same, what the hell. But I couldn't help myself. I was going to kill them, I was going to kill them both. Sure enough, I got to the crummy six-story taxpayer in the East Bronx where Pete and his old man had this sweatshop called "High Fashions, Inc." and Vickie's car was out in front.

I don't know whether you've ever been in a dress factory. It's a madhouse: long lines of machines for sewing, cutting tables, row on row of girls at the machines, fluorescent lights beating down, other girls, floor girls, walking around taking finished stacks of material from the sewing machines, bringing raw materials over so that the machines don't stop working, supervisors walking around, noise, noise, noise, machines going, people talking, people yelling, and at one end a short raised section, three or four steps higher than the rest of the floor, where there's the bosses, the office. That's where Pete was, so I went charging into the plant, then slowed down. I didn't want people looking at me. I knew I must have looked like some kind of wild animal. I went through the plant and up the steps and looked into the office—and there was Pete holding Vickie. She was sobbing, and he was holding her, so I went charging in and started punching, hitting, slamming, again and again as hard as I could, and after I'd slugged him again and again and again he started to go down, and I was still slugging him, and suddenly Vickie was on me, slapping and scratching and screaming, "You're killing him! Killing him! Killing him! *All for nothing!*"

I slugged her with the back of my hand and yelled at her, "Whaddaya mean, *nothing,* you stupid bitch?"

But instead of running away from me she was back on me, slapping and scratching again and yelling, "Nothing, is what I said. Go on, kill me, kill me! I'm not afraid of you anymore. I don't care whether you kill me like you killed the only guy who was stupid enough to think there was something to you, something to you instead of just being the kind of an animal that you really are!"

"Yeah, and chasin' around after you behind my back," I yelled at her. "Over the house every time I went out of town and I suppose all he came over for was to tell you what a great guy I am!"

"What do you mean?" she yelled.

"You know goddamned well what I mean, you cunt," I yelled back. "Don't give me that Miss Innocence shit!"

Suddenly she began to laugh, hysterically. "And you're not only an animal, you're a stupid animal! You're a fool on top of everything else. He was only over to the house twice, once when he found me . . . heard I was going to do something foolish, and once when Jacky had a fever and I couldn't get a doctor, so I called him to come over and see if we should take him to a hospital. Twice he was over to the house, and both times he behaved like a perfect gentleman because you were his friend!" Her laugh went even higher. "You fool, he's the only one of your friends who never did make a pass at me. That's the kind of friends you have!"

She was pushing and slapping me toward the door, when all of a sudden the hate and passion drained out of me and I felt—I don't know what I felt. Nothing.

My eye fell on the desk Pete had been standing at. On it was a long pair of tailor's shears. You know, the blades maybe sixteen inches long. The thought hit me, later, that if I'd been Pete and somebody had come at me the way I had, those scissors would now be hilt deep in his gut.

I felt like a zombie. Vickie was still hitting me and pushing me and I didn't do anything. I was like a sleepwalker. She pushed me out the door and screamed, "You're rotten, rotten, rotten! You're a sick maniac, a maniac! You belong in an asylum!"

I went out through the factory and down to the car and drove back home. It was late now and I just went into the living room and turned on a light and sat down.

I just sat there. After a long time—I didn't know how long it was—I heard a car come up the drive. Vickie let herself in.

"There you are," she said sourly. "Well, Pete isn't dead, in case you're interested, but after the way you acted I don't suppose you really care." She paced back and forth across the room and kept talking without looking at me. "And to bring you up to date on *all* the latest developments, I'm leaving you." She stopped and said it again for emphasis: *"Leaving you!* And I don't care if you do try to kill me. Go ahead, I'm not afraid of you any longer.

"There's worse things than being dead, and one of them is living with you. I'm leaving tonight. I must have been crazier than you are staying with you this long. . . . You'll destroy anyone who's too close to you, just like you would have killed Pete and me if you'd had the time. . . . You won't let anyone care for you, you can't believe that people truly care for you, and you know why? Because deep down in your heart you know that you don't deserve to have anyone love you!"

Ah, Jesus! This day just wouldn't end. I remember one of the Robinson fights, Robinson had me but I just wouldn't give the son of a bitch the satisfaction of knocking me down, so I told the referee I'd murder him if he tried to stop the fight. I got my arm wedged around one of the ropes and stayed there defying Robinson to knock me down. He couldn't, but I got about as bad a beating as I've ever had. So help me God, I'd rather take a beating like that than listen to my wife tell me she'd rather be dead than living with me. It makes you feel—well, the hell with it.

"I kept thinking that you'd change if you got to the top, if you got to be champ," Vickie said. "That maybe then you'd see that other people are people, too. That everyone isn't out to fool you or cheat you or clip you, but I can't stand it, I just can't take it anymore. . . . And you'll never be champ, I'm sure of that. Not now! You've just made too many enemies, too many people hate you. . . . I'm taking the children and leaving!"

I was on the point of breaking down. I couldn't take any more of it. It's like those nightmare times you have when you're a kid, like someone close to you dies and you know there's absolutely nothing you can do about it, no way you can change it, no hope of fixing it. You think of killing yourself, but it goes on and on and on. Nothing can change it.

Now I could hardly talk again, but for a different reason. Finally I got the words out. "Aah, Vickie," I said. "Aah, Vickie, please no, Vickie . . . no. Don't leave me. Christ, I'm pleading. I know, I know all the bad things, but I need you, I'm a bum without you and the kids. I'll change, I promise you. . . . I'll change. And I'm gonna be champ, I promise you that, too. . . . Aah, Vickie, maybe I don't do it the right way, but I love you, I love you. . . ."

There was a long, long silence. Then slowly Vickie said, "You know, if there's one thing—I just don't understand you, not one single little bit. . . . You love me?"

"Yeah," I said.

EIGHTEEN

Finally I was able to talk Vickie into not leaving me, but maybe she was right about me being a maniac. The only thing I really wanted was that title. I know what I said to Vickie, and I meant it—without her and the kids I'd be nothing but a bum—but the whole point of my life was being champion. Without that I wouldn't be nothing either. I *had* to get that title. I was making a hundred thousand dollars a year. I was rated number one, and I was fighting guys like Jimmy Edgar and Bob Satterfield and George Kochan, who are all top boys, and the reporters were saying maybe I'm not quite another Stan Ketchel—though how the hell they'd know beats me, none of them was around then—but I'm as tough as Battling Nelson. But none of all this was getting me a crack at the title. My old friend Rocky Graziano was off fighting Tony Zale, but was I going to get a crack at the winner? You can guess the answer, free.

One thing I did, my brother Joey blew his stack at. There was this real tough kid, Tony Janiro. So was his manager a tough kid, a wise guy. They figured Janiro could move up a little by beating me, but they had a gimmick that the mob put in. I would have to weigh in at a hundred and fifty-five. Now, remember that I could barely make middleweight. That meant my best fighting weight was around a hundred and seventy. And I'd been fighting light heavies, which is up to a hundred seventy-five. And taking weight off for a fighter is just like for you. Sheer torture. That's the way you take weight off, weight-watchers—torture.

I was maybe better than a hundred and eighty-five and had to get down better than thirty pounds. And to put the icing on the cake, there was a forfeit of fifteen thousand bucks.

Joey came storming into my room in the gym, where I was leaning against the rubbing table, bandaging my hands for a round of sparring. Joey had the newspaper with him and asked me, "This for real?"

"Yeah," I nodded.

Joey was close to going out of his skull and screamed, "Are you nuts? A hundred and fifty-five? What are you gonna do, cut off a leg? You must be outta your cotton-pickin' mind!"

What the hell, Joey had nothing to say about it. I just shrugged, but he was still steaming.

"And in the first place, you're gonna blow fifteen thousand bucks!" he yelled. "I know you're rich, but that rich?" Then he got sour. "Also, the least you could do would be to discuss it with me in advance. I'm your manager, you know, even if it is only for the record, and I'm also your brother and I like to hear about things before somebody shows them to me in the newspaper."

Well, probably I should have told him. It's just that I was so used to doing things for myself that I didn't think of it. But there was no use to say this to him, so I just didn't say anything.

"Will you at least tell me why?" Joey asked. "I think it's nuts, but you must have had a reason."

"Look, Joey," I said, "how long have I been the top contender? Four years at least, right?" He nodded. "And where am I gettin'?" I asked. "Nowhere, right? At least as far as the title is concerned. So what I'm gonna try to do is get every bit of screwy publicity I can. Half of these clowns think I'm a screwy jerk as it is. I can't do anything right for them, so I'm gonna do some things that will make them sit up and pay attention." I saw Joey getting a worried look, so I said, "Look, nothin' real loony, but these guys who own boxing now, I don't care how tough they are, they can't take the heat forever. Maybe it don't make any difference to them that all the newspaper guys say I should get a championship fight, but sooner or later, someone who matters is gonna say it and then it will mean something.

"Or even more than that," I went on, "sooner or later the heat is gonna get hot enough that some real Mister Big in the rackets is gonna get hold of these boys in fighting and say, 'Look, this La Motta boy is gettin' too big. Now the hell with what you think about giving him a title shot, too much more of this publicity can blow us all out of the water. And what the hell, he's not superman, put him in the ring with a real tough guy and there's no law that his head can't be knocked off. You know he's lost fights before.'"

Joey said, "But, Jesus, fightin' Janiro at a hundred and fifty-five. It ain't as if he was some pushover, you know. He's a tough kid."

"You don't have to tell me," I said. "I'm the one that's fighting him. But what the hell, it's gonna get me some headlines. I bet it gets more headlines than any other middleweight fight this year."

"Okay, so it'll get you headlines. But that's all it'll do. It won't make any difference."

Christ, this kind of talk, from my own brother.

I got up and went over to him. "Whaddaya mean, Joey? What ain't gonna make any difference?" I began to lose my temper. "Whose side are you on, anyway? You been talkin' to Nick and his boys, too? For Christsake, ain't there anybody with me?" I took him by the arms and shook him. "They been workin' on you, too, Nick and his boys? Come on, talk to me. Where'd you get that information from?"

He just shook his head. "No, no, Jake, for Christsake don't be so goddamn touchy. There's two things about this fight. First, it's very big all around town that you're gettin' a hundred thousand bucks to dump this fight and this weight bit is just to make it look right—that you was so weak you couldn't make your real fight. And the second thing is my own personal feeling that if you get yourself down to fifty-five you'll be so goddamned weak you won't be able to fight a ten-year-old boy. What'll happen is you'll weaken after five rounds and this Janiro will take you apart. You won't be able to fight for months. He's a tough kid, Jake."

I let go of him and went back to the rubbing table, and

he said, "Besides, I don't know if this great plan of yours will work at all. You know what the public's like. They're so stupid they couldn't pour piss out of a boot if you printed the directions on the heel and the toe. They don't give a damn whether you ever get a crack at the championship. If it ain't you they'll go to see somebody else fight. And they don't know what the hell is goin' on anyway."

He could have been right. I wasn't really counting on any great public outcry to get me a shot at the title or anything else, but I did figure that if there was enough stink in the newspapers sooner or later the mob would figure out that maybe the smart thing to do was to get rid of that stink no matter whose feelings were hurt in the process.

"Okay," I said to Joey. "Okay, we'll see how it turns out."

He gave me a funny look. "Is it okay to get a bet down?" he asked. This was a polite way of asking if I was going to dump the fight or not. I didn't know whether to get mad or to laugh.

"Get a bet down," I said.

Between starving myself and the steam bath I weighed in just under a hundred and fifty-five, but I was so weak I could hardly walk. I went home and my stomach was so shrunk I couldn't eat. I called my doc and he came over and started putting glucose in my veins. He was doing this when Rocky Graziano came by. Rocky, I knew, bet big on fights and he bet on me a lot.

He gave me the same look Joey had given me.

"You okay, policeman?" he asked me.

"I'm okay," I said. "Policeman" is a boxing gag.

"You gonna win?" Rocky asked me, still with that same look.

"I'm gonna win," I said. "Stop lookin' so worried."

In boxing a "policeman" is a top fighter who, for one reason or another, can't get a crack at the title. So the only fights he can get to make any money are with the real tough kids on the way up—the ones the champ himself would just as soon duck. Archie Moore was a policeman for years, and Rocky liked to use the tag with me because I was knocking off guys he would like to give a miss to.

I'm not bum-rapping Rocky, he's a friend of mine. There are always some kinds of fighters you'd just as soon not fight—the wild swingers, the butters, the ones you might just lose to, and the ones where you might get a broken hand or a real bad eye cut. Rocky called me policeman long before he won the championship because he didn't want to be eliminated before he won the title, and I took some fairly tough guys out of his way.

Speaking of Rocky, *after* he won the title he used to like to say to me, "Which do you want, a lot of a little bit, or a little bit of a lot?"

What Rocky meant was that I was fighting for purses of maybe ten or fifteen thousand dollars, out of which I was giving Joey ten percent as my manager of record, but when Rocky fought Zale there was a purse of a hundred and fifty thousand dollars, and the Rock still ended up with ten times what I ended up with.

Well, to get back to the afternoon of the Janiro fight, Rocky was still there at my house when Joey came in and said, "I got a bet down."

"Great," I said. "How much?"

With the rumor that a fix was in floating around, and a big deal being made about the weight bit, and the odds on the fight going up and down like a yo-yo, I figured maybe Joey had gone for a couple of hundred bucks.

I couldn't believe his answer, it made me want to split him in half.

"I had to put up forty-four thousand bucks to make fourteen."

"You what?" I screamed.

He went on the defensive.

"You said it was okay to get a bet down," he said.

"Jesus Christ, not forty-four thousand bucks!" I yelled at him. "J.P. Morgan don't bet money like that!"

Well, what the hell! There wasn't anything I could do about it. It's very hard to get money back from bookmakers once they've taken it. Between Joey and the weight problem and being on edge from all the training, I felt as mean as I've ever felt in my life.

By now it was midafternoon, time to eat, and Joey said he'd get me a steak.

"The hell with steak," I said, "I'm sick and tired of it. I'll fix something for myself." And I did. I fixed some real hot Italian sausages and some french-fried potatoes and poured me a pitcherful of chianti.

"You *are* outta your mind," Rocky told me. "Jesus, they don't need to fix a fight with you, just let you eat what you want."

Well, I beat Janiro.

Don't ask me how, it could have been the thought of that forty-four thousand bucks I'd be out. It took me the full ten rounds to get to him, and I just made it—and I spent a lot of the next day talking to bookmakers around Westchester and in the city and over in Jersey, telling them if they ever took another bet like that from Joey without an okay from me, I'd come down and take them apart.

The day after the fight, Joey came out to the house again. "I spent all morning on Jacob's Beach," he said. "Boy, Jake, you're the talk o' the town, they're all talkin' about what you did to Janiro, they couldn't believe it, you was so thin. . . . And, boy oh boy, you should've seen some of the long pusses on the wise guys who bet against you, they must've lost a bundle. . . ."

"And that's all?" I asked him. "Nothin' but Janiro and the dough they lost? Nothin' about who I should be fightin' next? Like maybe shouldn't I get a crack at the champ?"

Joey shook his head. "Look," he said, "can I talk to you without you blowin' your stack? You on edge again now or not? Half the time now it's even money you end up in a fight tryin' to talk to you."

"Talk away," I said, and threw myself down on the sofa. The floor was covered with newspapers and Vickie was going through them, setting the stories of the fight aside so she could cut them out later for my scrapbook.

"Well, Christ, I'm your brother," Joey said. "I'm on your side. And I don't think this plan of yours is workin'."

I guess if it had been another time I would have blown up, but how long can you keep on doing that? I could see myself spending the rest of my life blowing up because the mob wanted in. "Okay," I said. "Forget it for now. Who should I fight? Who's hot?"

Joey looked relieved, but he shrugged.

"The only guy you can fight is a light heavy. This one-fifty-five bit could kill you. When you get back in shape there's a red-hot kid in the light heavies named Billy Fox. He's got forty-three straight knockouts according to the papers and there's a lot of talk about him."

"Get him," I said.

Joey looked at me as if I was crazy. "For Christsake, you just finished shrinking yourself down to a living skeleton, now you want to go and fight a guy they say is the hottest light heavy around?"

I banged the couch. "Get him," I said. "Jesus Christ, you're supposed to be a manager, you're supposed to be able to get fights. Well, get Fox!"

"Okay. Okay, awright awready, okay!"

He charged out of the house, and I looked up to see Vickie staring at me. "You're all tied up in knots again," she said. "What's the matter?"

"Aah, Vickie, you know," I said. I laid on my stomach and put my chin on my hands. "I'm beginnin' to feel like I'm living in some world where nothin' is real. What the hell have I got to do? I'm the best middleweight there is. In a real world someone would say, okay, this guy has fought a lot of fights and knocked off the best of them, if he thinks he's so goddamned good let's put him in the ring with the champ and see just how good he is. Instead of which all I keep gettin' is this—shit!"

She looked at me and said, "I'm with Joey, I want to say something to you without you blowing your stack or slapping me around."

"Okay."

"Have you thought of going to see Pete?" I didn't say anything, so she went on, "I know how much you miss him, how much you depend on him. Maybe if you could patch things up and he and you could talk to each other again things would be better for you. . . ."

Still I didn't say anything. She didn't know how right she was. There was just about nothing I wouldn't have done to patch things up, but . . .

"I know," I said. "But look, Vickie, what do I say to him? I've thought about it, before God I have, but what do I do, call him up on the phone and say, 'Pete, I'm sorry about that little trouble we had, how about havin' dinner?' Is that what I say?"

She shook her head. "No, not that."

"Then what? What?"

She shook her head again. "I don't know."

So Joey was going after the Fox fight, and one day I was at the gym, lacing on my shoes in my room, and the door opened and there was Salvy with that goddamned toothpick of his. Just instinctively my hands went into fists.

"Jesus Christ," I said, "am I gonna have you on my ass for the rest of my life?"

He took the toothpick out and held his hands out in front of him. "Now, take it easy, Jake," he whined. "Why are you always givin' me a hard time. You know I'm just the messenger boy as far as you're concerned. I just got one thing to say to you, but it's important. It's important for you, not for me. . . ."

So I stood up straight, but my hands were still fists.

"Okay, okay," Salvy said. "Jesus, does everything have to be a torture test with you? What I came to tell you—you can have a championship fight."

I didn't believe him. Who would send Salvy with a message like that? "Aw, blow," I said. "Whaddaya mean, you rat bastard? How would you know, anyway? Who'd tell you?"

I guess he sensed I wasn't going to slap him around.

"Look, Jake, this is different," he said. "Siddown, huh? Siddown?"

What did I have to lose? I sat down. "So what's different this time?"

He kind of half-laughed and let out his breath. Then he went back to the door of the room and looked out, and he stepped back and stood where he could see if there was anyone coming. "This is what's different," he said. "You get a crack at the title . . . and a hundred grand besides . . . if you dump to Fox."

You know, as long as you live, you can't keep up with the mind of the good, ordinary, run-of-the-mill thief. If this Fox is so good—forty-three straight knockouts, remember, and he's a light heavy—what am I gonna get a hundred Gs for dumping for? And if he ain't that good, what is the mob building him up for?

Those questions have answers. In the first place, he wasn't that good—I should knock the poor son of a bitch, he ended up in the loony bin, his marbles jarred loose, that's what the mob does for you—he couldn't beat your sister Susie. He had two big weaknesses as a fighter: he didn't have a punch and he had a glass head. Every time you hit him, something jarred. But he was a colored boy out of Philadelphia and he looked good to the average slob in the three-dollar seat, plenty of action and a windmill style of fighting, a headhunter—he was always going for the other guy's chin—so that's why the mob was building him up, him and his string of knockouts.

And as for me, if I dumped and got the championship fight, naturally I had to sign up with the mob. I'd get up into the big money but they'd get half, plus all that was involved in the betting.

What was I going to do, fight the mob for the rest of my life? This was the establishment. What they said went. I'd been fighting them now for four years and where had it gotten me? Fighting guys like Janiro and another tough cookie named Cecil Hudson for purses of less than fifteen thousand bucks, that's where it had gotten me. But I wasn't going to let Salvy see what I was thinking. "Out," I said to him.

"But, Jake, look . . ."

"Out!" I repeated, and out he went.

What could have gotten me off the hook was that a few days later, when I started training for the Fox fight, I was sparring with a real tough colored boy and he hit me a couple of body licks so good that I could feel the pain all the way to my earlobes. I could hardly make it to the bell, and when the bell sounded I just climbed down out of the ring and got to Joey.

"Whatsa matter with you? You got five more rounds to go," he said.

I could hardly breathe. "I think he broke a rib or something," I said.

He looked at me and said, "Okay, we better get to the doc, get some clothes on."

It was the doc, Dr. Nicholas Salerno, who gave me what could have been an out for the Fox fight. When he got through giving me his examination, he said, "You got to call off that Fox fight, Jake. You've got a ruptured spleen. That means what you do is you get into bed and you take a complete rest. Starting as of right now."

"But look, Doc—"

"No," he interrupted, "I'm not going to give you any dope for a ruptured spleen the way I did for your fists. No, sir. This is entirely a different thing. My orders are for you to go to bed, and if you want to do something different you go find yourself another physician."

There was nothing I could say to him. I got dressed and me and Joey went home.

Vickie started giving me a little needle about the iron man finally turning up with some rust in him and I told her to shut up. I was in no mood for that kind of jazz.

"Well," Joey said, "I better call the Garden."

"You don't tell nobody nothin' till I tell you to," I told him.

"Now what? What are you thinkin' of now? Not some other nutty scheme?"

"Look," I said, "you heard me, didn't you? I'll tell you when to tell people, and I'll tell you what to tell them."

"Okay, okay." He shook his head at me. "I hope you ain't thinkin' of doin' what I think you're thinkin'." He started toward the door. "I might as well blow off. I'll be by tomorrow and see how things are. If you want me, just give me a ring."

Joey took off and Vickie asked if there was anything she could do. There wasn't. There wasn't anything anybody could do. Including me.

I don't know how Vickie put up with me. For one thing, I was on edge for the fight. For another thing I was going through the tortures of the damned about throwing this fight. Why the hell shouldn't I? An additional reason for the mob wanting to be sure that Fox won occurred to me, and that was—not to be modest about it—that back in those days, if you could beat Jake La Motta you had to be good, so this colored boy would be an even bigger drawing card. By now, though, I knew that the mob had me by the short hairs. Unless I gave somewhere, I never would get a shot at the title. And, what the hell, I'd lost fights before, and they were dead on the level. What was so bad about losing to a light heavy with a record of forty-three straight knockouts? And then I'd think, the hell with it, goddamn it, I'm not gonna throw a fight, I got too much pride. And then I'd think great, with your pride and a dime you can get into the subway. But pride don't show up in the record books, and it don't show up in the size of your purse.

I spent most of the rest of the day just trying to get comfortable, to find some way of sitting that wouldn't hurt me and pacing back and forth. The television was so lousy Vickie couldn't look at it and finally she said, "Jake, you're supposed to be resting in bed, why don't you try just lying down?"

"I can't," I said. "I tried it. I can't find a way to get restful. That's what worries me. I know I'll never be able to get any sleep tonight. I never felt this helpless before."

"What's wrong? I mean, I've seen you before fights before, but not like this. Can I do anything?"

"Naw."

"What is it, Jake?"

I shook my head. "I don't know what it is," I said. "I don't know, it's the kind of a thing that—the words won't come out."

"I know," she said. She paused for a second and said, "The only one you really ever were able to talk to was Pete. . . . Look, Jake, you know the saying about how time heals all things, why don't you call Pete and tell him how you feel. I'm sure he'll understand."

Somehow I felt a little hope inside of me. "Okay," I said. "Okay. The phone's beside you. Dial his number."

She dialed it, and when it began to ring she handed me the phone. Pete answered.

"Hello," I could hear him saying, "hello."

I couldn't say anything. I just stood there with the phone in my hand, looking at it.

"Hello," Pete said for the third time, "is anybody there?"

Then I heard the click as he hung up, and I handed the phone back to Vickie. "I wanted to," I said. "I tried. I couldn't. I couldn't."

Vickie didn't say anything. She just hung up the phone. "Okay," she said. "I guess I understand."

The old feelings came back over me, the uncertainty, the doubt, the feeling of being trapped, of not knowing what to do, not knowing which way to turn.

I said to Vickie, "I'm goin' out. I got to get out. I'm goin' for a walk."

"Jake, no," she said. "You can't, you shouldn't!"

But I knew I had to, I'd go nuts in the house, so I went out.

I don't know how long I walked. I walked and walked, and I don't know what I thought. All I know was thoughts kept boiling around inside me, I couldn't get them organized, they'd just keep coming back and back and around and around. I could hear all sorts of words inside my brain, things that I'd said or other people had told me— me telling Pete that I felt I was running out of time and me chasing Vickie in the car and beating Pete in the dress factory and then Vickie shrieking at me that I'd never be champ, never, I'd made too many enemies, and me saying I'd do it my own way and Joey telling me it wouldn't make any difference, the public was too stupid to care, and Salvy telling me I could be champ if I'd just go along, and Patsy telling me that in the ring I was a real tough guy but outside I was a slob.

After a while I could feel myself sweating, and I was saying to myself over and over again, what the hell, what the hell, what the hell, I knew I couldn't keep going on this way, I'd go crazy this way.

Then suddenly I knew what I was going to do.

There was only one thing I wanted out of life. That was to be the champ. I was going to be the champ no matter how.

All of a sudden I began to feel savage and better at the same time.

I knew where Nick hung out, at the old Debonair Club. I'd walked so far by now that it wouldn't take me any time at all to get there.

NINETEEN

Up to the time of the fight the big thing I had to do was keep my mind on the fact that I had made my decision. You know you can go back on it. Hell, I could have got out of the fight altogether if I wanted—all I had to do was bring up the spleen bit, which was no lie. But thinking of that brought all the doubts back, so I had to keep telling myself, the decision is made, stick with it.

In case you don't know, something like that gets around the world I live in like lightning. The first tipoff was the bookies. They got a sense of smell about things like that. In a sense they're part of the mob and in a sense they aren't. I mean the mob guy bets as much as the next guy or more, but also while the bookie had to rely on the mob guy for protection and the license to operate, still the bookie's not in business for the sake of making the mob guy rich. So when the big bets begin to come in the bookies begin to get the message of what's happening. The net result of this is that pretty soon, the Fox–La Motta go is out. That means the bookies won't take a bet on it.

I'll also tell you something else about throwing a fight. The guy you're throwing to has to be at least moderately good. I mean, this fight is in Madison Square Garden, and all the fight writers are there and a big crowd, so this little scuffle has got to look like a fight. But the mob guys, like lots of others, are plain stupid. Fox can't even look good. The first round, a couple of belts to his head, and I see a glassy look coming over his eyes. Jesus Christ, a couple of jabs and he's going to fall down? I began to panic a little. I was supposed to be throwing a fight to this guy, and it looked like I was going to end up holding him on his feet.

I don't know how we even got through the first round

179

without me murdering him, sometimes I thought the air
from my punches was affecting him, but we made it to the
fourth round. By then if there was anybody in the Garden
who didn't know what was happening he must have been
dead drunk. There were yells and boos from all over the
place. Dan Parker, the *Mirror* guy, said the next day that
my performance was so bad he was surprised that Actors'
Equity didn't picket the joint. Anyhow, at the time, all I
wanted to do with this fight was get it over. The only thing
I could figure to do was just let him hit me, but even that
didn't work too good because, like I said, this kid didn't
have a punch, and all around the Garden they were yelling, "Fake! Fake!" Finally the referee had to stop it—
what else could he do? I was against the ropes with my
hands down pretending I was taking a beating, and Fox
had hit me about fifteen times with everything he had,
which wasn't enough to dent a bowl of yogurt.

"Ladies and gentlemen!" the announcer blared, "the
time . . . one minute, forty-seven seconds of the fourth
round . . . the winner, by a technical knockout . . .
Billy Fox!"

I don't know how long it's been since you stood up on a
platform and listened to about twenty thousand people
booing you, but I personally didn't like it. And the knowledge that I deserved it didn't help. Well, it was done and
over.

Or so I thought, at that particular moment.

I was wrong. I suppose there's a way to fix a fight—I'm
sure a lot of them have been—but not by La Motta. I'm
too stupid. The way I fixed it was in Madison Square Garden in front of a packed house, and so phony that even the
New York State Boxing Commission caught on. *And* the
District Attorney. Now, I'm not knocking the boxing commission, then or now, New York or anywhere else, but
bright they're not. It's a nice payoff from the governor, not
in dough but in kudos, so people can say, "There goes Joe
Schmolowitz, he's a member of the state boxing commission."

Anyway, even those guys caught up to me, and there
were weeks of hearings and investigations and all the rest
of it, and what saved my life was the good doc, Dr. Sal-

erno. He testified that I had a ruptured spleen, and I said
Fox had hit me there and it hurt so much I couldn't even
lift my hands—and who the hell was there to deny it?
Nobody doubted the doc, so his testimony stood, and in a
fight, even the fighter can't tell you precisely where every
punch hit, so neither the DA nor the boxing commission
could prove anything. The boxing commission felt bad
enough about all the rumors of a fix, however, to fine me
one thousand bucks and to suspend me for seven months
on the grounds of concealing an injury.

The fine I could stand. The seven months was murder.
But the worst news of all was the fact that suddenly the
whole bit had turned around on me. The whole thing had
blown up.

After all this stink, how the hell could anyone think of
me for a championship fight? Every boxing writer and
sports columnist going was down on me. I was even
ashamed to be seen on the street. There was this time when
I was home, out in the backyard, and I heard the little kid
next door saying to some friend of his, "Next door is
where Jake La Motta lives. He's the fighter, but my father
says he's just a big phony." So what am I supposed to say
to that? Bust a twelve-year-old kid in the mush?

The seven months I stayed at home could be the worst
seven months of my life. There was nothing to do. I sort of
stayed in shape, but that was all. I wasn't training for a
fight, so I didn't have to go down to the gym and box
every day. I didn't want to talk to anyone, and most of all
I wouldn't talk to reporters. I wouldn't answer the telephone. I didn't want to see anyone. I didn't want to go
out. Everything was beautiful.

I suppose it was worse for Vickie. Who wants to live
with a wounded tiger?

Maybe there were only two things that made it at all
bearable. One was that I knew I had no one to blame but
myself. Sure, there were a lot of ifs, ands and buts, but
basically it was me, no one else. And also I was in sort of
a half-coma. I was positive I had blown the championship
bit, though I used to have dreams about some magic way
of waving away everything that had gone wrong and somehow the phone would ring and there would be an offer to

fight for the championship, all the past forgotten and forgiven. But realistically, I knew it wouldn't happen. I'd be able to get fights only because promoters would know that people would come to see me get knocked flat on my ass.

Thinking back, I'm glad it wasn't me who was living with me for those seven months, sitting around the house and brooding. Then one day I was out in back of the house throwing a stick for our dog Tami—named for Tami Mauriello—to fetch, when Joey drove up and got out of the car and came trotting across the grass, a grin this wide across his puss. "Hi," he says. "Or maybe I should start sayin', 'Hi, Champ.'"

It didn't sink in. "Okay," I said, "what gives?"

"What do you mean, what gives?" he asked. "I got a call at the gym. The man. Get it? *The* man. He asked me when you was gonna start fightin' again, when was the suspension finished. I told him in a coupla weeks. And he said, "Well, when he gets two–three good fights under his belt, provided he wins 'em he'll get his chance.'"

Again, for a couple of seconds, it didn't sink in, then suddenly it burst on me. This was it! This was my chance! This was my crack at the one thing I wanted! I jumped on Joey and began wrestling with him, and we both went down on the grass.

"This is great!" I was yelling so loud that Vickie and the boys came out to see what was happening. "This is great! This is it! This is it!"

"Awright!" Joey yelled. "I'm not your first match! Get offa me, willya!"

Vickie gave me a kiss, and the boys were running around the yard yelling because this was the first time in months they'd seen me do anything except snarl at them, and after a while things quieted down a little.

Then Joey said, "There's just one little thing."

I looked at him. "There always is. What is it?"

"Twenty thousand bucks in cash."

"All right," I said.

And that was that.

The guy I ended up signing to fight for the championship was the great French middleweight, Marcel Cerdan, and it was always my assumption that the twenty thousand bucks went to somebody in his camp, which consisted of his manager, the late Joe Longman, who was killed in the same plane crash that killed Cerdan in the Azores in 1949, plus Sammy Richman, another manager, and Lew Burston, who was the foreign representative of the IBC. Longman couldn't testify in front of the committee, of course, and Burston and Richman swore they never saw a nickel of the money. Joey took the Fifth Amendment all the way through. All I know is I took twenty thousand bucks out of the bank and gave it to Joey, and that was the last I ever saw of it.

I might mention that I only got nineteen thousand out of the purse, so I would have stood a loss on the fight of a thousand dollars if I hadn't bet ten thousand dollars on myself with me on the short end of 8–5 odds, so I picked up sixteen thousand dollars there. I only got fifteen percent of the gross to Cerdan's forty, which was less than the challenger's standard cut of twenty percent and a lot less than the thirty-five percent I normally demanded, but I wasn't going to jeopardize getting that fight by quarreling over details.

But I'm getting ahead of myself.

As soon as my suspension for the Fox fight was over, I fought a guy named Ken Stribling in Washington, which was a very good fight town then, and knocked him out in the fifth round. In the rest of 1948 I had a total of four real good wins, including two knockouts, and, in fact, up to the time I fought Cerdan, who got the title by belting out one of the toughest middleweights ever, Tony Zale, in Jersey City, the one real tough fight I had was with a rough French Canuck named Laurent Dauthuille up in Montreal. This character opened up a cut over my eye so big you could see the top of the eyeball—twelve stitches it took them to close it.

I lost the decision, and I thought maybe that would also mean I lose the crack at the title, but I got Joey on the phone and he told me that Mister Big figured, what the hell, anybody could lose a decision on a cut eye.

I had a couple of other good fights before the Cerdan

fight. One was with another tough guy named Robert Villemain in New York and the other with a brawler named Joey DeJohn in DeJohn's hometown, Syracuse.

I beat Villemain and knocked out DeJohn in eight, but now with my reputation the newspaper guys would claim there was something wrong with all the fights I had—even that the Villemain fight was fixed. How you fix a fight to win it, I don't know.

There was even gas about the Cerdan fight—not about it being fixed, of course. But before I get to that, I want to have a little fun reminiscing about the Cerdan fight. It was probably one of the happiest times of my life. In the first place, Vickie and I had just had a baby daughter. In the second, I was in maybe the best shape I ever was in my life. The DeJohn fight had got me down so that I came into training at maybe a hundred and sixty-two pounds, which meant no sweating. In fact, I had to be a little careful not to get down too far.

And it was for the championship. I was finally getting the crack I wanted. So how can you get any happier than that?

I was about to find out.

The fight was in Detroit, which was always a favorite place of mine, and Vickie came out with me, bringing the baby because it was so young. Even the reporters and me were getting along fine.

Vickie and me and the kid had a really fine hotel suite there, nothing but the best when you're fighting for the championship. The afternoon before the fight there was a knock at the door and I went over and opened it, and guess who was there.

Father Joseph. From Coxsackie. The chaplain.

I threw my arms around him.

"Dad!" I yelled. "You made it! Great, great, great! Boy, am I glad to see you."

He broke out laughing. "Jake," he said, "I thought we had it straightened out about calling me 'Dad.' But you look great. What I really came up for is to thank you for the train ticket and the ringside. You know, you shouldn't have done it. But if you hadn't, I was going to see you fight for the championship if I had to beg, borrow . . . or pray for the way to get out here."

I was feeling great. "Gee, Father," I said, "if you only knew how good it is to see you! You know, maybe you won't believe this, but there's been an awful lot of times when I've thought to myself how I wished I could talk to you. You know, I really even tried to talk to Him," I said, jerking my thumb skyward, "but it ain't the same thing somehow. Maybe I shouldn't say this to you, but the trouble is you don't get an answer. You get the feeling you're talkin' to yourself."

Father Joseph smiled at me. "Well," he said, "this isn't exactly the time or the place to have another of our chats, Jake. But I assure you that whatever words you direct to Him are not lost. Now, I want to meet your beautiful wife and the new baby, and your friend Pete. I heard so much about him from you, and yet I still haven't met him."

I didn't know what to say. What happened with me and Pete wasn't something I was going around bragging about, and Father Joseph was looking at me in a very odd way when I was saved by Vickie coming in with the baby, and there were introductions all around. "Hey, Father," I said, "someone sent up a bottle of brandy to toast when I win. How about a little glass right now just to celebrate? Come on, I've seen you take a nip of wine, right in the Coxsackie chapel, too."

He laughed and said, "All right, Jake. Theologically, it's not the same thing at all, but I guess on an occasion like this I can drink a little toast." So I poured him and Vickie a slug and about a teaspoonful for myself, and we stood there and had a toast, and the matter of Pete was forgotten. Except I wished he was around.

I guess you all know what a championship fight is like, the excitement it sets up. This was extra special on account of the fact that Cerdan was a Frenchman. Americans are so used to taking it for granted that they're the only top-ranked fighters, at least from the class of, say, welterweight on, that when a real topnotch foreign fighter comes along, there's a special atmosphere built up. A fight like that builds and builds and builds till finally it's the night of the fight, the hour of the fight and almost the minute of the fight, and now here's the time you've been waiting for ever since—well, in my case, ever since I can remember, ever since I was a kid.

It's hard to describe because it never happens to most people. When you were eight years old, did you know what you wanted to be, what you wanted to do? And except for a detour here and there, did you spend all your youth working toward that one single solitary thing, the thing that you'd literally give your life to get? And then did there ever come one final single solitary moment when you knew this was it? This was it! Now you either got it or you blew it?

Maybe I'm not explaining it too well, but if you can say yes to all that, I think you're lucky. Luckier than most people. From what I've seen of most people they just buck along doing what they have to do, driving a bus or working in an advertising agency, and what happens to them is a matter of luck. Either they get promoted or they don't.

So what would they know about how it feels to climb up the steps into the ring, the lights blinding white and hot above you, the yells of the crowd, see Cerdan over in the other corner, jogging a little and weaving his shoulders and sucking in as much air as his lungs will hold, doing everything a fighter does to get loosened up and ready in the last couple of minutes before the fight starts? Nothing.

I start warming myself up, hard and hot as I can, and I can feel the tenseness inside me that I haven't felt for a long time, and it seems to me it's forever before the bright arena lights go down, leaving only the lights above the ring on full, and the microphone comes down and the announcer takes it and begins the announcement:

"Ladies and gentlemen . . . for the middleweight championship of the world . . . at a hundred and fifty-nine-and-a-half pounds . . . the great French champion . . . from Casablanca, Morocco . . . Marcel Cerdan!"

Cerdan is a very popular champion around the world and gets a great roar of applause. Then the announcer goes on:

"And in this corner, from the Bronx, New York, the challenger, at one hundred and fifty-eight pounds, the Bronx Bull . . . Jake La Motta!"

I'm sorry to say that even though I got as noisy a reception as Cerdan, half of it was boos. You know the old saying about giving a dog a bad name. It had gotten so that no matter what I did, it was wrong. Six months before the championship I had fought Tommy Yarosz, and I stopped hitting him when he was helpless on the ropes. The crowd booed me and Jimmy Cannon, who was a columnist on the *New York Post* then, wrote that I was "probably the most detested man of his generation." Well, that covers a lot of ground. I could mention—well, never mind.

There I was in the ring with Cerdan and the fight started and it was one hell of a fight because we both had styles that were a lot alike—go, go, go, punch, punch, punch. Both of us were willing to take punches in order to hand 'em out, and both of us had a punch. The very first round was a lulu. I was charging out of my corner and fighting the only way I knew how, hard and fast. He came back at me good and hard, and somewhere around the middle of the first round he wanted to go into a clinch but I didn't, and I was half-punching, half-shoving him to get him off me when he went down. What caused it—whether it was a punch or the shoving or a slip, or a combination of all three—I still don't know. Anyway, he went down and the referee motioned me to a neutral corner, but Cerdan was back on his feet before the ref could start counting. Cerdan looked all right to me, but after the fight was over he claimed he hurt a muscle in his right shoulder when he fell.

Maybe he did, but it didn't feel that way to me from some of the lefts I took during the fight and there are still movies of that fight around, if you'd care to look at them and make up your own mind. Also, the records show that Cerdan won the second round on the cards of everybody who was scoring.

In the second round, as a matter of fact, I also got a knuckle pushed out of joint, and the trouble with a boxing glove is that it isn't easy to get out of in a hurry, or to manipulate. You can get your seconds to manipulate it, but if the knuckle doesn't go back in, you don't have the time to take the glove off and fix it up. Anyhow, this was

on my left hand, and I had enough confidence that I could
jab with it but not hook, and from the second round on I
was getting to Cerdan. That again is on all the record
cards. The third, fourth and fifth, I won on all the score-
cards, and in the sixth and seventh, Cerdan began covering up a little and I could hear my corner men, Al Silvani
and Al DeNapoli, yelling to me, "That's it, Jackson!
That's how to go, Jackson!"

By the eighth and ninth rounds, I knew I was winning. I
heard afterward that Joe Longman wanted Cerdan to quit
before both the eighth and ninth rounds and Cerdan told
him: "If you stop the fight I will kill myself."

He was both brave and proud, which is what a champ
should be, and if he was going to lose, he was going to go
down fighting.

But after the ninth round, the referee, Johnny Weber,
saw how much trouble Cerdan was in, and he went over to
his corner and took me by the wrist and led me back to
the center of the ring and raised my hand up and all hell
broke loose.

The noise was so loud you couldn't hear yourself think.
It sounded like it would lift the roof off the joint, and the
aisles were filled with people, and my brother Joey
jumped into the ring, and then the seconds, and they threw
their arms around me, yelling and screaming and pounding, and the cops piled up there all around the ropes to
keep these jokers from climbing in, and the bell kept gong-
ing away for silence till it quieted down enough so the announcer could get down the overhead microphone again:

"Ladies an gentlemen . . . Marcel Cerdan is unable to
answer the bell for the tenth round. . . . The winner and
new middleweight champion of the world . . . *Jake La
Motta!*"

TWENTY

I cannot describe exactly what I felt. I felt like, you know, God had given me the world. It was absolute pandemonium. There was booing, I could hear that, but the whole place was filled with cheering, cheering for me, the reform-school kid from the Bronx. It was for me they had all these cops out. The cops helped Father Joseph and Vickie into the ring. The referee, still holding my hand up, led me around to face all four sides of the ring and held me there so the photographers could get all the pictures they wanted. I was so happy and worked up I was crying right there in the ring where everybody could see me. I threw my arms around Vickie and squeezed her.

I can remember it even today, absolutely the happiest moment of my life. I went over and said something to Cerdan. Something about how he was a great fighter. The only fly in the whole jar of ointment was looking out at ringside and seeing Nick sitting there with Salvy and the rest of his gang, but even they couldn't ruin that moment for me.

Finally the joint started to quiet down a little and the cops got us out of the ring. I got back to the dressing room and went through all the business of talking to the reporters and getting a shower and a rubdown and finally getting back to the hotel. It was bedlam, of course, but the kind of bedlam you want to last forever.

What I had now was the gold and jewel-studded championship belt that Joe Louis presented to me, the belt I'd waited all my life for, and the crowd all slapping me on the back and telling me what a great guy I was, the kind of crowd that comes to a championship fight, from the judges and senators and other big shots with their dames in evening gowns, to the fast guys who want to look as if they're big shots, and the dames they have who're mostly not their wives and who are in evening gowns also but that are cut closer and lower. And, of course, as always there are the bums who are just hoping for something good to drop on the floor so they can pick it up.

One thing there is at a party like that, there's life. Vickie was at her best, in a dress that must have cost a damned fortune and that showed her off to her best. At one end of the room there was a bar set up where they were mostly pouring out champagne, and off on one side somebody had got a great big armchair that looked a little like a throne and they'd wound gold tinsel all over it and set it up on a little platform and there was a gold paper crown on the back of the chair.

They took me over to the chair and sat me down in it and one of the party girls who had a thirty-seven-inch bust in a thirty-six-inch dress put the paper crown on my head and gave me a real good kiss while the photographers took some more pictures, and everybody gave me a toast with the champagne and everybody was crowding around, the girls kissing me so their pictures would be taken, the guys shaking my hand or slapping me on the back, asking me all the jackass questions they ask you if they don't know anything about fighting:

"Did you have the fight planned that way, Jake?"

"When did you know you had it won?"

"Did he ever hurt you, Jake?"

"Did you ever have any doubt that you were gonna win, Jake?"

Then happened the thing that you won't believe—except that it happened.

These two guys pushed their way up through the crowd and one of them, an older guy, gray-haired and kind of pudgy and with a criss-cross of ugly livid scars on his forehead, got close enough so that finally he stuck out his hand to me and gave me a big grin and said, "Jakela, how are you?"

I looked at him—I knew him from someplace. And then I remembered.

"Jesus," I said. "Jesus Christ. Holy Mother of God—Harry Gordon. Harry Gordon! The book!"

The slob had a big grin on his face. He turned to his friend and gave him a nudge. "See," he said to the guy, "I told you Jakela would remember me. I told you Jake wouldn't forget old Harry!"

Jesus Christ, it was enough to make you gag! Here the last time I'd laid eyes on this guy I was beating his brains out with a lead pipe, and now he's proud as hell that I remember his name. Jesus Christ. And at my big celebration, which I bet he spent everything he had to get to.

I was so stunned I couldn't think of what to say. I couldn't say anything. Then, finally, I said, "Harry . . . Harry . . . you're dead. You're dead, you son of a bitch. I saw it in the paper myself! You're dead."

There was so much noise in the room I guess he didn't realize how much my voice was going up, or if he did, he figured it was just so I could be heard. It was like what I had always dreamed of, that I would get to the top of the heap, and something like this would happen. And right here and right now.

Except it couldn't, because here was Harry Gordon, but he was alive . . . and he was laughing at me. I mean really, literally, laughing.

"So if I'm dead, how am I standing here waiting for a glass of champagne for me and my friend?" he asked. "Oh, yeah, I know what you mean. . . ." And he laughed again. "The old thing back in the Bronx. Some schmuck it was wanted to hold me up and instead of saying, give me your money, which I would have been proud and honored to do with no trouble at all, he comes up behind me and hits me over the head and the result is he gets no money at all because he doesn't know where I keep it!"

All this is a riot. I've spent all this time worrying about him being dead, and he's breaking himself up with how funny it is, and I'm the schmuck.

Then he got serious. "What happened, Jake, was that it even came out in the paper wrong. They printed I was dead instead of only dying. I don't know, but they're entitled to a mistake, no? There was even telegrams sent out

to the relatives and friends, they come in to sit *shiva*, but I
fooled them all—and I bet some of them weren't too
happy."

I was listening to this in my hotel suite right after I'd
won the middleweight title, and I was beginning to think I
was losing my mind.

I put my hands to my head. "Harry," I said. "Harry,
what happened? I never saw you in the neighborhood
again, that was why we was all sure you was dead. I even
went looking for you."

He looked at me a little strange. "You went looking for
me?" he asked. "Now, why would you do that?"

"I couldn't believe you was dead," I said.

"Well," he said, "six weeks in the hospital and one step
from the morgue told me the Bronx was too tough for an
older man. . . . How long could I fight it? So I took
what money I had and moved to Florida. And I went legit
and started a little business, and I'm doing fine. The only
reason I ever think of the old Bronx is on account of you.
When I began to read about you in the newspapers, you
know, back in your first fights, I was your biggest fan.
. . . Why not—old friends from the Bronx, right, in the
same old neighborhood? People down in Florida, they
think I'm nuts. Every fight you fight, I got to see it or hear
it, and when I saw you was fighting for the title, I had to
see it in person. Me and my friend, we came up together.
. . . Jakela, I nearly yelled my self to death for you out
there." He patted me a couple of times, then he looked
around. "Hey," he said, "where's Pete! I got to say hello
to that big bum. Where is he?"

Aah, for Christ's sake. I could feel myself getting jittery.
Pete again. And this son of a bitch Harry Gordon! All the
torture I went through thinking he was dead, and that I'd
killed him, and here was the son of a bitch looking like
he'd live another sixty years.

The only thing I wanted to do was get rid of him, him
and his friend. I reached out and got a couple of the party
girls and pushed them at Harry and his pal. "Hey, girls," I
said, "these guys are friends. Treat 'em good. Be nice to
'em. The works. It's all on me!"

The girls didn't really jump at the idea, they'd naturally been figuring on making out with something in a little higher class than a sixty-year-old ex-bookmaker. But, after all, it was me talking, and after a minute or so they melted a little. "Sure, Champ," they giggled. "Anything you say."

And suddenly I figured I had to get outta there. I thought maybe I was going nuts. Here was the greatest night of my life and all I could think of was all the things wrong with my life. I got up out of the chair and charged into the next room, where there was only the baby in the crib, and I threw myself on the bed and shut my eyes. I could see myself on that street in the Bronx trailing old Harry as he was going home, hitting him with the pipe, pushing him into that vacant lot, hitting him again, taking his wallet and running off, throwing the pipe down the sewer, seeing the police car coming, tying my shoelace, finding Pete— and then I was up in the dress factory, hitting Pete as hard as I could and Vickie was screaming, and then I was beating Vickie and then raping Viola, and I found myself crying, sobbing, and I didn't know what the hell was happening, I thought I was going nuts, that I was losing my mind. I thought, Christ, is this the way it's going to be forever? Can't I ever get out of this? I ought to be happy, me and Vickie are getting along, we just had a new kid, I've just won the title, Harry Gordon is alive, so there ain't no murder rap against me, there never was one. Shouldn't I be happy, out there drinking and having a good time? Instead of which I was wracked with all this.

The door opened. Somebody took me by the shoulder and got me to sit up. It was Father Joseph, with Vickie standing behind him.

"Father," I said, "I'm sorry. I swear to God I'm sorry!"

Father Joseph nodded his head as if he knew what I was talking about. I didn't know myself. I just knew that I was crying about something. I didn't even understand what, and I was sorry for something. He got me to a chair and nodded at Vickie. "Would you . . ." he asked, "would you leave us for just a little while? I think it would be better. . . ."

Vickie went back out and I could hear the roar of the party rolling in. I even recognized my brother Joey's voice yelling, "Wow! My brother's king of the world!"

But Father Joseph was saying to me, "Sorry about what, Jake? What are you sorry about? Tell me about it, son."

And all I could do was shake my head. "I don't know," I said. "That's the trouble. I don't know. I don't know what's the matter with me, what's happening."

After a while Father Joseph said, "Jake, maybe you never learned to give anything. You take everything, and you take it with your fists."

This wasn't what I wanted from him, or anybody. "Nobody never gave me nothing!" I said. "Nobody! I had to get it all myself! And when I started to make it all of a sudden I had a million guys around me tryin' to take it off me! In this life you gotta take care of number one. That's what I done. Nobody else'd do it. . . . Aah, hell!" I stopped.

Neither of us said anything. Through the closed door I could hear the sounds of the party, the music and the singing and the laughing and the yelling.

"Father," I said finally, "what's happenin' to me? I know what the world is like, you know what it is, too, except you're a priest and I guess you really believe things that I think are a crock. But I don't understand it. Here I am just now world's champion and I feel like I'm goin' out of my head. I just want to get away somewhere, get away from everything, not feel the way I do."

He said, "Ah, Jake, it would be so much easier for you if you only understood that there are more things to life than just the desires of your body and the thoughts of your mind. God has given you a soul, but if you don't believe in God I don't know how to explain it to you. Some of the things you've told me in the past—it's not only that they're what society calls crimes, they're also what the Church calls sins. Maybe you feel you get away with them because no one knows about them, but our Lord does, Jake. And you know about them, too. I've always felt there were things you didn't want to tell me about and there's no way I can force you to. But I think the reason that you feel the way you do now, the reason you ran off from your party, is your inner knowledge of the wrongness of some of the things you've done. It's your soul, or your conscience, or whatever you want to call it, telling you that you can't go on forever taking anything you want with your fists. . . ."

His voice faded away, and I knew he couldn't figure out what else to say to me, and I didn't know of anything to say.

"Well . . ." I started, and there was a kind of hesitant tap at the door, then Vickie came back in.

"I couldn't wait any longer," she said. "Is it all right?" She looked at me. "I mean, how are you, Jake? Are you all right?" I didn't know exactly what to say to her either, so she turned to Father Joseph. "Is he all right?" she asked.

Father Joseph nodded. "Yes, yes," he said. "He's fine now, just fine. Oh, it was the fight, all the pressures and the training, you know, all the buildup. And some other little things, things that bothered him more than they should have that finally got to him. . . ."

I tried to give Vickie a smile. To Father Joseph I said, "So what should I do? What's my next move?"

Father Joseph said, "It depends on yourself. If you've gotten to the point where you realize that no one can stand all by himself, not even you, that none of us can stand all alone, then I think you ought to make your peace with God. You need Him, Jake, whether you know it or not, and I promise you He won't turn his back on you."

"I'll try," I said. "I promise I'll try."

He grinned. "Now you're talking like a pal," he said. "You'll be doing me a good turn, too, you know." He gestured upward. "If He sees a character like you walking into His pad because of me . . . well, that should get me some good marks up there, too, you know. Saving the one strayed lamb . . ."

I was feeling a little better. "Not that I'm much of a lamb," I said, "but you got a promise."

"A solid promise?"

I nodded. And I meant it. Then. "Yeah," I said. "Solid."

He broke into a great big smile. "Great, Jake!" he said. "You don't know how happy you've made me."

He clapped me on the shoulder and I jumped up and threw my arms around his shoulders.

"I better get started back," Father Joseph said. "I hope I've done all I can here."

Vickie came over and gave me a peck on the cheek and we all walked toward the door. Father Joseph had his hand on the knob, but before he opened it he said, "Jake, there is one more thing that I want to say before I go. I've thought about it a number of times, and I don't want to make any comment about it, but I want to put the thought in your mind and I want you to promise to at least consider it. Okay?"

I didn't know what he was leading up to. "Sure, Father, I promise," I said.

Then Father Joseph said, "I'd seriously like you to consider giving up fighting."

I couldn't believe my ears. It isn't often your mouth really drops open but I think mine did. "Give up fighting?" I asked. "Quit? Father . . ."

He raised his hand. "Yes, I know, Jake," he said. "I know. You're the champ. Well, I don't expect you to quit tonight. Or tomorrow or the next day. But you're well fixed. You've got plenty of money. And after tonight you don't know how to forgive yourself. You still blame yourself for—I don't know what. I think that in some way you're still trying to punish yourself. When you've fulfilled whatever your contract calls for, will you at least think about planning your retirement? You know, you could go off into boys' work or something like that, an undefeated champion. . . ."

I nodded. "Okay. I promise."

He looked at me again. And I could see he didn't really believe it, and he was right. He was right in two ways. He was right in that I wouldn't really seriously consider retiring, and he was right that retiring and going into boys' work might have been the best thing that could have happened to me.

But Father Joseph went along with my second false promise. "Great, great," he said, and he shook my hand. "Let's not get out of touch again. Okay? Let me hear from you soon and we'll talk about it a little more when you've thought about it. Right?"

He went out through the door and I turned to Vickie. "Punish myself?" I asked her. "Quit fighting? What was he gettin' at?"

And all she could do was shrug, so I grabbed her and tussled her over to the bed.

TWENTY-ONE

Whatever my promise to Father Joseph, I couldn't even begin to think about quitting fighting—if I ever would—till after the return match with Cerdan. There was a return-bout clause in the contract for the fight, and the return was set for the Polo Grounds on September 28, but I got hurt in training and the fight was rescheduled for December 2 at Madison Square Garden.

And almost everybody who knows anything about fighting knows what happened. On October 27, 1949, while flying back to the United States with his manager, Cerdan was killed when the plane crashed in the Azores. It was a national tragedy in France, where Cerdan was as famous as, say, Joe Louis or Jack Dempsey in this country.

Well, a substitute fight was arranged with Robert Villemain, the Frenchman I had just barely beaten earlier in the year, and the date was changed to December 16. I lost.

Fortunately, it was a nontitle fight. Of course, with my track record, there was a lot of talk about how I happened to lose, but I'll say again that the only fight I ever dumped was the Fox fight, and if I had wanted to dump to Villemain, I'd have done it early, because especially in the closing rounds I was taking about as bad a beating as I've ever had in the ring. What happened was that besides being my own manager, trainer and pastor, I was also my own doctor. The day before the fight I felt a cold coming on and I had read a lot in the papers about some new miracle drugs called antihistamines that were supposed to cure a cold right on the spot. They were all the rage then. So I sent Joey out to get some and dosed myself up with them real good. I forget now what they did for the cold, but I still remember what they did for my reflexes. I was way off my timing. Villemain beat me to the punch so often it was pathetic.

Still, I know now that the antihistamine pills were just an excuse. Yeah, I know it's been proven that antihistamines can dull your reflexes—in fact, they advise you, right on the box, not to drive a car while under their influence. But I know it wasn't so much the pills as it was me. I didn't realize it at the time, but overnight I was changing.

I now had the title and the knowledge that I was not the rotten, sneaky murderer I had thought I was. Gordon hadn't died. I hadn't killed a man. Something was still eating me, but at least I felt a whole lot cleaner than I had. But somehow, I also felt a lot less vicious as a fighter. I think that the moment I discovered I was not really a murderer, I also stopped being a killer in the ring. Something had gone out of me. It started in the gym. Where I'd used to rip into my sparmates trying different moves and punch deliveries, now I was making like a showoff, with fancy moves and flurries that really had nothing to do with true conditioning and timing.

The drive had gone out of me and, worst of all, I was beginning to get bored by it all. But I was still going to remain champion for as long as I could. I felt that if I had to, I could always push the right buttons and become as vicious and mean as I had to be. I had been conditioned too long and too hard to suddenly lose that. But it just wasn't the same as being a mean, cruel bastard every minute of the day just because you believed yourself to be.

I admit I looked terrible, losing to Villemain, and there was a lot of talk that I was ready to be taken. So immediately there was a lot of pressure on me to defend the title. I was willing enough, but a title means a lot, you know, more than just the money you get for winning. You get invited every place, people want you to make speeches or just make an appearance, they want to be seen with you, they say hello when you walk down the street. It makes you feel real good. Here I used to be a punk kid in the Bronx, fighting on street corners and stealing plumbing fixtures out of empty houses, ducking around corners every time I saw a cop, and now I could walk down Fifth Avenue and perfect strangers would give me a "Hi, Champ" and shake my hand, and if I saw some living doll a "Hi, babe" was even money to get a smile instead of that "Drop dead, creep" look.

But most of all I wanted to be as much in command of the situation as I could be for any fight where the title would be up. You know, if you got as much as twenty bucks, there's a positive minimum of six guys figuring out how to get it away from you, and if what you got is the middleweight title, then there's a million.

Also, when it came to defending the title, I was really having trouble with the weight. I know, the smart thing is not to let yourself balloon up between fights, but for Christsake, since when is a prizefighter supposed to be Saint Francis of Assisi? You get through two, three months of tough training and all the edge you build yourself up to for a fight, then you have the fight itself, all the busting around you get up in that ring—and I don't care how easy it looks to you sitting out there in a fifty-dollar seat. If you're in with a pro you're going to take a busting around—hell, after the fight, aren't you entitled to let down?

Anyhow, I decided that what I needed was to get a couple of over-the-weight bouts under my belt. I figured to fight at a hundred and seventy pounds, which meant light heavies. I fought Dick Wagner at Detroit, and the referee had to stop it in the ninth because Wagner was helpless. Then I knocked out Chuck Hunter at Cleveland in six, and took a decision from Joe Taylor at Syracuse.

Finally the powers that be in boxing decided that my first defense of the title would be against Tiberio Mitri, an Italian who was the European middleweight champion and—according to the publicity—a pretty good fighter, a lot like Cerdan.

Like Cerdan he wasn't. He would get off balance, and one thing a top fighter rarely is, is off balance. The fight was at Madison Square Garden and it went the full fifteen rounds, largely because it's hard to fight that kind of fighter, and I was piling up points so fast, why should I risk busting a hand on his head trying to nail him?

With the Mitri fight over, now all the wiseacres were

setting up the dream match—me and Sugar Ray Robinson, who, according to the record books, had won four of our five fights. I say he has won two of them, or at the very most two-and-a-half, and I have the movies of the fights to prove it, along with the day-after stories of a lot of the sports reporters.

My own feeling was that Robinson could wait. Mostly it was a question of money. There was a lot more dough to be made, was my feeling, for all concerned, if I fought Rocky Graziano and then Robinson. I had wanted a Graziano fight before Mitri. All the fans knew Graziano, Robinson and me. And, as impartial as I can be, I would say that any one of us at the top of our form can probably take either of the others. Robinson did just as much horsing around as me, and I was no bargain, but he had one of those physiques that you could abuse again and again and then train back into shape and he was as tough as ever.

The minute I even mentioned a Graziano fight, all I got was static—first of all from Rocky, of all people. I couldn't figure him out. I told him he had his chance to win back the title he lost to Tony Zale, and what did he say? "I don't want no title. I had too much trouble when I had it."

Then the newspapers were on my back again. They wrote columns that Rocky was only ranked number nine on the list of contenders in *Ring* which was another thing I couldn't understand because he'd won every fight he fought since he lost to Zale except for a draw with that kid Tony Janiro.

There was also trouble with the political side of boxing. The Managers Guild was trying to negotiate a new television pay contract with the International Boxing Club, and for its own purposes the guild did not want the IBC to have a real big moneymaking deal till after the contract had been signed.

But I was convinced that a La Motta–Graziano fight would be a natural, and also would make a fortune. And just personally, it was the kind of fight I'd like after all those kid-stuff slugging matches we'd had back on the East Side. This would be a real fight. Finally, to set it up, I offered Rocky thirty percent of everything instead of the forty-twenty split that would be natural between a champion and a contender, and finally the contract was signed.

There was a curse on that fight. I was always a great believer in the play-it-cool bit—if it is to happen, it will happen. And maybe the fact that I wanted it so much and did so much to swing it put the curse on it. At any rate, I'd only been training for a few days at the Concord, a resort up in the Catskills, when I got the word that the fight was off. Rocky had broken his hand.

After Mitri, I signed to meet Laurent Dauthuille, the Frenchman who had beaten me two years before at Montreal. The fight was for September 13, 1950, at the Detroit Olympia, and it was while training for this fight that I began to get the idea that I couldn't go on with this life forever. Somehow before I had always been able to get myself down to the hundred-and-sixty-pound limit, but this time, to use the phrase again, it was sheer torture.

In fact, I remember one afternoon I was lying on the rubbing table in my private room in the gym, twelve pounds overweight and staring at the ceiling, and Joey was sitting in a chair and trying to get me to put off the fight. "We'll say you pulled a muscle in your shoulder," he said. "Put it off for a month. Who the hell can prove you don't have a pulled muscle?"

"Forget it."

"Aah, Jake," he argued, "you had to lose over twenty-five pounds. That's too goddamned much for a guy your size who's supposed to be a fighter."

I was in no mood for that kind of shit from Joey or anybody else. I was one hell of a lot more worried about the weight than he was. I'd gotten to the point where I felt it was either do what Father Joseph had suggested—quit—or move on up to the light heavies. I couldn't keep doing this.

"What's this 'supposed to be' crap?" I asked him. "Who's the champ here, you or me?"

"Aw, Jake, I'm your brother," he said, "and I'm supposed to be your manager. You should see yourself in the ring. You look terrible. You can't punch your way out of a wet paper bag. If you wasn't my brother, I'd bet against you."

"Forget it, I said!" I snapped at him. "Make any goddamned bet you want! If you get caught bettin' against me, I'll break your back!"

"The trouble is," he said, "you get through a fight, you chase around too much, you eat too much of that pasta, you drink too much booze. . . ."

"I said forget it!" I yelled. "How many times do I have to say it? You're a great one to be talkin' about living the Boy Scout life!"

"Awright!" he said, throwing his hands up. "I ain't fightin' for the title! Go ahead and blow it! See if I care! Aw, what the hell's the use, you're gonna blow it to somebody sometime, anyway." He looked at me and started to get mad. "What the hell has got into you, anyway? You're not the same fighter you used to be. . . . You got all the dough, why don't you retire?"

I sat up quick. "Whaddaya mean I'm not the same fighter I was? What the hell is all this?"

"I mean you act like something has happened," Joey said. "You got no zing. Why are you lettin' these sparring partners bomb you around the way they do? Look, Jake, I don't know what's wrong, but I got a feeling there's somethin', and this kid Dauthuille is a real good fighter. He's got class. He beat you the last time. . . ."

"It was the cuts," I said. "You know that. You was there."

"I know. But he's still a real good fighter. Why go up against him if you're not ready? And I say you're not ready."

"And I say I am! For Christsake, who's fightin' this fight, you or me? I'm ready I tellya! Quit worryin'."

But Joey had a lot of right on his side. I came into the ring at the Detroit Olympia really feeling weak, and instead of charging out with the usual swarming windmill style that was the only way I could really fight effectively, I tried to turn boxer, jabbing away at his face, looking for a break that would let me bring over a haymaker. But it wasn't my style of fighting, and I didn't know how to set him up.

Dauthuille kept coming in, throwing punches all the time, and while he wasn't really a knockout fighter, he was hitting me again and again and again.

Later Pete told me—yeah, Pete, you'll see—that he heard this fight over a car radio and that never in his life did he hear a radio announcer so close to going out of his skull. Because when Pete began to listen, the announcer was saying something like:

"Ladies and gentlemen, I've sat in front of these microphones for twenty years describing fights for you and I'm sure we both remember moments in the past that were strange . . . unusual . . . but this, ladies and gentlemen, is the strangest championship fight I've ever seen. . . . Ever since the opening bell, the champion, Jake La Motta, has simply been wading into the punishing punches that the young and perfectly conditioned challenger, Laurent Dauthuille, has been throwing at him . . . I've never seen anything like it . . . I don't know how to explain it . . . No man actually seeks punishment . . . but it seems to me this is the way it is . . . because it looks from here that there are a lot of punches the once mighty bull from the Bronx could have avoided. . . . And there's the bell for the end of the fourteenth round!"

I could have told him what was happening. I wasn't ducking because I didn't have the strength to spare, and along about the twelfth round it had dawned on me that I could lose this fight. I pretended to be in trouble, and when Dauthuille charged in to finish me off, I opened up a barrage of punches to his head and body, but it wasn't enough. Like I said, it's very hard to finish off a trained fighter with one punch or even with a set of punches. During the fourteenth round I was trying to keep my left in his face but he got past it a couple of times, once with a right that almost knocked me down and once with a good solid left.

Even over the radio, Pete told me later, it sounded like a real beating, and the guys who were listening to the fight were telling each other, "Well, that's the end of La Motta, he's blown this one, he's really had it."

In the corner between the rounds Joey was almost crying, he was so desperate.

"Whatsa matter with you?" he yelled at me. "You look in a daze! You know you're blowin' this fight? You know you're losin'?" He slapped me across the face. "It oughta make Nick and his pals happy!" he yelled. "They seen you in trainin' and they got a big-bite bet against ya. You got a piece o' that action?"

I didn't even get mad at him. I was thinking that I only had just one chance to win this fight. I had to have a knockout. And I had one little thing in my favor. Dauthuille was pretty near the end of his rope. He'd been doing all the fighting for fourteen full rounds, while I had some energy left.

I came out for the fifteenth knowing what I had to do, charging at him, throwing lefts and rights. He knew he had the fight won and he tried to cover up against me, and I tried to keep boring in, getting more and more desperate as the round went on, and suddenly in the midst of one mixup I threw a left hook, one of the few I'd thrown all night, and by pure luck he was wide open at the moment and the hook caught him flush on the point of the jaw. I saw him sag and start to back away and I followed him, throwing punches as hard and as fast as I could, and I saw he was gone. I almost knocked him through the ropes, but he was a very game guy, and as the referee was counting he tried to pull himself up by the ropes, and when the referee got to ten, he was actually up on one knee. And there were thirteen seconds left in the fight!

Ed Sullivan later wrote, "Of such extraordinary doings are champions made."

Pete told me the radio announcer was so excited he thought he was going to come right out through the loudspeaker:

"Ladies and gentleman, what a finish! What a finish! You should be here with me, this place is going mad, it's pandemonium! With only twenty-three seconds to go— that's right, twenty-three seconds to go—Dauthuille went down under a savage, slashing attack by Jake La Motta, the Bronx Bull. We've seen fights turn around right at the end, we've seen fights pulled out at the last minute, but ladies and gentlemen, we've never seen anything to match this. . . ."

And so on.

Well, it made me feel pretty good, winning a fight that tough and knowing that Nick had gone for a bundle, and also knowing nobody could fault me for that fight, nobody. It gives you a good feeling to be a champ and know that people think you're worth it, that you're the toughest guy there is.

That great feeling didn't last forever, of course, because the human animal of the fight fan, once you've done the impossible and he's given you a great big hand, asks, "Whaddaya gonna do for an encore?"

In this case the encore had to be Robinson. He was welterweight champ at the time, so the fight had a natural title: "The Battle of Champions."

The fight was also a natural for Robinson. I think now that if I was smart, if I had it all to do over, what I should have done was to go for the light-heavy title and leave the middleweight title undefeated. Then they could have had an elimination and someobdy else could have fought Robinson. Because that was what Robinson was doing. He had grown into a natural middleweight, and when he fought me his welterweight title would be vacated.

To this day I don't know whether it was Robinson or weight that actually licked me. When you're young you can reduce yourself to a shadow and still keep at least some of your strength; as you get older you can't. When I fought Robinson the first time, back in 1942, I had made the hundred-and-sixty-pound limit and three weeks later I was up to one eighty-two. Here I was now, nine years later, faced with the same old problem, except multiplied by nine. I had to get down to a hundred and sixty, and when I started training I weighed one eighty-seven. Christ, I was even above the weight limit for a light heavy, and I was going to fight middleweight!

I swear to God, never had I gone through the hell I did then. For the last two weeks of training I was eating almost nothing. Five days before the fight I went to Chicago—where the fight was to be held—so I could do some training in public and help build up the gate. Almost as soon as I got there, I collapsed. I was so weak I could barely walk, much less train. They put me to bed and put out the story that I was in such perfect shape that to do any more training would only dull the edge.

The way a fighter normally takes off weight is by training—roadwork, sparring, gymnastics, bag-punching and the like. But to do that, you have to eat a high-protein diet. My problem was that every morsel I ate put weight on.

The night before the fight, with the weigh-in scheduled for the next morning, I weighed one sixty-four and a half—almost five pounds over the limit. If you're nothing but blubber, you can take off five pounds overnight. But if you're a fighter, mostly bone and muscle, *Jesus!* My handlers decided I had to go to the steam baths.

Over the years I had naturally developed a phobia about steam baths, but what the hell else could I do? Forfeit?

I took the steam as long as I could and staggered out. My trainers pushed me back in. Again I took it as long as I could, and again I staggered out. And again they pushed me back in. It went on for hours. I was dying. No fight was ever so bad. I wanted water so bad I told them I'd quit, I wouldn't answer the bell, and all they'd let me do was lick an ice cube.

The only smart thing I had done during the whole operation of setting up the fight was, I had figured when we signed that I'd have trouble making the weight—though not anything like this—so I had a clause put in that the weigh-in would be at ten in the morning instead of the usual time of noon. That would give me an extra two hours to build up my strength before the fight.

When it was time to go to the weigh-in, our scales showed me at one sixty, and I went over pretty worried. There's often as much as an ounce difference between scales, and I was worried about whether ours and those of the Illinois Boxing Commission would be the same. I even took off my socks and my boxing trunks for the weigh-in, and I hit one sixty on the nose. I could hear my cornermen let out their breaths. One of them had a bowl of beef broth he'd been warming, but my stomach was so nervous that I could only swallow a couple of mouthfuls. We went back to the hotel and I began to drink orange juice. Late in the afternoon Joey ordered up a rare steak and I could only eat half-a-dozen mouthfuls.

I must have known that defeat was coming, even though I wouldn't admit it to myself, because I even began to think about the possibility of hedging the bet of ten thousand dollars that I'd made on myself. Then I thought, Christ, that's all I'd need, to have something like that on my record. And that is not the sort of thing that can be kept quiet.

Then I did something I'd never done before. I told Joey to get up a bottle of brandy. The only good thing about doing the amount of drinking I used to do between fights, you get to know exactly what any given amount of alcohol will do to you, and how long its effect will last. I wasn't going into the ring with Robinson even a little tight, I'll tell you that. I didn't want to commit suicide. But I figured the brandy woud give me a little strength.

I was kidding myself, of course. The brandy wasn't to give me strength. It was to give me false courage. And what false courage is really is true fear. What the brandy was really doing was helping me avoid the fact that I was in absolutely no shape to go up against an opponent as good as Robinson.

The fight was held on February 14, which, besides being Valentine's Day proper, is also the anniversary of the St. Valentine's Day massacre of 1929. Well, Robinson didn't have a submachine gun and there was only one victim but it was still a massacre. Actually, the fight didn't start off too bad for me, even though my timing was off—the records show that for the first ten rounds I was ahead. If the fight had ended at the end of the tenth round, I would have won, but the fight still had five rounds to go and I could feel I was beginning to run out of gas. I kept thinking, all right, you son of a bitch, you're not going to put me down, nobody's ever decked Jake La Motta, and it's not going to be you. If that's as hard as you can hit you must have been fighting pushovers all this time, let's see how hard you can hit, you son of a bitch.

Well, Robinson couldn't hit me hard enough to put me down, but the only thing that was holding me up in the thirteenth round, when referee Frank Sikora got between us to stop the fight, was the fact that I had one arm wrapped around the ropes. It looked just like the Billy Fox fight, except that this one was for real.

Al Buck wrote in the *New York Post* that "the bleeding, bruised and battered Bronx Bull was still on his feet, but nobody would want to see that slaughter again."

I didn't know it then, but that was really the end of my career.

TWENTY-TWO

I was to have ten more fights. One fight too late, I decided that I *had* to move up to the light-heavy class—not only couldn't I go through the torture I had gone through for Robinson, but I wouldn't have the strength to beat a fourteen-year-old boy. In 1951 I was almost thirty years old, which is getting on for a fighter, and if there was a chronometer to measure my real age I was probably somewhere between thrity-five and forty because of those alternating periods of fasting and feasting I went through. I guess any doctor would tell you that the human body isn't built to take that kind of treatment.

Anyhow, my first fight as a light heavy matched me up with an up-and-coming tough young kid named Irish Bob Murphy, and here again I made another of my patented mistakes. There was four months between the Robinson and Murphy fights and I had let my weight balloon up to around one ninety-five, figuring that getting down to one seventy-five would be a cinch. What I had on my side was logic and stupidity. I had almost as much trouble getting down to one seventy-five as I had to get down to one sixty for Robinson, and I went into the fight feeling almost as weak as I had before. The fight was at Yankee Stadium, and Murphy stopped me in seven rounds. Practically everybody thought I was over the hill, and the headlines in Dan Parker's column read "Wanna Know Whatta? La Motta No Gotta."

It killed me to admit it, but Dan Parker was right. I had lost that self-image of indestructibility. I guess I was beginning to turn into an ordinary human, and to see myself this way frightened me.

I took a long layoff, seven months, in which time I did a

lot of thinking, positive thinking I guess you'd call it. And it came easy because during the layoff, I laid more chicks, put together, than I had ever laid in my life. This seemed to do wonders for my mixed-up thinking about my manhood. I came back with a new belief in myself, and I devoured everything good said about me, trying to make that belief even stronger.

I fought Norman Hayes in Boston. He got the decision, but it was straight highway robbery, the way it often was up in Boston. When I fought him in Detroit a couple of months later, I won easy. I fought Eugene Hairston in Detroit and it was called a draw, so I fought him again, and again I won easily. Then I got another crack at Murphy, and this time I came out with the win.

I now had the feeling that I was, as the sportswriters said, on the comeback trail. Joey Maxim was the light-heavy champ then, and since I had knocked off a couple of the leading contenders, I figured I had to aim for him. I may have been fooling myself about how good I was doing, but I wasn't fooling myself about how much more time I had left to win fights.

And who was in the way of me getting to Maxim? It was Robinson again. He was getting greedy—hell, he was always greedy. Not that I'm knocking him, mind you. I was greedy myself, I'd take anything I could get or steal. But Robinson was overreaching himself in kind of the opposite way from me. In other words, like I'd stretched myself to the breaking point trying to get down to middleweight, he was trying to build himself up to light heavy. It didn't work, even though Sugar Ray got the fight. He fought Maxim in Yankee Stadium on June 25, 1952, which, as it turned out, was a very hot day—night actually—and he was counted out in the fourteenth. It was a very odd count-out. Like, Maxim wasn't the greatest light heavy who ever laced on gloves. The popular version was that Robinson collapsed of heat stroke and exhaustion, which I guess I'll buy, even though there was a rumor that Robinson quit because he didn't want to have the light-heavy title to defend. That rumor was wrong on two counts. I wouldn't say Robinson and me are bosom buddies, but I don't think he ever quit in a fight in his life.

He's got too much pride, and like I say, he'd take anything not nailed down he could get.

Well, all that's slightly beside the point. The point is that because Robinson was fighting Maxim, I was put off onto a siding. Another point is, as I say, I didn't realize that basically I was through as a fighter.

Look back at your own life and you'll see it's a succession of highs and lows. You had things you wanted so much you felt you'd be willing to die for them—at least I hope you did—and either you got them, which would be a high, or you didn't get them, which was a kind of a low. Or you got them and then lost them, which would be a bottom low.

Well, I think my highs and lows were higher and lower than most people's. There can't be a high any higher than being a world's champion and—though I didn't recognize it then—I was on my way to my lowest low.

I was only going to have four more fights, all with guys you never even heard of, and I was going to lose two of them. The first one was with a guy named Danny Nardico, and what cost me that fight was my own stupidity. Nardico was probably a nice guy, kind to his mother, but when it came to fighting he was strictly from Peoria. Not a bum, mind you, but not a guy where you lie awake nights figuring strategy. The fight was for New Year's Eve in Coral Gables, Florida, where Jim Norris had a winter home. A couple of days before the fight I managed to get the flu, and I called up Norris—you remember I had to sign with him to get the Cerdan fight—and he said, "What the hell! You can beat this guy with one hand. It's the first fight ever that's going to be put on the coaxial cable from Florida." There's enough of the ham in me, so I said, "Okay, the hell with the fever I got! I'll fight him."

And old stupid got his block knocked off in the eighth round. I laid off for a year, then I fought and beat Johnny Pretzie at West Palm Beach and Al McCoy at Charlotte. Finally, on April 14, 1954, I met Billy Kilgore at Miami Beach. I lost in ten rounds.

I'd been fighting professionally since 1941, and now I was through.

You know, it's easy enough to say, but what does it

mean? Here I was an uneducated kid and the better part of a million bucks had gone through my hands and I was only a little better than thirty years old, and now what? What was I going to do? Where was I going?

The first thing to do is forget, and to do that, I was going to make a short trip through hell.

Oh, it looked great at first, trying to see how many dames I could lay in any given twenty-four hours, and how much booze I could drink. But maybe it was the old thing about retribution. Sooner or later you pay for what you get.

Right before the Nardico fight, Vickie said that what I needed was a vacation, and I couldn't have agreed more. We already were in Florida and what we'd seen we liked. The sunshine was terrific and a lot of people we knew lived there. We went to Miami Beach, and we decided to live there. Beautiful climate, action—what more could you want? We found a beautiful house out near the LaGorse Golf Club, and I bought it. Thirty-five thousand bucks, cash, which is what I later sold the Westchester house for. For a while I had the two houses, and the fight club I had in the Bronx, which had been the old Blenheim Theater that I used to get thrown out of as a kid for roughing it up, and I had a fair wad of straight cash, better than a hundred thousand bucks, and other property. From one piece of property alone, if I never earned another nickel all my life, I would have an income of ten thousand a year as long as I lived. That was from a parking lot right near Yankee Stadium, for which I had paid $62,500.

Okay, so I was getting this minimum of ten thousand a year. The problem was that I was spending about twenty-five, just as if I was still at the top of the boxing heap.

Vickie and I became well-known characters all over Miami Beach. We each had Cadillacs, which we called His and Hers. I had a real bright convertible that I'd drive around with a big cigar in my kisser, wearing shorts and those real loud Miami Beach sportshirts. I bet there wasn't a nightclub or cocktail-lounge bartender in town who didn't know Jake La Motta.

Okay, that's the happy side. But no matter how much

you try, you can't stay in the sack *all* the time. While I was a fighter I had some control over myself, but after I lost to Kilgore I seemed to lose everything. I was like a caged tiger around the house. I don't know how much Vickie knew about how much I played around, but I guess she had to guess.

Finally she said to me one day, "Look, Jake, we can't go on like this the rest of our lives. We're too young. You got to find something to do. Something that gets you out of the house, where you got something to do. And I don't want to do nothing but nag, but you'll also drink yourself to death the way you're going."

How could I argue with her? She was absolutely right. So, I bought a cabaret.

Having a guy like me running a saloon is like having a tiger guarding your sheep. I didn't expect to make a killing with the saloon, but I wanted to make enough to cover that gap in my income. About the only smart thing I did with the saloon was to pick a location where nobody except somebody as stupid as me could blow the deal. The spot I picked was Collins Avenue, which is the main drag in Miami Beach, right at the corner of Twenty-third Street and directly across the street from one of the Beach's most famous hotels, the Roney-Plaza. The nightclub front was on Collins Avenue, with a big neon sign saying JAKE LA MOTTA'S, and I also had a package store, part of the same building, with the entrance on Twenty-third Street. I spent a fortune on that joint—a hundred thousand bucks at the very least. I put another mortgage on the house and a mortgage on the parking lot. I had the inside of the club fixed up with no expense spared. There was a great big lobby with heavy leather chairs and couches, and pictures around the walls, mostly of me with sports guys and politicians and movie and theater people—once you get famous it's amazing the number of people who want their picture taken with you. Then inside that was a big bar and cocktail lounge, and beyond that was the nightclub part, also very plush.

One of my troubles, I found out later from talking to a real nightclub operator, was that I was booking acts at a thousand bucks a week when in a place that size I never should have paid more than three hundred.

That was only one of the troubles, though. The other was that I really began to play around too goddamned much. Oh, for the first six months or so I was pretty serious about the place. Actually it was quite a spot. Everyone knew about it, and everyone used to drop in—Walter Winchell, Joe DiMaggio, Joe E. Lewis, Milton Berle, Kay Starr, Rocky Graziano, Phil Silvers, Johnny Ray, Perry Como, Buddy Hackett, Frankie Laine, Martha Raye. And lots more.

But now I didn't even have the discipline of boxing to keep me even moderately straight, and running a saloon isn't a twenty-four-hour job. Or maybe it is and I was too dumb to know it. Anyway, I was meeting an endless succession of broads—society dames, movie starlets—and they almost all wanted to meet the champ. And I was drinking more and more, and I began to go out with these dames. You know the old story about the guy that was a real success with broads and finally a friend asked him his formula and the first guy says: "Easy. Every good-looking dame I see, I ask her if she wants to get laid." And his friend says, "Boy, you must get your face slapped a lot." And the first says, "Sure, but look at the number of times I get laid."

Well, it's true.

So I was doing great, I thought, till this night Vickie came in. I had about four or five of these broads around, and a couple of guys, and I'd had about a pint and a half of liquor. Vickie said, "Jake, I want to talk to you in private. Outside. Can you come outside for a minute?"

I still remember that night as clear as if it was yesterday.

Like I said, I was a little drunk, and Vickie had almost won the Mrs. America contest awhile before, and I said, "Aah, you sound mad again. . . . Ah, Vickie, you always sound mad nowadays. . . . How about sitting down a minute and meeting these good people?" I swung my arms out. "I want you folks to meet my wife, the best wife in the whole country . . . the whole world. . . . You folks know she almost won the Mrs. America contest? Well, maybe that's what she's mad about. I wouldn't let her win, even though she's the most gorgeous broad you ever seen, ain't see? But if she won, she woulda hadda travel, and I ain't about to let anything as gorgeous as her go travelin' around the country. Do any of you folks blame me?"

But Vickie wasn't having any of this drunken crap and she waited till I was all through, then she said, "Are you coming outside or not? I have something to say to you, something important, and I want to say it in private." And she turned away and walked off.

Well, even through all the booze I felt sick. I had a feeling of doom, like that sense that was always at the back of my head, or way down deep, that the time would come when I'd turn a corner and there would be Fate. And I knew what he would say: "Okay, Jake, this is it. Now's the time for paying up. Now the fun and games are over and done."

Anyway, I got up and followed her out. "Vickie," I said, "Vickie, baby, you look so mad. Whatsa matter, baby. What's up?"

She looked at me and suddenly she sighed real deep. "Ah," she said, "what's the use?"

I knew what the use was. "Honey," I said, "you're not mad are you? What are you mad about? You know what a saloon is like. . . . You know, it's a place where people go to have a little fun. . . . You can't have fun without having some dames around. . . ."

She didn't say anything, and my voice sort of trailed off. I didn't know what else to say. Finally she said, "I'm sorry, Jake. I'm leaving you. I mean it. This is the end. Everybody in Miami is talking about all the whoring around you're doing. . . ."

"Aw, come on, Vickie. Dames like to brag too, you know. If I'd laid all the dames . . ."

"No, Jake," she said. "I've talked to some of them. I'm going to get a divorce. They've made sworn statements to my lawyer." She looked away from me. "I don't even care anymore," she said. "I haven't cared for a long time. Things have been dead and buried between us for months.

Now I'm not thinking about anything except the children. You're never home, and when you are, you're either drunk or irritable. . . . You use language in front of them that you wouldn't use in a fight camp."

I started to break in but she turned and looked at me and shook her head. "And you can't come home again, either, Jake," she said. "I have a court order. You can't come home because if you do I'll go to court and have you adjudged an unfit father."

And suddenly she turned and ran over to where her car was and shot out of the parking lot.

That marked the real end of my marriage to Vickie, even though we did see each other again and God knows she tried to help me. As far as I'm concerned, she's a great dame. She had her faults, but who the hell doesn't? After she booted me out I began to spend almost all my time either horsing around or at my club. I even slept on a cot in my office.

I didn't realize that Fate was now setting me up for a real belt in the mouth.

TWENTY-THREE

There is one thing you've got to understand about Miami Beach. You don't go there for culture. You go there for a good time, which means broads and booze to start with. Then some betting of one kind or another, and from there on, you're on your own. Now, the city fathers of the Beach, elected or not, understand this perfectly. The problem they face is that if things get too rough, the local yokels who pay the taxes start raising hell and something has to be done. A little scandal and sin they don't mind because that's what brings tourists down. Take my word for it, whether you arrive in Miami Beach when everything is running wide open or whether a reform wave is rolling high, you can get anything from babes to dope, if you know where to look. You don't have to look too hard, either.

What the cops do to walk this very narrow chalkline— or, anyway, what they used to do—to strike a balance between keeping the town looking clean but still keeping the tourists coming in, was to make a couple of sensational raids either at the beginning of the season or at the end, depending on conditions. It was all a matter of how things were going. There might be, say, two hundred joints operating, some of them operating way outside the law, some with maybe just minor technical violations of the law. The idea is to pick the ones that will yield the most publicity for the raids. The cops knock off one or two, there's a big splash, then people settle back to enjoy life again. Everybody understands this. The guys who are in business expect an occasional pinch, they set up front guys to take the rap so that business can go on as usual. It's a nice arrangement. The Beach gets the appearance of decency without the hardship of it.

Since all my business depended on my name, I couldn't have a front man. I was the front. Now, there is a law in Miami Beach that if there is a prostitute in a nightclub the owner of the club is responsible and he can be charged with abetting prostitution. If that law was really enforced every other saloon keeper in Miami Beach would be spending his life in jail. My place wasn't too big; the night-club part of it seated only eighty-two people. There was good entertainment, pleasant surroundings, quiet atmosphere and not too stiff a check, considering. I don't deny that guys could meet dolls there, just as they could anywhere else in the Beach. Single guys and single gals often came into my joint, just as they did everywhere else, and if they wanted to talk to each other, what was I supposed to do, tell them to get out? And how in the name of Christ can you tell what any given doll is up to, or whether she's a pro—go up and ask her? And after she finishes slapping your face and says no, she's a perfect lady, how do you prove it? It was a crazy law. Some of the girls who came into my joint were pros, I have no doubt of it. The girls stopped in just about every bar on Collins Avenue on their rounds. But, what the hell was I supposed to do? Plenty of dolls come down from New York on their vacations, dolls who are perfectly respectable on Madison Avenue, but they get down to the Beach and they don't mind playing around a little. Guys would pick up gals in my place, and how was I to know whether it was a Miami Beach pro or a secretary from some Manhattan advertising agency? And what they did was their business, I always figured. The only person whose sex life I'm interested in is my own. In my place, I've introduced guys to gals if I knew them both. But I sure as hell wasn't running any whorehouse.

The first thing I knew that anybody had anything against me was one morning when I woke up because some guy was shaking me.

The place was a mess. Like I said, I was living in my office above the nightclub, and when you live alone—or when *I* live alone—I'm a slob. I clean up only when things are so bad I'm even ashamed of it myself and I only send out my laundry when I don't have anything clean left to put on. So there's dirty socks and shirts and shorts thrown over on the side, there's empty whiskey bottles in the wastebasket, there's empty beer cans in the corner. Besides that, I had had a bad night—I always had bad nights in those days. I couldn't get to sleep unless I was bombed, so that when I woke up in the morning the first thing I had to do was have a shot so I could operate, which meant I was always going around at least half-stoned. And these guys had come in about ten o'clock, which was at least an hour before I got up, and my mouth felt like an outhouse.

"C'mon, Jake, get up!" one of the guys said, and even before he showed me the piece of tin I knew he was a cop. All alike, the whole world over. They got this look, and they all say the same thing.

"Whaddaya mean get up," I said. "How'd you get in here, anyways?"

"The porter let us in. We're from the sheriff's office. They want you downtown."

"At this hour? For Christsake, what for? What've I done now?"

"Look, Jake," the guy said. "I don't know. I don't run the joint. All I know is, they say bring in La Motta. You wanna make a federal case out of it?"

"Shit," I said. I figured I was a taxpayer with a business. What would I gain by fighting? "Lemme get dressed," I said and I went along with them.

You wouldn't believe it. At least, I couldn't believe it. There was this fourteen-year-old broad. That's right, fourteen. They get ripe early down south. She testified at the trial that she had been in my place twice. Let me repeat, *twice*—which hardly rated her as a regular at Jake La Motta's. She said the first time she was with her madam and I had come over and asked her why she wasn't drinking and that she said she was over twenty-one but she didn't have anything to prove it. She looked over twenty-one now. The size of her chest and the amount of makeup she had on, she could have been *thirty*-one. She said I kissed her and told the bartender, any doll who can kiss like that has to be over twenty-one. So she had a drink and, she testified, later I introduced her to a man and the man took her off to a room and swung around with her and paid her twenty bucks. Two or three weeks later, she said, she came back in and met another guy, and another twenty bucks in her kick.

The way this doll got into the act in the first place was that the police had decided on one of their big raids and they had picked her up and she had listed every bar on Collins Avenue as a place where she had picked guys up, but they hadn't paid any attention till she said Jake La Motta's. That was their meat! This would get headlines all over the country. It did.

LA MOTTA HELD ON COMPULSORY PROSTITUTION CHARGE

FORMER CHAMP HELD ON PROCURING INDICTMENT

SEIZE LA MOTTA AS PROMOTER OF MIAMI BEACH PROSTITUTE, 14

Well, after they booked me and all the rest, I got a lawyer and got out on bail, and Joey was waiting for me. I was still in a kind of a fog. Joey was waiting down at the foot of the front steps of the courthouse and all I could think of to say to him was, "What are you doin' here?"

He looked at me. "Where else would I be?" he asked. "Jake, what is this? It's all over the papers, the radio, everywhere—everybody up in New York is talkin' about it and, brother, it sounds horrible."

It was horrible. They had thrown every charge they could at me: maintaining a place for the purpose of lewdness or prostitution; encouraging a minor female to prostitution; contributing to the delinquency of a minor; permitting a minor to be served alcoholic beverages.

All I could say was, "Honest to God, Joey, I have no idea what the hell it's all about."

Joey shook his head. "Jake, they're charging you with being a pimp for a fourteen-year-old dame."

"I know it, I know it, for Christsake!" I yelled at him.

"What I'm saying is I don't remember this dame, I can't remember ever having seen her. For Christsake, even if people can't understand that I'm not foolin' around with any fourteen-year-old kid under any circumstances, what the hell would I be doin' with any fancy stuff that would endanger a place that I got a hundred thousand bucks tied up in? Do they think I'm crazy?"

Joey shook his head again. "I been talking to the assistant state attorney," he said. "He told me he doesn't think they have too much of a case, unless he's givin' me a snow job. He showed me pictures of this dame—dressed up, she looks older than my wife. It's a whore's word against yours. But the publicity—wow!"

What made it even better was that this doll showed up in court looking like a fourteen-year-old kid—bare legs, short dress in the days when grown-up dames at least covered their snatch with their dress, not like today, no makeup, demure-looking, hair done the way a kid would do it. My friends the prosecution did that.

My lawyer did bring out at the trial that the girl's own father had broken her in as a prostitute, that he had done five years for incest, and that he had turned her over to the madam to manage her. Somehow that seemed to make the jury madder than ever at me. They were really mad at the father, of course, but they couldn't do anything to him, so I was the guy to pay for ruining this nice, decent young girl.

Maybe I made a mistake not taking the stand at my trial, because I was sure I could convince the jury I wouldn't do anything that would wreck a hundred-thousand-dollar operation. But my lawyer thought I shouldn't, and the jury was out two hours. When they came back they found me guilty of "keeping, maintaining and operating a place for the purpose of lewdness or assignation, and aiding and abetting a female in prostitution or assignation."

The sickening thing about it, much worse than the six-month jail sentence and five-hundred-dollar fine, and even the publicity I got all around the country, was the knowledge that I didn't even know this little broad. I mean, if I had set her up, I would have said it just goes to prove how stupid I was. But not even to know her!

I got out on three thousand dollars bail awaiting appeal, and even I was amazed at what the newspapers can do when they go after you. I remember Joey came home with me, and there was one paper that had a picture of this broad, you'd swear she was eleven years old.

"Them bastards," Joey yelled. "They don't print any of the pictures they took of her the night she was arrested as a whore, when she looked twenty-five!"

"Stop aggravatin' yourself," I said. "I'll beat this on the appeal."

"So what?" Joey asked. "You're ruined. Everybody in the country is going around sayin' what a bum you are."

I nodded my head. "And I'll tell you what kind of folks they are down here," I said. "They got this phony rap on me, and now they want ten thousand dollars."

"They want what?"

"You heard me. Ten thousand dollars and they'll guarantee a reversal in the upper courts, then they'll have it thrown out of the trial court."

Joey opened his eyes. "You're not kiddin'?" he asked.

"For Christsake, why would I kid?"

"Christ, they're worse down here than they are in the Bronx."

I shrugged. "The same everywhere," I said. "This guy comes to me, he's a friend of the pol who knows the judge . . ." My voice trailed off.

Joey said, "Well, that's a load off my mind. It's a holdup, but it's better than goin' to the can. Let's get it up and get outta this goddamned city."

I can't describe how old and tired I felt. How I didn't give a damn. "Fuck it," I said. "The hell with them. I ain't gonna pay it."

"You nuts?" Joey yelled. "Get up the dough. Don't be so goddamned—whatever you are."

"I don't know," I said. "I'm probably just as well off in jail as the way I am now." Maybe I was punishing myself for everything I did that was wrong. You ever get that feeling, that things are so wrong you won't do a goddamned thing to set them right? You want to see how bad they can really get, you even want to help them get worse. It's irrational, insane, like the army that's losing and leaves its guns so the enemy can have them. The only thing I didn't do was commit suicide.

I had to sell the saloon and I moved back in with Vickie and the kids, though the divorce suit was under way, and I slept in a spare room.

Vickie couldn't have been better. She stuck by me, even if she was divorcing me. And I've got to say this—my marriage to her, especially after the disaster with Pete and after I began to grow up a little, was a good marriage. It produced three fine children and a good home, and she stayed with me all those years until, like I said, I began to go Miami and whore around.

While the appeal was going on, one night at Harry's American Bar in Miami Beach, I saw a girl who I later found out was called Sally Carlton. She was gay and pretty and young and I had had enough to drink to be convinced that I was pretty goddamned charming. I went over to her table and introduced myself, but at this point introducing me was like introducing Jack the Ripper. Sally Carlton asked me to leave. So I did. She already knew about me, obviously, and my rep at that time was the biggest bum on the eastern seaboard. A week or so later she came into a joint called the Pin-Up, where I was sitting, and this time she was a little more friendly. Some friends of mine, who also knew her, had told her that I was getting a bad rap. She had a couple of drinks with me and we left together.

Sally was a great girl, and she proved it that first night. I was so bombed that I couldn't see straight—never mind drive straight—so she made me stop the car and got out and flagged a cab for herself. But I guess she had second thoughts after she got in the cab, because the next thing I knew she had pushed me over in the front seat and taken over the wheel. Then she drove me home, undressed me and put me to bed.

That was, as I remember it, the only other fairly decent thing that happened during that time. I was like a man living in hell, and it didn't make it any less hell to know that I'd made it myself. At any rate, all that time Sally was very sweet and sympathetic, and night after night she listened to me telling her my troubles, and somehow, just be listening, she gave me courage.

With me not getting up the ten grand to pay off the powers that be, naturally my appeal was denied, and I had to serve the six months. The night I turned myself in to start the sentence I brought some of the clothes I would need over to Sally's apartment, and she made dinner for us, and ironed five shirts for me. It was a sad meal, and when it was time to go, I was sitting on the couch feeling about as low as you can get, and I said to her, "Aren't you going to kiss me good-bye?"

She shook her head. "I don't think we better," she said. "Just go."

She was right, I guess. If I'd kissed her, I probably wouldn't have left. I went over to see Vickie and said good-bye to her and the kids. And then Vickie drove me to jail.

So here I was at thirty-five, right back where I was at fifteen—in the can. Except this was worse. Back when I was fifteen, who the hell ever heard of Jake La Motta? Now everybody in the world knew that Jake La Motta, once the world's middleweight champion, was a real bum. A first-class bum.

What they put me on was what was called a chain gang, though actually the only time we were chained was when we were in a truck being taken to or from our tour of what they called hard labor—which was actually things like digging trenches, mowing grass in the parks or along the sidewalks, cutting up trees, things like that. It wasn't easy at first, partly because of the years of drinking and late hours, and partly because it used different muscles than the ones you use for fighting. I'd go to bed at night drunk with weariness, and get up in the morning sore from head to foot.

I put myself on a diet, too, which wasn't hard to do, as you can find out for yourself by treating yourself to a meal in any given prison, but partly because I had a wild idea that maybe if I could get into shape I could go back to fighting. It was a wild idea, all right, but it did one good thing. I went into the can at two hundred and ten, and I came out at a hundred and sixty.

I can tell you one thing about jails, if you're interested. They're pretty much alike. The one in Florida had all the basic elements of Coxsackie. Coming in as a name had both its advantages and disadvantages. A prison is like a jungle, somebody's going to rule. With the other prisoners I didn't figure to take too much shit. Maybe I was out of shape, but I figured it would take four or five of them to take me, and they'd only take me when I was dead. With the screws it was a different problem. The average screw has the job becase he isn't smart enough to wash automobiles. And these screws were Florida crackers. Rednecks. Peckerheads. Dumb, mean and dirty. But they knew that I could buy and sell their whole joint, them and the warden included.

You could get anything you wanted if you had the cash. Sally would come up on visiting days, and she was allowed to bring up a package once a month. I always staked the screw that examined the incoming packages so that he never examined mine too closely. I don't think he would have found anything, anyway, but I didn't want to take a chance of getting Sally in trouble, because if they ever opened up the sealed container of orange juice she always included in the package, we would have made new headlines like, LA MOTTA SWEETHEART CAUGHT SMUGGLING LIQUOR INTO PRISON. What Sally and I worked out was that she would take the container of orange juice and, leaving the seal unbroken, would make just one little hole at the top of the container with a very thin-needled syringe. Then she would siphon most of the orange juice out of it and inject it full with gin or vodka through the same tiny hole. After that she would scrape enough of the wax from the bottom of the container and, real carefully, plug up the hole. Well, you can believe that made a few days a month bearable in that lice hole. I nursed that beautiful container of cuckoo juice carefully, and for a couple of days a month I would float around feeling no pain at all, smiling at everyone and everything cause I was crocked out of my skull.

Then there was the pothead who had worked out a hell

of a scheme. His girl always brought him up a hundred-bag box of teabags every month. When that box came in every teabag had been emptied of tea and refilled, jam-packed with pot. I don't know how she ever worked it out, but she would reseal that box with cellophane so that it looked like it was just taken from a shelf at the supermarket. Well, that sure helped kill three or four days a month more. The pothead would sell me five or six teabags, and that amount was tough to get because he had steady customers, but I got my share.

And there was Sally. She would look so fantastic on visiting days and my hunger for her would get so great that I had to do something about it or go nuts—I'm not the kind of guy that could ever make it with one of those jailhouse queens. So, with a heavy payoff to two screws and a civilian hospital attendant, I worked it so that I "hurt" my back at a time when there was no bed space in the hospital. They ordered complete bed rest for a few days and put me in an empty barracks adjoining the hospital. They chained my leg to the bed just to remind me that I was to stay put—though I don't know where the hell I could have gone with gun-carrying screws on every tower.

Sally came to see me and, with a little more cash under the table, they let her visit me in the barracks. Of couse, she had my container of orange juice along, and, man, did I go after her. Poor Sally was scared out of her mind at first. I hadn't mentioned or suggested anything to her, I just started ripping at her clothes, and she almost had a fit—especially with a guard a short distance down the corridor.

Well, I went into that barracks with a phony back injury, but both Sally and I came out of it with aching backs for real. I think what added real spice to it was the surroundings and the possibility that the warden and his crew might come storming in on us while we were making love.

But creeps like Florida screws never stay bought. You know how their minds work. Maybe on the outside I'm a big shot, but in here I got to snap shit when they say snap. And, of course, it was more fun for them to let me get this far and then say snap.

Well, they were about to have a lot of fun.

TWENTY-FOUR

One day we were all on the work gang cleaning up some trees that had been blown down by a hurricane—I think it was a hurricane. Anyhow, they'd all fallen over, and we'd hacked off the branches and cut them into logs, and we were loading the logs onto the truck. As usual, the one thing you got in a prison that you don't need is manpower, and the result of that was that here you had about twelve grown men dealing with a log that four could handle. There was no room for me—not that I was pushing—so I was standing off to the side and the screw came up and said, "What's with you, helpless?"

I said, "You got eyes. There's no room." Of course what I should've said was, "I'm sorry, sir, I tried to help, but there's no room."

You ask for trouble, you get it. The screw grinned at me and said, "You're supposed to be Mister Tough Guy. Go over there and make room for yourself."

So I went over and in the course of trying to get in on the act, I was kneeling and somehow the log dropped and pinned my arm to the ground. Now this log, it was about ten feet long and better than two feet in diameter. I moaned as I took most of the weight on my arm. The other cons start to lever it off and one of the screws, shotgun in the crook of his arm and fat red face in a smile, strolled over, squirted out a shot of tobacco juice and said, "Well, Champ Pimp, what's wrong now?"

He could see.

"Log fell on my arm," I said getting up.

"Well, now . . . whaddaya know. Champ Pimp got himself another boo-boo. . . ."

"Lay off the name," I said.

228

He just gave me a bigger grin as they got the log off and I got up. "Riles ya, does it?" he said. "Grabs ya where it hurts, huh? That's what you are, aincha? That's what you was convicted of, ain't it?"

"Knock it off, you fuckin' cracker," I snarled at him.

He aimed the shotgun right at me. "You goddamned Yankee!" he screamed. "Get in the truck! Get in the truck!"

So they got me back to the warden's office and shoved me in so that I stumbled across the room and halfway across his desk. The warden got up and said, "All right, what is it?"

"He called me a 'fuckin' cracker,'" the guard said, "and he doubled up his fists like he was gonna slug me!"

I don't think that was true, but what the hell difference did it make? I was in for it anyway, I knew it.

I said: "Would it make any difference that this particular cracker takes a personal pleasure in ridin' me? Even since the first day I got here—"

But the warden cut in: "Would it make any difference that in this prison you don't double up your fists to him?" he asked, loud and hard. "Would it make any difference that here you're just another number! You're here to serve time like everybody else. We got a perfect democracy here, everybody equal, all the scum treated exactly alike, no privileges!" He motioned to the guard. "Take this particular piece of scum and throw it in the hole!"

And throw me in the hole he did. That peckerheaded, rednecked bastard took me down, and I was standing by the cell door while he opened it, my mind a complete blank because I still couldn't believe all this was happening to me, when all of a sudden I was sent hurtling and stumbling into the cell, and this heavy wooden door with the tiny cross-barred window was slammed at my back. He snarled at me through the window, "This oughtta cool ya—ya champeen pimp."

He left and I was in this dark, gloomy cell, and all I could hear was him cackling as he went down the empty corridor. It was like a black curtain being rung down over my life, like this was it, this was the end, no beating the count this time, no matter what.

Well, I never was a quitter, and I'll never forget that day. As I looked around that stinking little cell, something happened to me. Maybe it was my fighting instinct, my survival instinct, I don't know—all I knew was that the fucking system, whatever it was that had shoved me into this hole, was not going to have the last say—not this way, anyway.

It started in me as a silent scream and then it burst out in one long, screeching "*No-o-o-o-!*" And the wall closest to me became the whole stinking world. I doubled my fists tight and lashed out at it, at them. I hit them where it hurt—in the gut, in the windpipe, on the chin. And I just kept on doing it, hitting a wall that was about as thinking and as feeling as the world.

The adrenaline was gushing through me like an animal all keyed up for the kill. Like the way it had been in the ring when I had one of those big, mean light heavies going and knew at last I had him and the killer in me drove me to move in and kill him—kill him like he'd been trying to kill me. Finish him off and walk away!

I felt the way I had the night I kept hitting Harry Gordon again and again and again. And when we raided the crap game and I was busting everybody's head. And I'm sure that if at that minute that bastard screw or nitwit warden had walked in, I'd have probably torn out their jugulars with my teeth.

I guess the thing that finally stopped me was that two of my knuckles crunched deep up my fist. I could always stand pain, it's part of fighting. You condition yourself against it. But my fists just wouldn't clench anymore.

I stopped, and all I could hear was the blood from my hands plopping to the floor. I slumped against the wall and sucked air into my burning lungs. Then, all of a sudden, the rage exploded in me again. And this time I really lost control. I screamed, "Why? Why? Why this? Whaddaya want from me? What the fuck do you want from me? You know, you know I'm not what they all say I am! You know I'm not that guy! I'm not an animal! Why? Why the top and now this? What did I ever do that was so bad? I'm as good as anybody in this fuckin' world today!"

And I lunged at the wall again, punched at it with more

hate than I ever felt for anything in my life. And, at that moment, I felt the worst, most shocking pain of my life. It may have been because of my already damaged fists, but I like to think different, because I never expected that anything could be so bad, so punishing. I yelled and moaned.

Then I started to cry—bawl like a baby is more like it. I dropped down to my knees and held my fists up and pleaded, "I'm not like that . . . please . . . not like that." And, for the very first time in my whole life, I prayed.

And while I was praying—begging is more like it—something started to happen. The tightness in my gut started to let go—and when it did, it was then I realized that there was never a time I didn't remember having that uptight gnawing feeling in my solar plexus. And I knew what had been causing that grip on my insides—fear. Not the fear I mentioned inside the ring, the one I finally beat and actually managed to turn to my advantage. This was something different, something that was a part of me. Because the fact was that Jake La Motta, the so-called toughest guy that ever jumped into a ring, ready and able to tear apart the roughest fighters that ever lived, had always been afraid of everything in life.

And at that moment I also knew that there wasn't anything for me to ever be afraid of again. Because what the hell else could happen to me. My home, Vickie, my wonderful kids, were my whole life to me and I had been terrified of losing them—and I had lost them. I had always been in a constant sweat that I would wind up broke—and I was. I had always been afraid of losing my rep as a fighter, and now it was as black as coal and everyone believed not just that I was a bum, but worse, a convicted pimp.

Most of all, I'd been afraid of God, fate, life—something—getting me all my life, and it finally had. I had never really believed in God—at least, I told myself I didn't—and I laughed at guys who went to church. I was too smart, too hip for religion. I would never admit to myself that I had any regard or fear of God. I had to think that way. First, because of all the rotten, terrible things I had done in my life; second, because how the hell is a guy supposed to get along with a God who tells you that harming another human is a cardinal sin, when all the time you're thinking of dozens of ways of hurting, punishing, cutting up some guy to make a living.

But let's face it, my mother, like most Italian mothers, had drummed into me so hard and so often the fear of sin and the law of retribution when I was a kid that it became one of my biggest fears. I don't care how tough a guy is, if you're brought up by a parent who is always on her knees, praying for forgiveness for having had some silly thought, or for being forced to do some stupid little thing for the sake of the family that she thought was wrong, it gets to you, and it sticks with you forever. You know you're going to get it—sooner or later. And I'd been looking for it all my life.

Well, I'd gotten it all right. I figured He had his revenge. I felt paid up completely to man and God, and I had stopped being afraid. There was only one way to go now, and that was UP.

TWENTY-FIVE

I guess if there's such a thing as a turning point in a man's life, that was mine. Everything changed after that. I don't think it's too much to say that the man who got thrown into that hole was not the same man who came out.

And I did get out—forty-eight hours later. I think part of the reason was that I had told the warden I'd hire ten lawyers and blow his graft-ridden hole sky-high when I got out. I mean, regardless of what had happened, if I started spilling what that jail was like, there were plenty of places it would be printed.

When the day came for me to be sprung, after six months in that prison, Sally went over to Vickie's to get my stuff. After a couple of weeks I was still horsing around Miami Beach, figuring out what to do next, when one night I was with Sally and we came out of a delicatessen and were about to get into the car when a guy walked into the delicatessen. He didn't see us, but I recognized him. Pete.

Suddenly something came over me. I leaned into the car and said to Sally, "Look, sweetie, be a good girl and drive home, willya. I . . . I just want to walk around a little and sort of unwind, get it? I'll see you later."

She didn't get it, but what the hell else could she do? She nodded her head and started the car engine and backed out.

I went over near Pete's car and waited till he came back out with a paper bag. "Hey, Pete . . ." And I walked toward him, putting out my hand.

He looked at me and didn't say a word. Then he turned his back on me and started to get into the car. I ran over to him and grabbed his shoulder. "No, Pete, no," I said. "Look, wait a minute, please . . ."

He looked at me like I was shit and threw my hand off his shoulder and started into the car again.

I threw out both my hands to him. "Aah, Pete," I said, and then I stopped. I guess I had gone over what I would say to him a thousand times in my mind, but now that the time had come to say it, nothing would come out. All I could do was trail after him, grab his shoulder and stop him from getting into his car. Then I started to say the same thing over again, real fast. "You're right! You're perfectly right! You got every right in the world to hate my guts!"

But he wasn't having any of it. He shrugged my hand off his shoulder and tried to put the paper bag on the car seat. "No, please!" I said. I knew that once he got into his car, he might pull away and I'd never get this opportunity again. "I know I'm a suspicious, treacherous bastard. You're right! I know I acted like the prize cock of all time. I should have never raised my hands. . . ." I guess this reminded him of the terrible beating I'd given him and he kind of half-pushed me away and started again into his car. But I pulled him by the arm and yelled, "No, Pete, listen to me!" I guess I pulled him a lot harder than I thought because the paper bag slipped out of his hands and fell at his feet—the containers of coffee and tea bursting open and splattering his shoes and pants legs. This triggered something in him, and suddenly his fists came up and he belted me with a left and a right to the jaw. He caught me by surprise and I automatically backed off to get my own hands up.

But Pete kept pouring it on in the way we were both taught—once you belt a guy, keep up the punishment till he's helpless, and he sure was trying to do it to me. All the anger and hurt that I had caused him he kept giving back to me with his fists. One . . . two . . . three . . . Punch after punch tagged me and, while he was hitting me, I felt good inside . . . because somehow I knew it was going to end okay.

I dropped my hands and just stood there, taking it. After a while I was saying, "Go ahead, hit me again. . . .

I deserve it. . . . Pay me back. . . . More. . . ." Pete stopped in midpunch and stared at me like he couldn't figure it. I nodded and tried to smile but my chin started quivering and I got all choked up and, before you know it, I was bawling and holding out my chin for that big fist that Pete was still holding in midair, and I was blubbering, "More. Go ahead, Pete, I deserve it."

Well, he finally threw it but very weakly, to my shoulder, and he left it there. He stared at me, then tears were flooding his eyes, too. His fist on my shoulder finally opened and he curled it around my neck and tugged me close to him and we went into the tightest bear hug you ever saw—clutching each other and bawling like two little children, hugging each other, not saying anything.

It seemed that everything began to go right after that.

Fighting was out forever, I knew that, but I began to get some jobs acting. Before I had gotten into all my trouble, I had done some shows on television. The first one I got through Rocky Graziano. He had got on television through Martha Raye, who put him on her show. That's where Rocky got started in his career as an actor—if you can call him that. Martha had a show of her own then, and Rocky was on it every week. I'm not getting in a knock about the actor bit, God knows neither him or me is going to make John Barrymore turn over in his grave, but Rocky got a lot of laughs on account of the strictly New York City accent he had, like me, and the way he mispronounces words and blows his lines when he's got a part he's supposed to learn. But he did have a good instinct for comedy, and back then he came to me and said, "You wanna do a Martha Raye show with me?"

"What the Christ do I know about actin'?" I asked him.

"What the hell, they're not askin' you to play Hamlet," he said. "You been on television enough fightin'. If I can do it, you can do it."

Sure I was interested, and what made it real big was that Margaret Truman, the daughter of the former President of the United States, was going to play my date on the show. If you remember, there was a time when she wanted to be a singer and an actress. I went up to New York for the show, and they handed me a lot of lines to memorize. I took one look at them, and the director of the show took one look at my face.

He was a pretty smart guy. "Okay," he said, "don't try to memorize them word for word. Just read them through so you know what the skit is all about, and say what comes natural to you. Just stick with the plot and don't give us something brand-new."

I think the best scene we did was just me and Rocky, in which Rocky was helping me get ready for the show. There's something pretty funny to the public about a couple of characters like Rocky and me who never did anything except go to reform school and fight making each other up so we'll look pretty.

Well, the television show went off pretty good, and I began to get offers to appear in plays. I was in the play *The Milky Way* at the Miami Springs Villa Playhouse, a part that called for me to memorize six hundred lines, and George Bourke, the critic for the *Miami Herald*, said I did a "superbly good job."

After that I began to get pretty serious about becoming an actor. I played the part of Harry Brock in *Born Yesterday*, which was put on at the Roney Plaza Hotel, and Walter Winchell said I was "surprisingly good." I went to New York to see what the score was on Broadway. I enrolled in the Bert Lane Theater Workshop near Times Square and started learning. The only way you learn fighting is by fighting, and the only way you learn acting is by acting. I would act every day—act, act, act. I did an episode for *Naked City* but they cut it, and in 1959 I went on the road with Lloyd Bridges, playing Big Julie in *Guys and Dolls*. I was picked from the theater workshop to play the co-lead in a movie called *Rebellion in Cuba*.

But there was still another bad period I had to go through. It started with my appearance before the Kefauver Senate subcommitte that was investigating boxing. By now, like I said, Pete and I were friends again and we were seeing a lot of each other. During all that time that Pete and I were separated, Pete had made good in business and settled down with a very pretty and sweet Vermont girl named Eleanor, who everyone calls Pinky. Anyway, Pete told me that the way he got filled in on what I better say or not say in front of the Kefauver committee came from our good friend Nick.

Pete was pulling into his dress factory this day, a week or so after the papers had all been full of how the committee was going to investigate all of professional boxing and how far into it the mob had gotten, and he heard this auto horn blow and turned around and there was Nick in the Cadillac sitting in front beside Salvy, who was driving, and Patsy, the pistol-shooter, was in the back seat—things don't change much. Pete went over to the car and Nick gave him the old grin.

"Hi, Petey," he said. "Just wanted ta talk ta ya for a second, if ya got a second. How about hoppin' in?" And he gestured to the back seat. Patsy reached and opened the door for him. Pete shrugged and got in. "How are ya, Pete?" Nick asked. "You look real good. How are things goin'?"

"Okay," Pete said.

Nick gave his hard, cold laugh, and said, "Same old Pete, always fulla conversation and wisecracks, never able to stop talkin'. Okay, eh? That all you can say?"

Pete shrugged again. "Come on, Nick. You know how things are. What's up? What's on your mind? You're not waitin' here for me to ask me how I am."

"All right," Nick said, "I'll tell you what I wanna talk ta you about. It's about your great old friend, the fighter who's now the actor, him and his big mouth."

Pete still didn't know what he was talking about, and he said so, and that got Nick mad. His face started to get red and his voice rose. "Are you tryna kid me? Don't you ever read the newspapers or listen to the radio? It's all over town, for Christsake!"

Nick was so mad that Pete got a little worried. "No, Nick, honest, I don't know what you're talkin' about. I got a little business problem I been worryin' about and I ain't seen the paper today. What's Jake up to?"

"What's he up to?" Nick screamed at him. "He's blowin' the whole thing, that's what! He's turning over the whole can o' worms! He's voluteerin'—volunteerin', mind you, for Christsake—to testify in front of that goddamned Kefauver committee, how he dumped the Billy

Fox fight, how he got the title shot, the whole bit!" He was yelling so loud that he ran out of breath, so he stopped and sucked in a chestful of air and then started again, lower.

"Now, look, Petey," he said, lower, and shaking his finger under Pete's nose, "this kinda talk could hurt a lot o' people, a lot o' people we both know—nice people, real folks with families. You know that and I know it. I'm lookin' you up because you seem to be the one person that this madman will listen to." He stopped and looked at Pete, cold and hard. "If he blows his mouth off down there in Washington, I give you my personal guarantee that I will personally deliver his body to the Jersey dump myself. Do you understand that?"

Pete nodded.

"He's dead," Nick said. "Dead as of the minute he opens his yap! You think you can give him that message in words he can understand?"

Pete just nodded again, and the car started slowly off with Nick shaking his head and saying to Pete, "I swear to God in all my life I never seen anyone as stupid as that thick-headed nut."

Pete got hold of me. "Dead," he tells me, "that's what you're gonna be. These guys are positively not kiddin', Jake, I know them. Kiddin' they're not, and bulletproof you're not. You want to end up in the garbage dump? And what the hell are you gonna prove anyhow? You know what those hearings down in Washington are. They never do anything except get publicity for a lot of jerk senators."

As I said, I figured Pete was right. I went down to Washington and—well, it's in the record. I admitted throwing the Fox fight, I admitted the hundred-thousand dollar bribe offer, plus the twenty thousand I paid for the shot at Cerdan. But when it came to where the bribe offer came from, I just kept denying that they had ever tried to bribe me. I kept saying that the only way I heard about the bribe offer was through my brother Joey and nobody else. This was safe because I knew that Joey was going to take the Fifth the whole way.

How much, if any, good those hearings did, I don't know. But for me they did nothing but bad. It seemed that everyone misunderstood my reason for appearing before the committee. I was a hated, despised guy again—"despicable," I think I was called. My image, well, forget it. Everyone, all of a sudden, was acting as if I had leprosy.

To give you an idea—I was a surprise guest on the Barry Farber radio show one night not long after the hearings, and Jersey Joe Walcott, the old heavyweight champ who was booked for the show, suddenly got up and turned his back on me and walked off the show. I'm still bugged over that. Didn't he ever read what they had to say about his managers and their affiliations in some of the press releases of his day?

I mean, didn't anybody ever give a thought to the damn reason I appeared before that senatorial political ladder—because that's all those committees really are. *Nothing* ever really comes out of those investigating committees except that a lot of little-known senators get to appear on television and get a lot of great publicity. Name one bad guy that all those good guys ever punished or sent to jail after any of the investigating committees have run their course.

There was one thing that really hurt deep. It was when the boxing world gave a big farewell to Ray Robinson. He had finally made up his mind to quit boxing. It was about time, I thought, because he had just gone through his eleventh comeback. Don't get me wrong—Ray is one fighter that I would never knock. I never minded saying he was the greatest. He was lucky in a couple of fights with me, but there's no question that he's one of the best.

Robinson's farewell to boxing took place in the old Madison Square Garden before a packed house. The Garden promoters brought in, at their expense, all the former middleweight champions that Robinson had fought: Bobo Olsen from San Francisco, Gene Fullmer from Nebraska, Carmen Basilio from Syracuse, Paul Pender from Boston, Rocky Graziano from Long Beach. They even brought in Randy Turpin from England Who was the only former champ they excluded? Jake La Motta, that's who! And how did Jake La Motta figure in Robinson's life and boxing career? I was only the first fighter to lick him when he was on top! I was only the guy he defeated for the middleweight title, and I was also the guy he waltzed with in six slambang wars, and—what the hell—I was the only former champ who could have walked to the Garden! I lived ten blocks away. I still ask myself, what the hell did I do so wrong that deserved such treatment?

So I threw the Billy Fox fight—okay, that's the cardinal sin in sports, and it should be. But did anyone think about the cardinal sin that was being committed against me for so many years? I couldn't get a title shot unless I threw the fight. Why did I finally admit it? Because those phony senators were going through the motions of cleaning up boxing. I thought I owed it to boxing and the sports world to tell what I had to go through. Boxing was the greatest thing that ever happened to me. I had and still do have a great loyalty to the sport. I figured—and you may not believe this—why should a country as great as ours have corruption in any competitive sport? But before you laugh at the idea of Jake La Motta having even a tiny iota of this type of idealism, ask yourself who I hurt or seriously damaged, except myself, by making that admission. What did I have to gain, damn it?

About three months after the investigations, I married Sally. It was another of my mistakes—even though we had two great children—and it convinced me that there's a hex on me as far as getting married is concerned. Again, I can't blame Sally for what happened. It was the worst possible time to be married. I was broke and getting broker. I made a couple of bad investments in Broadway shows and other places and pretty soon we were moving to cheaper and cheaper hotels, and what dame is going to put up with that forever. I was so busted that at one point I was working on a maintenance gang in Central Park.

When you're living in crummy eight-by-ten hotel rooms like I was, you need something to keep you from going nuts with boredom. From the time I was a boxer I used to read a lot, but now I went crazy, reading all the paperbacks I could get my hands on—stuff like *The Territorial Imperative* and *African Genesis,* books on art, hypnosis, meditation. I guess it kept me going.

But things didn't stay black forever. I've got to credit

two people with helping me out of my hole or at least seeing that I didn't sink any deeper into it. One of them was Teddy Brenner. About six years after the investigations, when I was a leper, an untouchable, Teddy Brenner, a top promoter, came through. Teddy is a guy that really knows and understands boxers and what makes them tick. He decided one day to go against all standards and policy and, on his own, had me introduced on one of the Emile Griffith–Nino Benvenuti title fights.

It was a thrill, down to my toenails. I was thrilled because, believe it or not, I got a helluva hand. No, it wasn't a hand, it was an ovation, and it choked me up to find that more people seemed to like me than I thought didn't. What was still greater about it was that the next day it was televised all over the country—and after all those years of probably being near-forgotten, I was again being introduced from a ring, and at a championship fight. For me, it was like a symbol of acceptance, and it helped open up a lot of doors that would have stayed shut.

Another great guy that helped me, and this is going to surprise you, is a former cop. A former police lieutenant yet, and a New York congressman—Mario Biaggi. He used to be called the toughest cop in the world, and I believe it. Just to show you what kind of guy Mario is, when that guy Tony, the one who had tried to set me up in the whorehouse to get me knocked off, was brought in for questioning in the Maitland Brenhouse murder, he, being a prime suspect, used me for his alibi. Bang! Headlines in every paper and radio news every hour on the hour, and every one of those publicity-hungry officials involved in the case were off in corners rubbing their hot little hands over the field day they were going to have. They gave out sneaky little hints about that notorious scoundrel Jake La Motta. It didn't matter to the press how remotely involved I might have been with Tony—there were these scandalous rumors being whispered about Brenhouse, and what better way is there to get sensational publicity than to involve an already disreputable guy like me.

The papers were ready to start rehashing my whole background again. It would have set me back a lot of years. But Mario walked in and asked me for the level-up story.

I told him and he believed me, and from that point on everyone stuck to the facts and everything just died a natural death, like it should have in the first place.

Well, lately I seem to have finally lived down my bad reputation and my career's started going up again. I've been getting dinner-speaking dates and nightclub dates. They've started calling me the Georgie Jessel of the sports circuit.

But more important, I'm really beginning to take off as an actor. A few years ago I did a program at the Barbizon Theater where I memorized ten thousand words, to play nine scenes from nine major plays. It was called "A Dramatic Concert with Jake La Motta," and the reviews were great. And I went over to Rome to play in a movie called *Ex-Americans*. Then I got a real break.

What happened was that Pete got bit by the show-biz bug—he figured, you know, why should so many people be making so much money out of movies and not him. So he bought a story by Peter Rabe called *A House in Naples,* got together with a producer named Joe Justman and we went to Italy and filmed the story. Pete seems to have a great instinct for directing and, of course, he cast me as one of the leads.

When we finished *A House in Naples*, Pete went on to a bigger production starring Jane Russell, Lee Meredith, Rocky Graziano and me. The romantic lead, if you're interested, is played by Peter Savage, who is my old friend Pete himself. There are also four other world's boxing champions in the film (six in all), including Tony Zale, Willie Pep, Paddy De Marco and Pete Scalzo. We called it *Cauliflower Cupids*.

While we were working on *Cupids*, Marty Heller, a lawyer Pete hired to bail him out on some legal problems with the picture, and I had a lot of dinners together and we'd talk. Well, I told him my whole life story—the complete truth—with no holds barred. The thing I'm most grateful for is that even though I'm sure he believed my story, he still believed in me. He kept saying, "Jake, this story is your life, it should be in a book." Well, he kept the idea going. He would say things like: "Your story would be something that people would understand—the violence, the way some people exist, how they stay alive. It's a story that should be in a book."

While he was talking, I kept thinking back to two things, two things that I'll never forget, that I remember most often. They were both during absolutely the lowest period of my life—when I was in that jail in Florida.

They used to take us out to the work site at the crack of dawn every morning, and like I said, this was the only time we were really chained. This truck was naturally a broken-down, beat-up old piece of machinery, and it was driven by one of those Florida cracker guards who wouldn't know his right hand from his left, and part of the drive was along this river, which was maybe not very big—I don't even know the name of it—but it was deep and kind of slimy and filled with moss and mud and all sorts of weeds and branches.

And every time we drove along that road in the early morning, beside the river, the truck groaning and lurching and speeding, in my mind I could see that redneck cracker losing control of the wheel because he drank like a fish and had a hangover every morning, and the truck catching its wheels off to the side and suddenly lurching down as it went off the road and turning over a couple of times and rolling down into twenty-five feet of river water and all of us chained inside so there wouldn't be a prayer in hell of getting out. I used to think to myself, Jesus, what a way to end it. God, gimme one more chance, just one more chance to get outta here.

The other thing was what I mentioned before, when I was in the hole in that Florida prison, pounding the walls and screaming at God and finally feeling all the fear that had built up in a lifetime drain out of me. I remembered being in a ring, the lights bright and the ref holding up my bruised and aching fist and saying I was the middleweight champion of the world, and how everyone went wild with screaming and cheering, and afterward how all the radios and newspapers in the world had stories about me, the slum kid from the Bronx. And how sometimes, when I'd pass a crowd and they recognized me, they'd all start cheering and run over to pat me on the back and jump all over themselves just to shake my hand.

Okay, here I was, in a hole as close to hell as I'll ever want to get again, but I knew that I was going to get out of there. I was going to fight my way out, but this time I wouldn't be fighting with hate and fear *against* someone or something, but *for* myself. I wouldn't be fighting to destroy anymore, but to build. And, maybe, if I fought hard enough and long enough, I would get people to cheer me again.

Who knows, maybe I will.

RELAX!
SIT DOWN
and Catch Up On Your Reading!

Hey There Sports Fan!

We have something just for _you!_

THE PRIVATE LIVES
BEHIND PUBLIC FACES

These biographies tell the personal stories of these well-known figures recounting the triumphs and tragedies of their public and private lives.

☐	14167	**BURIED ALIVE: The Biography of** Janis Joplin by Myra Friedman	$2.95
☐	13592	**CHANGING** Liv Ullmann	$2.75
☐	13150	**DON'T FALL OFF THE MOUNTAIN** Shirley MacLaine	$2.25
☐	13310	**THE SECRET LIFE OF TYRONE POWER**	$2.75
☐	14378	**HAYWIRE** Brooke Hayward	$2.95
☐	13648	**THE TWO LIVES OF ERROL FLYNN** Michael Freedland	$2.50
☐	14130	**GARY COOPER: INTIMATE BIOGRAPHY** Hector Arce	$2.75
☐	13824	**ELVIS: PORTRAIT OF A FRIEND** Lackers & Smith	$2.95
☐	12942	**JOAN CRAWFORD: A Biography** Bob Thomas	$2.75
☐	12000	**THE KID** Pete Axthelm	$2.50
☐	12455	**MONTGOMERY CLIFT: A Biography** Patricia Bosworth	$2.75
☐	13030	**SOPHIA: Living and Loving,** Her Own Story A. E. Hotchner	$2.75
☐	14551	**AN UNFINISHED WOMAN** Lillian Hellman	$2.75
☐	13206	**A ROCKWELL PORTRAIT** Donald Walton	$2.95

Buy them at your local bookstore or use this handy coupon!

Bantam Book Catalog

Here's your up-to-the-minute listing of over 1,400 titles by your favorite authors.

This illustrated, large format catalog gives a description of each title. For your convenience, it is divided into categories in fiction and non-fiction—gothics, science fiction, westerns, mysteries, cookbooks, mysticism and occult, biographies, history, family living, health, psychology, art.

So don't delay—take advantage of this special opportunity to increase your reading pleasure.

Just send us your name and address and 50¢ (to help defray postage and handling costs).

BANTAM BOOKS, INC.
Dept. FC, 414 East Golf Road, Des Plaines, Ill. 60016

Mr./Mrs./Miss_____
(please print)

Address_____

City_____State_____Zip_____

Do you know someone who enjoys books? Just give us their names and addresses and we'll send them a catalog too!

Mr./Mrs./Miss_____

Address_____

City_____State_____Zip_____

Mr./Mrs./Miss_____

Address_____

City_____State_____Zip_____

FC—9/78